THE WORLD'S
ECONOMIC DILEMMA

THE WORLD'S ECONOMIC DILEMMA

by

ERNEST MINOR PATTERSON

Professor of Economics

UNIVERSITY OF PENNSYLVANIA

WHITTLESEY HOUSE

McGRAW-HILL BOOK COMPANY, INC.

NEW YORK · 1930

Published by

WHITTLESEY HOUSE
Trade Division of the
McGraw-Hill Book Company, Inc.
370 SEVENTH AVENUE, NEW YORK

Printed in the United States of America by
The Maple Press Company, York, Pa.

PREFACE

IN RECENT years the study of international affairs has greatly increased in the United States, a change that is due to the new position in which we find ourselves since the World War. Some of the problems that we are facing were gradually appearing and we would have been compelled to attempt their solution in a few years even if we had remained at peace. The war merely accelerated the movement and by so doing has introduced complications. Also some of the problems are more acute because they have developed so rapidly and their sudden appearance has not given us adequate time to adjust our thinking.

What is true of the people of the United States is true in varying degrees of people in other parts of the world. There are many changes elsewhere as well as here. The increasing economic interdependence of all countries has presented an entirely new set of facts and forces. Many of them either are unknown or else are little understood. This has been particularly serious since so many of them are economic while those entrusted with the conduct of public affairs and with the responsibility for making decisions have lacked economic training. Economists without political training might have done still worse. There certainly has been a crying need for a blend of the two.

When we turn to the literature in the field we are struck with the lack of any broad treatment of many of the issues involved. There are many volumes appearing, particularly in these postwar years, but they fall into two general groups. The first are written by historians, by journalists, and by political scientists and reflect the specialized interests of their authors. Some treat current events in a most valuable manner, but with a minimum of background. Others present the principles of international law and of politics. The works of the historians are apt to place emphasis upon political matters and even when economic considerations are introduced they are not always presented with enough of the economic principles involved to make the treatment adequate.

Another group of books on international questions has been written by economists but most of them are narrow in scope and for the most part technical. Some treat of foreign trade, others of foreign exchange and of foreign investments. There are some also on world population questions. Nevertheless, it is not inaccurate to say that there is a dearth of literature in the field of international economics.

In our colleges and universities this lack is now being felt. For a long time the teaching of courses in international affairs has been in the hands of historians and political scientists. In the last few years the economists are being called upon to give such courses but the material needed has not yet been satisfactorily assembled. It is to be hoped that it will soon be made available.

This volume is not written with the thought that it will fully meet that need. The author hopes that it may prove valuable as collateral reading and in that way stimulate interest in a field of outstanding importance. He also hopes that it may be of significance to the general reader in presenting some of the fundamental facts and forces that make international relations of today so difficult.

E.M.P.

PHILADELPHIA, PA.
August, 1930.

CONTENTS

THE WORLD'S
ECONOMIC DILEMMA

Chapter I

INTRODUCTORY · THE DILEMMA
SUMMARIZED

THIS volume analyzes the world's economic dilemma. Economic interdependence is universal. Every part of the world now depends on every other part, and complete cooperation in carrying on business seems, at first thought, both desirable and necessary. Yet numerous obstacles exist due to an organization under which limited areas of the earth's surface are separately organized for political purposes. Each of these states must perform many economic functions that place it in opposition to other states similarly organized. The free movement of people and of goods so necessary to economic welfare is thus checked and a dilemma is created from which it is not easy to extricate ourselves.

Yet it is a dilemma that is not incapable of solution. Instead, the answer is already in process, but since the solution has been found only in part, there are many reasons for uncertainty as to the outcome. Years may pass before success or failure will be clear.

In the first section (Chaps. I to IX) the fundamental factors in the problem will be presented. They are economic and they are well known. In fact, most of them are so familiar that mere reiteration seems commonplace. No reader will be surprised to learn that the world is an economic entity, that each part is to a high degree dependent on every other part. Yet there are some phases of this dependence that call for more emphasis than has yet been given them and there are other phases that up to the present have not been clearly presented at all.

Mere interdependence, however, does not create the dilemma, although it does give rise to problems. There are difficulties of adjustment and opportunities for friction, but these are to be found in economic life everywhere. The additional perplexing fact is the existence of national units. As a matter of administrative necessity governments are organized, each directing many phases of life within its own territorial jurisdiction.

A nationalism develops that is more than a sentiment. For centuries such peace as prevailed was dependent on the strength of national governments and on the devotion of citizens and subjects to the state. Today, peace depends far more upon adjustments between states, upon concessions, upon modifications of sovereignty. In these adaptations a rigid nationalism hinders rather than helps.

Sovereignty may be a legal fiction but its reality is thoroughly believed in. Both government officials and common people insist upon it and contend that it must not be violated. International lawyers refer to it. Disputes between nations are "justiciable" or "non-justiciable." Treaties are made providing for the amicable settlement of questions that do not affect vital national interests. Especially since 1914 are there strong evidences of an excessive nationalism.

There are, however, some signs of a modification in viewpoint. More and more adjustments have become imperative and the interlocking of interests is more generally acknowledged. The necessity of mutual concessions is everywhere admitted and an international viewpoint is in evidence even though the nationalistic spirit seems stronger than ever.

[4]

Introductory. The Dilemma Summarized

Yet there is a complication in modern growth. The state today performs more functions than ever before. Not only have problems world wide in scope been multiplying but also those of more limited importance. Life is increasingly complex. Industrialization, urban concentration, the annihilation of time and space by telegraph, telephone, railway, radio, airplane, and television, the development of vast networks for the transmission of electric current—all these and other forces have compelled social action. Competition has disappeared over wide areas, and to talk as did the late President Wilson of the "new freedom" is futile. Social welfare cannot be trusted to the guidance of the "invisible hand" upon which Adam Smith was willing to rely. The state has intervened, and *laissez faire* is profoundly modified.[1]

This growth of state control over many phases of economic life accentuates the dilemma. Governments assume, in fact must assume, definite responsibility for the organization of economic activities within their respective jurisdictions. Nationalism is more than a state of mind and is not to be exorcised. It cannot be dismissed by incantation.[2] Under twentieth century conditions the state must organize and direct a maze of social life within its own borders and for the welfare of its citizens. This compels activity on a national basis. Ordinarily it goes so far as to undertake protection of the national economy against the world economy which is pressing on it from all directions. Says Josef Grunzel: "Economic protectionism . . . is neither more nor less than the sum total of the measures adopted by the national economy unit for

[1] See KEYNES, J. M., "The End of *Laissez Faire*," London, 1927.
[2] Nor is the situation accurately expressed by the title of Francis Delaisi's excellent volume "Political Myths and Economic Realities." The title of the original French edition is a better one: "Les Contradictions du Monde Moderne."

[5]

the purpose of advancing its interests in the field of world economy."[1]

This dilemma having been stated and its difficulties emphasized, illustrations will be presented (Chaps. X to XV). The United Kingdom, France, Germany, Italy, Japan, and the United States will be examined in turn. The dependence of each, the difficulties of its present situation, and some of the recent attempts by each to find a solution for its predicament will be shown.

Finally, in the concluding chapter there will be recorded some of the progress that is being made. To state the dilemma is not to suggest that it cannot be solved, for distinct gains can be recorded. The difficulties are greater than is generally realized. The obstacles to a solution are not to be removed merely by appeals to goodwill. There are plenty of people in the world who desire peace. The time has come for the expert in social science, and he is at work in many directions. Old political behavior is rapidly being modified, and a new type of diplomacy is gradually being evolved. Business men and bankers of widely separated countries are learning how to work together—not merely for sentimental reasons, although many of them are idealists of the highest type, but for mutual gain. The concluding chapter will attempt to record some of this progress.

[1] This quotation is from his "Economic Protectionism," which is probably the strongest and most scholarly defense of protection since "The National System of Political Economy" by Friedrich List.

Chapter II

POPULATION AGAIN AN ISSUE

O^NE of the most interesting developments of postwar discussion is the attention being given to problems of population. Book after book has appeared and the magazines are filled with articles on the subject. The thinking world seems suddenly to have become population conscious. Only a few years ago other questions were to the front and such matters as the Malthusian law of population and the law of diminishing returns were presented more as formal facts of economic theory than because of immediate human interest in them.

It is desirable to state the reasons for such a revival of interest in the subject, but the analysis will be aided by a reminder that population has always been a problem. Often there has been a belief that numbers were excessive but just as often the other view has prevailed. Social practices and theories as well as religious dogmas have expressed the convictions held at different times and places. The Romans, the Spartans, the Athenians—as well as Egyptians, Assyrians, and others—faced the issue of the proper numbers for their respective communities. The well-known scriptural injunction "Multiply and replenish the earth" is an expression of one solution for a meager population, while infanticide and certain other social practices were designed to reduce or to prevent excessive numbers. Both civilized and savage groups have undertaken answers and these answers have varied with the conditions that confronted them. Readers who care

[7]

to pursue the subject further are referred to the comprehensive study of Carr-Saunders. [1]

There is no occasion to dwell here on earlier views. Instead, it will be better to note briefly that about one hundred years ago there was a particularly active agitation which found its leading expression in England but attracted the attention of students and writers all over the world. Malthus' great essay was but one statement of this interest which affected much of the thought not only of that immediate period but also of many succeeding years. His theory of population growth has ever since been a necessary part of every survey of economic doctrines, and in recent times those who have revived the discussion are frequently styled Neo-Malthusians.

An interest so widespread is not to be explained as due merely to the writings of any one person. In the economic conditions of that time the growth in numbers of human beings was fundamental and extremely serious. Out of it arose many of the most acute of the current problems and on it were based many of the explanations of social and economic life. The "dismal science" of economics was particularly permeated by this one fact.

Less than a century before, the Industrial Revolution had begun, a movement of such broad significance that the word "industrial" is too narrow for its complete description. As machines supplanted human beings, men became aware of their own numbers. To substitute water power or steam (and later electricity) for human drudgery seems a gain, but in a complex world, functioning under a wage system, where one man hires many others, the machine may, for a time and for many, be a menace, not a benefactor. Displaced workers felt the tragedy most keenly, but all thoughtful observers became conscious that numbers

[1] CARR-SAUNDERS, A. M., "The Population Problem," London, 1921.

create problems. The beneficence of a high birth rate was questioned. Exhortations to replenish the earth lost some of their appeal.

Under these conditions the economists developed three fundamental and closely related dogmas. One was the law of diminishing returns, as applied to land, a statement of the physical limitations of the earth. No given area of land can produce an indefinitely large amount of food per capita even with the application of additional amounts of labor and capital. If an acre has been cultivated very superficially, extra attention, more labor and capital, may perhaps give a return more than proportionate to the additional outlay. But there is somewhere a limit. Assuming no improvement in method, a point will in time be reached where extra units of labor and capital will give less than proportionate returns.

From this clear limitation there are three possible forms of relief. One is to improve methods, advance the arts, find ways by which each unit of effort and expense can be applied more effectively and bring a larger return. A second is to put under cultivation larger areas of land. A third is to limit the growth of population.

A second theory advanced was the Malthusian explanation of population growth. Everywhere in the plant and animal world is found the tendency to multiply. Increase of numbers is so rapid as to be effectively pictured by the use of a geometric rate of increase, *i.e.*, such a series as 2, 4, 8, 16, 32, 64, etc., or 4, 16, 64, 256, 1,024, 4,096, etc. Among human beings this results in a tendency to increase at a rate that varies from one country to another and from time to time. Combined with the law of diminishing returns which explains food supply as limited, increasing more nearly as does an arithmetic series, *e.g.*, 2, 4, 6, 8, 10, 12, etc., the outlook is clearly discouraging. In the absence

[9]

of relief, population will outrun food supply or tend to do so. Positive checks such as disease, famine, and war will destroy men and women already born, or negative checks such as delayed marriage, sexual continence, and birth control must and will appear.

From these two theories there followed a third, the iron law of wages. Large numbers of people struggling against the niggardliness of nature can have only a limited and perhaps declining amount of wealth and income per capita. If anything temporarily increases the output per person and permits higher wages, the tendency to multiply numbers soon reduces the gain. A larger population appears among whom the increased output is divided and the per capita amount is no greater than before. Wages are constantly forced down to the level of subsistence.

These three dogmas were disheartening. The outlook they brought was a black one, discouraging not only to Carlyle, whose dictum regarding the "dismal science" of economics is familiar, but also to everyone else. The facts seemed to coincide with theory, and real progress appeared impossible. John Stuart Mill felt in 1848 that "it is questionable if all the mechanical inventions yet made have lightened the day's toil of any human being." Engels' account in "The Condition of the Working Class in England in 1844" is appalling. Macaulay, Carlyle, Ruskin, Toynbee, and Booth have given pictures of the general poverty that are among the literary classics, and countless later writers such as the Hammonds have made abundantly clear the low standards of living and the distress in town and country alike.

But with the passage of decades conditions altered. Industrialization concentrated millions into the cities where they worked raw materials into finished goods. To an increasing degree these materials came from the far corners of the earth and the resulting manufactures were sold over an equally wide area. In western Europe, and to a lesser extent elsewhere, numbers grew but were maintained, and even at rising standards. Their food was imported from the less densely populated regions—from the Americas, from Australia, and from Russia. It was paid for out of the profits of manufacturing.

As these newer areas were brought under cultivation and yielded their huge supplies of food to the old world the economists turned their attention to other matters. Population no longer seemed redundant and for many years the Malthusian theory and the law of diminishing returns were a part of formal economic doctrine, but little more. The "iron law" of wages was displaced by other wage theories. The burning issues of this succeeding period were of a different kind. Heated controversies raged over the distribution of the economic output between the productive factors rather than over the inadequacy of the amount available for division or the large numbers among whom it was distributed.

But since the end of the war in 1918 another change has come. Once more the growth of human beings is engaging attention. In prewar days so-called "Neo-Malthusianism" was active but the discussions were mild compared with the present agitation.

This revival of interest is not surprising. In any case it was bound to come but the dislocations of the war hastened it. Although strain was to be observed before 1914, the world economic machine continued to function. That the United States had reached the point where food imports about equalled food exports was noticed by only a few. Russia was not a dependable source of wheat supply for western Europe, though not many realized it. Demand for certain raw materials was growing more rapidly than

[11]

the available supplies, but only on infrequent occasions was this brought vividly to public attention. Distress in Lancashire during the American Civil War reminded the British of their dependence on a commodity whose supply was beyond their control, but this was the unusual rather than the ordinary. Other exceptions may, of course, be found, but for the most part the raw materials used in manufacturing seemed to appear as needed.

Strain was showing itself more clearly in the struggle for markets, the rivalry of financiers, the scramble for concessions, the partition of Africa and of a part of Asia. How much of this movement after 1870 is to be explained in economic rather than in political terms is debatable, and for the most part an argument would be futile. Politics and economics are closely related, and many of the problems faced by the statesmen have an economic origin.

Tendencies well under way were hastened by the World War. For a time they were hidden or only slightly in evidence because of universal absorption in the conflict, a condition that was generally maintained until the collapse of 1920. Up to that time inflation continued and with the rise of prices concern was felt over supplies of raw materials. An agitation for a continuance of the war control of food products, oil, and important commodities was started but it proved futile. Investigations were begun,[1] but since the business crisis of 1920 and 1921 public interest has shifted to the question of markets, where it still (1930) remains. For a time supplies of food and raw materials

---

[1] Note, for example, that by Prof. Corrado Gini made for the League of Nations appearing in 1921 under the title *A Report on the Problem of Raw Materials and Food-stuffs.* Another highly valuable study is Raw Materials and Foodstuffs in the Commercial Policies of Nations, by William S. Culbertson, published March, 1924, in The *Annals of the American Academy of Political and Social Science.*

seem more than ample. At a later date raw materials will again be discussed but at present manufacturers do not know where to sell their output. Millions of workers are in a precarious position even when they are not entirely out of work.

As a result there is a keen interest in the whole population issue. Is population becoming too large? By what standards shall we determine the desirable number of human beings? How many people can be supplied with a suitable amount and kind of food and how soon will that maximum be reached in view of the present rate of growth? One of the most recent evidences of the importance of the subject was the World Population Conference held at Geneva in 1927 and the permanent organization brought into existence at that time for the scientific study of the complicated issues involved.

With the larger question of world population and food supply this volume is not directly concerned. Readers are referred to the extensive literature—to Haldane, Carr-Saunders, Raymond Pearl, Harold Wright, J. Russell Smith, E. M. East, to the *Proceedings* of the World Population Conference. The issue they raise is highly important but there are others to which our attention will be given. Even if we believe that our earth can care for any number probable in the next 500 years, that belief rests on a highly important assumption—namely, that business can be kept functioning smoothly. That raw materials and foodstuffs must be kept freely moving from the country into the cities and from the great agricultural regions to the industrialized areas is clear. That manufactured goods must similarly make their way freely to markets is no less certain. If these conditions cannot be met, then even the present numbers are too large in many areas to be maintained under present standards of living.

To put it differently, we shall not discuss the number of people that can be maintained by the world's resources. There is not one saturation point for population, but several. The maximum numbers may perhaps be those who can be kept alive; or the numbers that can be kept in a determined condition of physical or mental effectiveness; or the numbers that can be maintained at a "subsistence" standard or a "living" standard or a "comfort" standard. It may be the numbers that combined with the existing volume of natural resources and the available supply of capital will produce the largest economic output in the aggregate; or perhaps the largest output per capita. It may be the numbers that can be maintained in accordance with standards set by one or another group of eugenists. And any one of these limits is subject to alteration as we improve the arts of cultivation, as we harness better the forces of nature, as our standards alter, as our ideas of decency and comfort change.

But no matter what standard we choose one assumption will be found to underlie it. Life is organized. Labor is specialized and its products are exchanged. The ability to acquire and to maintain any agreed standard is dependent on the continued free operation of business processes. As large numbers of people concentrate in given areas they become dependent and their dependence is roughly related to their numbers per square mile. The law of diminishing returns is a fact. In many areas no extra application of effort can maintain the output of the soil at a given per capita amount as population increases. City dwellers must get their food from outside their borders, giving their own attention to manufacturing and trade. Raw materials, too, must come from elsewhere, while the products of city toil must be sold in external markets and at a profit out of which food may be bought.

[14]

What is so obviously true of a city has in modern times become true of great areas. Great Britain is one outstanding illustration of dependence and Belgium is another, although there is no section of our globe that is not today dependent on nearly all others. It is most vivid, perhaps, in the case of cities, but the agricultural areas also are dependent. It is from the industrial sections that they must secure the manufactured articles which they need and, under modern conditions, much even of their food. Grain is not consumed in its natural state on the farm but is sent to the cities to be ground into flour and perhaps even changed to bread or boxed cereals for return to the farm. To grain may be added nearly all the other raw materials of food and clothing which are not transformed on the farm but are often sent many miles, perhaps even overseas, for manufacture to be distributed later over a wide area in a form ready for consumption.

This fact of interdependence is so well-known that any statement of it seems trite. In these postwar days it is a common theme. But what is not realized fully is the extreme difficulty of distribution and of organization which it creates. There is a general appreciation of the dependence of one part of the world upon the rest and of the importance of international cooperation and goodwill. But there is an almost universal failure to understand the difficulties that must be faced in maintaining the free functioning of business. That friction exists is understood and that something ought to be done about it is realized. And, as usual, panaceas are much to the front. Universal peace, possibly effective through a multilateral declaration against war, seems adequate to some. Others rely on the League of Nations or a World Court (including, of course, the adherence of the United States). Another group contend for the lowering of tariff barriers, believing that more

[15]

complete freedom of trade will furnish the solution. Socialism, single tax, prohibition, and other proposals all have their devotees; while many, even in high places, fall back in rather obvious despair, on the assertion that all we need is a different outlook, more idealism, more good-will, a revival of religion, the spread of the gospel of Christ.

Each of these proposed remedies is difficult, and some are almost impossible of application. But unfortunately no one of them nor even all combined would be adequate. Each conceives the problem as more simple than it really is. None appreciates its complexity. Most of the remedies, if not all of them, are admirable in themselves, and the writer advocates the adoption of a number in the list, as well as of several others.

At the beginning of the second quarter of the twentieth century the disorganization that prevailed from 1914 to 1924 has been partially overcome and the larger features of the world problem are beginning to appear more clearly. The remainder of this chapter will sketch it in broad outline. There are two main aspects. One is the number of people, their locations, their occupations, and their needs, or rather their desires. The other is the earth with its resources from which human desires must be met.

It is well to repeat that many of the current difficulties have been developing for decades. Some have arisen directly from the World War but most of them are far more deep-seated. The conflict disorganized for a time the functioning of the world's economic machinery and in so doing has brought to our attention difficulties that in any case would soon have become apparent. A realization of this is important if the situation is to be faced with a proper perspective.

One outstanding fact regarding population is that the trend discussed by Malthus has been very pronounced during the last century. The number of people in the world

today is perhaps 1,948,000,000 as contrasted with 600,000,-
000 or 700,000,000 in 1800. In Europe numbers have
perhaps trebled. For particular countries the gains vary
and it is to be remembered that for none is statistical
knowledge very exact. In all of them there is an increase
during the period covered. Even in France there is a gain,
though a slow one, the slight growth being due not so
much to a low birth rate as to a high death rate among
infants. The particularly rapid gain in the United States
is, of course, due to "immigration from abroad as well
as from heaven," to quote one writer's way of expressing it.

Even since 1913 there has been growth. For the world as a
whole the estimated population was 1,786,826,000 in 1913
and by 1927 was 1,948,526,000, a gain of 9 per cent. Even
for Europe (including Asiatic Russia) the numbers for
the two years were 487,179,000 and 520,164,000, showing
a gain of 6.7 per cent. If Russia is excluded there is a gain
of 6.4 per cent, or from 347,479,000 to 369,664,000. Even
the slaughter of the war only slightly retarded the growth.

Available knowledge of birth rates and death rates,
moreover, confirms the other data. Everywhere the former
exceed the latter with consequent gains in numbers. A
glance at the accompanying table makes this clear. In it
19 countries are listed, the order being that of the excess
of births over deaths in 1927. Japan leads with a gain of
15.2 per 1,000, followed by Poland and Canada. Last in
the list is France with a gain of 1.6 per 1,000. The United
States is ninth with 8.4 per 1,000 in 1926.

A number of interesting facts can be gleaned from a study
of this table. For example, in the period 1905 to 1909
France had the lowest birth rate among the countries
listed, *i.e.*, 20.1 per 1,000. Even in 1921 to 1925 there was
only one country, *i.e.*, Sweden, that had a lower rate,
although Switzerland was close. But in 1927 Sweden,

[17]

England and Wales, and Switzerland had lower rates, while Belgium, Denmark, Germany, and Norway were almost as low.

Births, Deaths, and Annual Increases of Population per 1,000 Inhabitants for Certain Countries

Country	Average birth rate			Average death rate			Excess of births		
	1905–1909	1921–1925	1927	1905–1909	1921–1925	1927	1905–1909	1921–1925	1927
Japan..................	31.9	34.6	35.0	20.9	31.8	19.8	11.0	12.8	15.2
Poland.................	....	34.7	31.6	....	18.5	17.4	....	16.2	14.2
Canada................	....	27.1	24.6	....	11.1	11.1	....	18.0	13.5
Netherlands............	30.0	25.7	23.1	14.7	10.4	10.3	15.3	15.3	12.8
Bulgaria..............	42.5	39.0	32.9	23.5	20.8	20.2	19.0	18.2	12.7
Roumania..............	40.1	36.6	34.1	25.9	22.2	22.2	14.2	14.4	11.9
Italy..................	32.6	29.2	26.9	21.7	17.0	15.7	10.9	12.2	11.2
Spain.................	33.7	30.1	28.6	24.5	20.4	18.9	9.2	9.7	9.7
United States..........	....	22.6	20.6[1]	15.4	11.9	12.2[1]	....	10.7	8.4[1]
Denmark..............	28.4	22.2	19.5	14.1	11.3	11.5	14.3	10.9	8.0
Hungary..............	36.3	29.4	25.2	25.7	19.9	17.6	10.6	9.5	7.6
Czechoslovakia.........	33.0	27.0	23.3	24.1	16.2	16.0	8.9	10.8	7.3
Norway...............	26.7	22.0	18.2	14.1	11.5	11.0	12.6	10.5	7.2
Germany..............	32.3	22.1	18.3	18.3	13.3	12.0	14.0	8.8	6.3
Switzerland............	26.4	19.4	17.4	16.5	12.4	12.3	9.9	7.0	5.1
Belgium...............	25.1	20.5	18.3	16.2	13.4	13.5	8.9	7.1	4.8
England and Wales......	26.7	19.9	16.6	15.1	12.2	12.3	11.6	7.7	4.3
Sweden................	25.6	19.1	16.1	14.6	12.0	12.7	11.0	7.1	3.4
France................	20.1	19.3	18.1	19.5	17.3	16.5	0.6	2.0	1.6

[1] For 1926. The 1927 figures are provisional only for France, Germany, and Hungary.

Relative death rates are also of interest. Again comparing the others with France, since the slow increase of population in France is so often discussed and deplored, it will be noticed that in 1927 the French death rate of 16.5 was exceeded only by the death rates of Bulgaria, Hungary, Japan, Poland, Roumania, and Spain. Italy had a death rate of only 15.7, while the Netherlands with a rate of 10.3 was the lowest on the list.

Caution should, of course, be used in interpreting this table. It shows clearly a decline in birth rates, although to this general tendency Japan is an exception. There is also a downward trend of death rates, though this decline is clearly being retarded in countries like the Netherlands, Norway, Germany, and England whose death rates were already low and where the age distribution of the population complicates the interpretation.

This point should not be overlooked. It is easy to assume that as long as birth rates are higher than death rates this excess demonstrates a growing population. But Dr. Kuczynski has pointed out the incompleteness of such reasoning.[1] In his study of population tendencies, only a part of which has been published, he says:

> If each woman has two children who become parents in their turn, the population will hold its own. If she has three such children, the population will increase by one-half within one generation. If she has less than two such children, the population will sooner or later decrease. With a fertility and a mortality as they prevailed forty or fifty years ago, the population then would have increased by about one-half per generation in all countries of western and northern Europe with the exception of France and Ireland, where the population about held its own. With a fertility and a mortality as they prevail at present, the population of some smaller countries still shows a genuine growth, but the population of the larger countries, France, and especially England and Germany, is doomed to die out.

It will be noticed that Dr. Kuczynski's final conclusion is carefully stated. It applies only to a limited number of countries and is true only if birth rates hold at their current level. But even if these low birth rates are maintained in the few countries where they now prevail, the area with

[1] Kuczynski, Robert R., "The Balance of Births and Deaths," vol. I (Western and Northern Europe), p. 4, New York, 1928.

[19]

higher rates is the larger part of the world. Moreover, even though the decline in population comes at the rate suggested by his data, the reduction will be a gradual one. Numbers will be great for decades to come.

Next to be noticed are certain human characteristics. Just how many persons can subsist on a square mile of land of a given fertility is not easy to say. Everything depends on the standards of living, and standards differ widely. As already pointed out, there is no single saturation point for the world and there is none for a given country. The average Italian seems contented with less than the amount insisted upon by an Englishman or by an American but would doubtless protest against living on the sum available to a Spaniard or to a Japanese.

And whatever standards may exist at a given time and place are not permanent. Human wants are indefinitely expansible. Only a slight amount is essential to bare existence. But luxuries quickly become comforts and soon comforts are necessities. There are subsistence standards, living standards, decency standards, comfort standards, Asiatic standards, European standards, American standards. A necessity can be defined only as any article to whose use one has become accustomed and which he will surrender with great reluctance.

This last point is an important one. Whatever standard has been attained will be retained if possible. And the higher the level the more effort will be made to maintain and to raise it. Attention will later be drawn to the fact that the world strain of recent years is not between countries whose people have the lowest incomes but just the reverse. It is the high-income countries that are the leaders in the modern struggle for supremacy. The present contest is largely though not entirely among the peoples of the United States and western Europe.

[20]

As the years have passed, the old iron law of wages has become thoroughly discredited. Wages clearly have risen. But this does not carry with it a denial of the law of diminishing returns. That law is a physical fact—a commonplace to every farmer, since he does not dream of concentrating all his labor and tools on a single acre but distributes them over the farm.

It must be remembered that this law is just as true for fertile as for impoverished soil. It has nothing to do with soil butchering, which occurs through a period of time. The law of diminishing returns applies to the potentialities of any land at any time. If a given region is so fertile that there is no occasion to cultivate it intensively the law is not a matter of immediate concern. Given enough people, the law is a grim limiting factor.

Then, too, its significance (not its truth) is altered by the changes in human knowledge and in methods of using the land. The art of rotating crops, irrigation, better choice of seeds and improved cultivation do not literally make soil more fertile but they do increase its effective productivity.

As the years pass, these changes in the arts are appearing more and more rapidly. There has come, too, an amazing growth in the supply of capital, in human ability to organize effectively, in all of the factors of production. And with these gains the power of man over nature has grown. Each year adds to the victories of humanity in its struggle against the niggardliness of nature.

To return to an earlier statement, the question is not one of the capacity of the earth to support a given total population. Presumably there is somewhere a limit, but we shall concern ourselves instead with the attempts of human beings to maintain or to raise their present standards and with the difficulties they are facing in their endeavor to do so.

[21]

Chapter III

HOW POPULATION PRESSURE APPEARS

WH N difficulty is experienced by any people in the maintenance of their standards, relief can be found either (1) through an improvement in economic methods or (2) in a shift in consumption, *e.g.*, from beef to pork or from wheat to potatoes, or (3) in a change in the nature of their economic activity, *e.g.*, from agriculture to manufacturing, or (4) by emigrating to another area where conditions are more favorable. Or, if the trouble is due to a temporary dislocation—to a stoppage in the free flow of commodities and services on which standards depend—relief may be found (5) by removing, if possible, the causes of friction in order that freedom of contact may again be resumed.

Economic strain is occasionally evidenced in a spectacular manner, perhaps by a breakdown such as occurred in the Ruhr district of Germany in 1924 or by many actual deaths from starvation as in the Russian famine of 1921. More often the strain, though real, is less obvious to the naked eye. It may come gradually and almost imperceptibly, the results being small economies, delayed marriages, crowded housing, a slightly higher death rate. In these days of statistical evidence it is often vividly revealed by reduced figures for bank clearings and freight-car loadings, a smaller volume of trade, more unemployment, and more business failures.

It is the purpose of this chapter (1) to elaborate on the growth of population in many parts of the world and to

[22]

indicate its density in certain countries and regions, (2) to observe the relief that has in the past been secured by emigration from the congested areas, (3) to note the current reaction against this movement, particularly in certain immigrant countries, and (4) to stress the extent and the nature of the dependence of certain countries on the rest of the world.

In 1800 there were probably 600,000,000 or 700,000,000 people in the world. Today the number is perhaps 1,800,-000,000 or 1,900,000,000. One hundred years ago so much of an increase would not have been thought possible. At that time the standards of living were low in Europe. The pressure of numbers was felt and in the judgment of many there was already serious overpopulation. Yet there are far more people in Europe today than there were then.

This again emphasizes our contention that there is no fixed number of people that saturate a country. The small population of the United Kingdom in 1825 was more than could be well cared for at that time. In 1913 there were 41,483,000 living on the same islands at a much higher standard, but now a slightly larger number seems too many. At least the reports in 1929 were to the effect that in certain of the coal areas anemia, rickets, and other evidences of malnutrition were increasing.

This world population of nearly 2,000,000,000 is not evenly distributed. There are vast areas in which there are but few people and there are huge cities in which millions are huddled together, entirely dependent on outside sources for all their material supplies and often lacking even air suitable for breathing.

To make comparisons by taking entire countries as the areas to be examined is hardly fair, because the density of population varies so much within each of them. In some parts of China the numbers of people per square mile are among the greatest in the world, yet the average for the entire country is lowered by the fact that some sections are sparsely inhabited.

Because statistics are available chiefly by countries it will be necessary to use them in that form, but we may first speak of great areas regardless of national boundaries. The accompanying map,[1] showing the distribution of world population, reveals three areas where the concentration is greatest: eastern Asia, including Japan and a part of China; India; and Europe. There may, perhaps, be added a section in the eastern part of the United States.

The visual impression received from this map is valuable, but statements in statistical form, though often misleading, are available only by countries and so must be used. Conclusions must be carefully qualified, but even so our impressions of the problem will be more vivid than if we should content ourselves with the map already noticed.

The most noticeable difficulty is the lack of precise knowledge regarding numbers of people. Gross land areas are well known, but census returns for some countries are entirely lacking or, when available, are not always reliable.

In lieu of census returns there are usually intelligent estimates of the population, and for such rough comparisons as we desire to make they are perhaps sufficiently accurate. We may accordingly use them and with the following results: The numbers of persons per square kilometer in 1925 in certain European countries were:[2] France, 74; Switzerland, 95; Italy, 131; Germany, 132; the United Kingdom, 191; Holland, 217; and Belgium, 257. In this list France is lowest and Belgium is highest. In Asia the

---

[1] Taken from "Commerce Yearbook, 1926," vol. II.

[2] Square kilometers are used rather than square miles, since the figures given in succeeding paragraphs are from reports issued by the League of Nations and are given only in square kilometers.

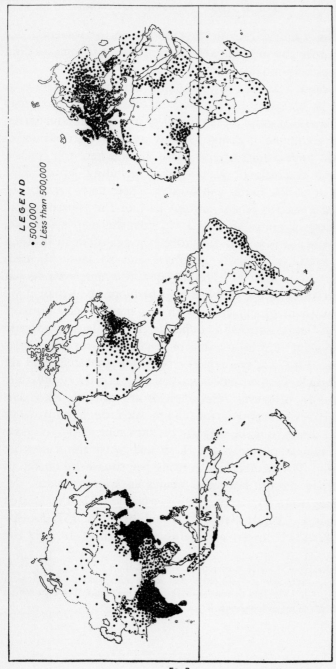

LEGEND
• 500,000
○ Less than 500,000

Fig. 1.—Distribution of world population. (*Commerce year book, Vol. II, 1926.*)

British provinces of India had a population density of 89 per square kilometer, and Japan had 154. The figure for the British provinces of India was lower than that for all of the European countries except France, and that for Japan was smaller than those for the United Kingdom, Holland, and Belgium. The United States had a population density of only 15 per square kilometer.

But such a comparison, while the simplest, is not very he pful and may even be misleading. Thus, Japan is a country with many mountains. Much of Japan is not cultivable or in any other way productive, and the number of people in that country as compared with the land from which a living can be secured is much greater than the 89 per square kilometer just given. Accordingly, we should make the proper allowances, but in practice this is not easy. What should be the basis of comparison? Perhaps it should be the area of arable land. If so, estimates of this are available and seem to be fairly reliable. But there are some disadvantages in using merely arable land, since timber lands, pasture lands, etc., should doubtless be included. Or, still better, we should, if possible, allow for productive land of all kinds including mines, water-power sites, and all other areas from which a living can be secured. But definitions of "productive" either are lacking or else vary widely, and comparisons are, therefore, misleading and perhaps mischievous.

Nevertheless, other figures than the crude ones just quoted should be given. Population density per square kilometer of arable land in 1925 was, for France, 178; for Germany, 305; for Italy, 307; for Belgium, 640; for Switzerland, 772; for the United Kingdom, 800; for Holland, 802. The British provinces of India had 205 persons per square kilometer of arable land, and Japan had 993, with the United States only 85.

[26]

The numbers per square kilometer of agricultural land show, of course, fewer persons per square kilometer, since the area of agricultural land is larger than that of the arable land. In Europe they are: for France, 112; for Switzerland, 171; for Italy, 188; for Germany, 215; for the United Kingdom, 242; for Holland, 327; and for Belgium, 435.

Estimates of density per square kilometer of productive area are not available for many countries and, for the reasons already given, are not very helpful. A few of them may be quoted, however, from the *Memorandum on Population and Natural Resources* prepared for the World Economci Conference at Geneva in 1927 and from which our other population figures have also been taken. In Europe the estimates for 1925 are: for France,79; for Switzerland, 123; for Italy, 143; and for Holland, 251. For the British provinces of India the numbers are 122 and for Japan, 199. There are no estimates furnished for Belgium, Germany, the United Kingdom, and the United States.

No hasty conclusions should be drawn from any of these figures. It must be remembered that many of them are confessedly nothing but estimates and that the bases employed are not in all cases the same. They cannot, moreover, possibly inform us with any precision on the matter that is really interesting, *i.e.*, How serious is the pressure of living conditions in these different areas, what world problems does this pressure create, and what solutions should be applied?

Thus, a population density of 89 per square kilometer of superficial area for the British provinces of India tells nothing of living conditions, and the figures of 205 for arable land and 122 for productive land tell little more. The intelligence and education of the people are almost as important as the fertility of the soil and the richness

[27]

of mineral deposits. The degree to which transportation has been developed and to which modern methods of cultivation are employed are important, and so, also, is the extent to which the population relies on manufacturing, as do the people of England and Belgium.

Then, too, arable land, timber land, pasture land, and mineral deposits vary widely in fertility or in richness. There is a vast difference between the fertile lands in the river bottoms of the Danube and of the Mississippi and the made land on many of the mountain sides of Italy—yet both are arable. There is likewise a difference between the coal deposits in some of the British areas which are a mile below the surface and the more accessible deposits in the Ruhr and in many parts of the United States or even in China.

In each of the groupings used, one fact stands out. There are two main areas of very acute congestion—one in Asia and one in Europe. They are alike and yet they are a contrast. In each there are large numbers per square kilometer, but in Asia standards of living are low. Poverty, distress, and squalor abound in India and in China and to a somewhat lesser degree in Japan. In Europe there is an abundance of poverty, especially at certain times and in particular places, yet the standards of living are much higher.

Comparisons are not easily made, but there have been studies attempting to state per capita incomes for some countries. Only a few seem sufficiently reliable for our use. One of them was by Sir Josiah Stamp of England and appeared in the *Journal of the Royal Statistical Society* for March, 1919. He presented his findings cautiously because of the difficulties in such an inquiry and because of the great opportunity for inaccuracy in drawing conclusions. His estimates were used by the National Bureau of Economic Research of New York and presented by them in an adapted form which is the one we shall employ. The method used is first to ascertain the probable total national income for each of the countries concerned and then to divide that amount by the population of the country. It is to be remembered that even population is often only a rough estimate and the determination of national income with precision is quite impossible. The figures presented, therefore, must be accepted by us with the same reserve and caution displayed by Sir Josiah Stamp and by the National Bureau of Economic Research.

Estimated Income of Various Countries at the Outbreak of the War in 1914[1]

Country	Approximate accuracy, within	Income	
		Total, billions of dollars	Per capita
United States....................	10 per cent	33,300	$335
United Kingdom.................	10 per cent	10,950	243
Germany........................	10 per cent	10,460	146
France..........................	20 per cent	7,300	185
Italy...........................	40 per cent	3,890	112
Austria-Hungary.................	40 per cent	5,350	102
Spain...........................	40 per cent	1,120	54
Australia........................	10 per cent	1,260	263
Canada.........................	40 per cent	1,460	195
Japan...........................	30 per cent	1,580	29

[1] Adapted by the National Bureau of Economic Research from a study by Sir Josiah Stamp in the *Journal of the Royal Statistical Society*, March, 1919.

It will be noticed that these estimates give the highest per capita income to countries with a low population density. The figure for the United States is $335 per capita, and for Australia $263 per capita. The European countries in order are the United Kingdom, $243; France,

$185; Germany, $146; Italy, $112; Austria-Hungary, $102; and Spain, $54. The only Asiatic country is Japan the estimate for which is $29 per capita.

It will be remembered that these are only estimates and are for the days just before the World War when price levels were lower than those of today. A later and less comprehensive study by Professor Seligman of Columbia University for the year 1918 to 1919 gives $635 for the United States, $403 for the United Kingdom, $256 for Germany, and $247 for France. The amounts are larger in each case, but the relative positions of the countries are much the same.

These comparisons are necessarily crude but seem ample warrant for the conclusion that we may divide the inhabitants of densely populated areas into two groups. First, there are those who have as yet developed only a moderate amount of dependence on other countries. There is some dependence but, comparatively speaking, only a little. Food and raw materials are found largely at home, and the urge to market products abroad is only slight. Pressure on the home soil is serious, the law of diminishing returns is an important fact, and the average income is low. A crop failure or a flood means quick death for thousands or even millions unless relief can be quickly secured from outside sources.

The second group is located chiefly in western Europe. Larger incomes are found, a higher standard of living— in most cases a much higher one. But this has not been secured by the use of domestic food supplies or domestic raw materials, especially in those countries whose standards are highest. In part, local food and raw materials are drawn upon, but to an important degree outside sources are utilized and the products that are manufactured must find foreign markets. This has made possible a higher

[30]

standard of living but it has also created a condition of extreme dependence.

One economist, Dr. B. M. Anderson, Jr., of New York, has estimated that even in prewar days some 38 per cent of French trade, about 54 per cent of German trade, and 62 per cent of British trade was foreign. We might add that the English people import from one-half to two-thirds of the food they consume and the Germans some 20 per cent, in which is found about one-half of their fats.

This arrangement has permitted a large fraction of the population to dwell in cities and give their attention to manufacturing and commerce rather than to agriculture, fishing, and the extractive industries. Incomes have been higher and crop failures and floods do not mean such havoc as in Asia. Supplies are regularly drawn from all parts of the globe and a shortage in one region is apt to be offset by an abundance from some other source. There is consequently a greater stability.

Yet there is another kind of uncertainty. In war especially there is danger that food from the outside may be cut off. Raw materials must be imported from sources that may be inaccessible in time of war or pass under unfriendly control even in peace. Markets may be disturbed by hostile tariffs, by boycotts, by economic crises and by other influences. Or a difficulty may appear of the kind faced by England today. A period of leadership and remarkable growth lasting through decades may be followed by one of serious decline through the rapid development of the strength of other countries.

Nineteenth century Europe cared for its growing numbers in three main ways. First, by industrialization, which meant a dependence as described and was possible on a grand scale only because there were great undeveloped areas from which food could come. Second, by a modification of habits that made possible the maintenance of good living standards on a limited area of land. Illustrations are found in the use of pork instead of beef and of potatoes instead of corn and wheat. The Germans found that pork and potatoes gave good nourishment and called for a smaller area for their production than did beef and wheat.

The third method by which relief was secured was emigration. During the nineteenth century the outward movement was a strong one. W. G. Sundbörg, a Swedish investigator, has estimated that from 1816 to 1910 there was a total overseas emigration from Europe that aggregated 41,814,000. From 1881 to 1890 the annual average of emigration from 13 leading European countries was 648,383; from 1891 to 1900 it was 537,218; from 1901 to 1910 it increased to 998,756; and from 1911 to 1913 the annual average was 1,368,367.

For Europe as a whole with its nearly 450,000,000 of inhabitants even this last figure—1,368,367—is not large, being less than one-third of one per cent per annum. This is so small a fraction of the total that the relief given to crowding seems slight.

But while the emigration was small when compared with the population of all Europe it was not so unimportant for particular countries. Toward the end of the prewar period there were 408,550 persons less each year to be fed in Italy, nearly 400,000 less in England, nearly 250,000 less in Austria-Hungary, and over 160,000 less in Spain. For these countries the relief was appreciable.

This movement may be contrasted with that from the Far East. The Japanese emigrated in considerable numbers to the mainland of Asia and in a few other directions. The Chinese, too, found some outlets, but, generally speaking, overseas emigration gave less relief to the Oriental peoples than to Europeans. The reasons are well known. Hostility in the immigrant countries, expressing itself in prohibitive legislation, was the chief barrier.

But in recent years even the European movement has been retarded. During the war it was, of course, checked but shortly after the end of the conflict the outward flow again started. Conditions in Europe were, of course, bad, and there were reasons for believing that the exodus might be a larger one, perhaps unprecedented in volume. In the United States particularly great alarm was felt lest the numbers should become greater than ever before, and there developed rapidly an insistence that restrictions should be imposed.

Some years ago an American author, Herbert Quick, wrote an interesting little volume entitled "The Good Ship Earth." In it he described our planet as a ship sailing through space from an unknown origin to an unknown destination, carrying as its passengers hundreds of millions of persons whose numbers rapidly increase. Sustenance for these passengers is necessary, and on the decks of the ship there grows a peculiar green rash—vegetation—on which they subsist. This rash is more abundant on some parts of the deck than on others, especially as compared with the number of people in each section. Because of its vital necessity, since life cannot be maintained without it, there is an intense rivalry for its possession. The passengers push and crowd, surging back and forth, at times even fighting to the death.

This allegory is vivid. Throughout all known and doubtless throughout all unknown time, peoples have migrated in search of food. But in modern times the direction and the volume and in many ways the nature of the movement have changed. There is a particularly striking difference due to the complexities of modern life. The standard of living today cannot be expressed merely through the supply of food. It is a complex of food, of clothing, of shelter, of transportation, of illumination, of recreation, and many other groups. It is a highly intricate blend of necessities, comforts, and luxuries.

As a consequence, migration occurs for the purpose of maintaining or of raising this complex standard. An emigrant does not leave his native land because of his difficulty in securing food in particular but because he believes that he can in the new environment secure a monetary income that will permit a higher standard. As conditions seem better elsewhere, he moves.

In the postwar period European overseas emigration was resumed but not on the prewar scale. In spite of the reports of millions ready to leave, the movement proved to be less than was expected. This was due to a variety of reasons. To start with, there had been an exaggeration in the stories that were circulated, the sort of exaggeration to be expected under such circumstances. Then, too, the mere desire to emigrate is not enough in itself. A voyage overseas is expensive and cannot be undertaken merely because of one's desire for it. Rather does it illustrate the real nature of what the economist calls "demand." Demand is made up of desire plus purchasing power. Emigrants must have passage money and an additional amount as a margin for temporary support in their new location.

More important, however, in checking the movement was the official attitude in both emigrant and immigrant countries. An illustration is the policy of the Italian government. It is understood that that government desires to retain to a high degree the allegiance of its citizens, an allegiance that is weakened or lost by residence overseas.

[34]

Also, there is a contention that Italy needs a larger population, an increase being desired in the next few decades from the present 40,000,000 to 60,000,000—a gain of 50 per cent. Emigration from Italy, while not absolutely forbidden, is at the best merely tolerated. Outside observers of Italy have not found it entirely easy to pass judgment on this policy. The population per square kilometer is about 131 for the total area and about 307 for the arable area. Besides, the soil is for the most part not very fertile and natural resources are scarce. There seems, in fact, to be considerable warrant for Mussolini's reminder that Italy must "expand or explode." The policy of discouraging emigration and of encouraging larger families, if viewed merely as an economic matter, is not easily reconciled with the fact of existing congestion. Perhaps the reconciliation is to be found in the political realm and hence in matters entirely outside the field of this book.

Another check on European emigration has come from the changed attitude of the immigrant countries. Some of them have for decades shown a tendency to debar Orientals. Their attitude has perhaps been due in a slight degree to racial prejudice but is probably due far more to economic considerations. In the United States, in Canada, and in Australia there has been a feeling that the living standards of the Orientals are low and that by accepting employment at meager pay they would depress the standards of American, Canadian, and Australian workers. Consequently, the barriers to Oriental immigrants have been raised higher and higher to the point of virtual exclusion.

Also, there has been for many years a tendency to scrutinize more and more closely the immigrants from other parts of the world—which means Europe in particular. Literacy tests, economic tests, and moral tests have been applied with increasing rigidity. Attempts were made even in such undeveloped areas as Canada and Australia to get settlers who were suited to local conditions. Even where immigration was in general encouraged there was an attempt to pick the newcomers.

But after the war the United States in particular imposed rigid restrictions. The barriers had been rising gradually over many years but the stream of immigration had kept increasing. From only 8,400 in 1820 the numbers had grown as the decades passed. They fluctuated chiefly with varying economic conditions in the United States but reached their largest amounts only in the early twentieth century. From 1900 to 1909 the immigrants varied from 448,000 to 1,285,000 per annum, and from 1910 to 1914 they varied from 838,000 to 1,218,000 per annum.

For many years Americans had spoken proudly of their country as the "refuge of the oppressed," and Israel Zangwill had designated it as the "melting pot" for the mixed groups who came from all parts of the world. But doubts regarding the policy of unrestricted immigration began to grow and during the war and early postwar years were expressed with more and more emphasis. The war had brought to public attention a series of facts that to many were very disquieting. Examinations of recruits drafted for the army showed an alarming number not only of physical but also of mental defects. Large numbers could not read or write. Many could speak only the languages of the countries of their birth. There was a lack of familiarity with American institutions and ideals.

The significance of these facts was exaggerated and distorted by many Americans, particularly by certain superpatriots who are as much of a nuisance and even a menace in the United States as their counterparts are in other lands. To other influences this group added the "Nordic myth" for which there is no adequate scientific support. Certain writers, among them Madison Grant, Lothrop Stoddard, and Albert Wiggam, became concerned over the "Passing of the Great Race," as it was called by Mr. Grant, and the "Rising Tide of Color," as it was styled by Mr. Stoddard. Such views were readily accepted and widely repeated.

Their application to the problem of immigration restriction was possible because there had been a pronounced change in the origin of the American immigrants. In earlier years the larger numbers had come from northern and western Europe, in more recent years from the southern and eastern countries. A tabulation of this change shows what had occurred.

Percentage of Immigrants by Countries of Origin by Decades[1]

Country	1861–1870	1871–1880	1881–1890	1891–1900	1901–1910
Austria-Hungary............................	0.33	2.6	6.7	16.0	24.4
German Empire............................	35.00	25.5	28.0	14.0	3.9
Italy, Sicily, Sardinia.....................	0.51	2.0	5.9	18.0	23.3
Russia Empire and Finland...............	0.20	1.9	4.4	14.0	18.2
United Kingdom...........................	38.00				
England...................................	....	15.6	12.0	6.0	4.4
Ireland....................................	....	15.5	12.0	10.0	3.9

[1] Taken from FAIRCHILD, H. P. Immigrations, revised edition p. 135, 1925

There should be added also the influence of organized labor which was anxious to limit the entrance of newcomers who would help to keep down the wage level. Many immigrants accustomed to the lower real wages as well as to the lower money wages of their home countries would readily accept employment for less pay than the American-born worker desired to take. Then, too, every addition to the numbers available for employment tended to lower wages.

The barriers were raised by the Act of 1921 and then still higher by the Act of 1924, which limited the annual

[37]

quota of immigrants of any nationality to two per cent
of the number of foreign-born individuals of such nationality resident in the continental United States as determined
by the United States census of 1890. The numbers admitted
were thus proportioned to the numbers from the different
countries resident in the United States in 1890, that year
being chosen in order to reduce the number who could
come from southern and eastern Europe and raise the
proportion who might enter from northern and western
Europe. Another section of the Act of 1924 provided that
beginning July 1, 1927, the annual quota of any nationality
should be a number which bears the same ratio to 150,000
as the number of inhabitants in the continental United
States in 1920 having that national origin bears to the
number of inhabitants in the continental United States in
1920. This provision was not carried out until 1929 but was
then made effective. It reduces somewhat the total entrants
and readjusts markedly the numbers from certain countries.
There is a sharp reduction in the quotas allowed to Germany, the Irish Free State, and the Scandinavian countries
and a large increase for Great Britain.

Since this chapter is not attempting an analysis of
American immigration, discussion of the present law need
not be continued. We may merely note that this action
by the United States is the most important check that has
occurred to emigration from other parts of the world.
In time, other outlets that already exist will be enlarged,
but the tendency of American legislation is to dam the
flow of considerable numbers whose emigration to the
United States might otherwise give a measure of relief
to their own countries.

A further word ought to be injected in explanation of
the action of the United States. Her restrictions on immigration are not merely arbitrary. Population density in

the countries named is still far less than in Europe and in Asia, but there are difficulties in assimilating and controlling an influx each year so large and heterogeneous. Then, too, the economic situation has altered. An economist would state it for the United States by pointing out that 150 years ago or even 50 years ago that country had a vast area of undeveloped natural resources and a shortage of capital and labor. Both capital and labor have rapidly increased until the resources are more fully utilized. To get the maximum output the importation of additional labor is not needed and American laborers prefer that immigration shall be sharply restrained. At least a rigorous choice will be exercised over both the quantity and the quality. What is perhaps most obvious and significant for the United States is true also of many of the other new countries.

That these restrictions should irritate the older countries is not surprising. For of course the issue is by no means clear. One expression of it has been this. Have the people in the densely populated areas of the world a "right" to go on multiplying in numbers with the expectation that their overflow will be taken by other countries? Some of them have this opinion On the other hand, have those who dwell in the sparsely populated parts of the world any right to oppose the immigration of those so unfortunate as to be born in the more crowded sections? Apparently they believe in such a right, as is shown by the restrictions they have imposed.

But it would be folly to suppose that either group will be convinced by the arguments of the other. In the United States it is contended that immigration is a domestic issue and protest is voiced against its consideration in international gatherings, yet it is highly probable that in a few years the whole question will be under acute discussion in the field of international politics.

And in this discussion the United States will be clearly, though perhaps tactfully, reminded of some of its inconsistencies. For example, Americans are contending for the right to restrict their own natural resources—their land—to use by themselves when after all a large percentage of Americans were born or their parents were born elsewhere, chiefly in Europe. For those whose parents were alien born or those who have just arrived or whose parents immigrated only one or two generations ago suddenly to oppose any further immigration seems strange and not entirely logical to Europeans.

Americans object to the Mexicans placing restrictions on exploitation of their oil by United States citizens, they criticize the Brazilians for valorization of coffee and refuse them financial aid, they contend that the British should not control the supply of rubber under the Stevenson plan. Yet all of these actions by the people of other countries are merely assertions of their right to do as they please with their own resources. They, in turn, oppose American insistence on limiting its density of population and criticise proposals formulated for restricting in the States the output of cotton or of copper and for controlling prices. We may as well admit that the issues are not clear and attempt to prepare our minds for the controversies that are sure to come soon.

In the meantime, America suggests little of real value to the people of the Old World or of the Orient. One possible form of relief or of alleviation would be the restriction of the rate of population growth, the practice of birth control. But Americans are strangely hostile to the idea and as yet the transmission of information regarding contraception is generally illegal in the United States. As far as population growth is concerned, public sentiment still approves gains and deplores losses. Any decline in the birth rate, though it appears in a world possibly becoming overpopulated, is viewed with alarm. In the Far East opposition to birth control propaganda is even greater. In Europe most of the official pronouncements are likewise in favor of growing numbers, even in countries like Italy where the crowding is greatest.

Since the war there has been a smaller emigration from Europe and the trend as yet is a downward one. The stream is partly diverted to other overseas countries than the United States but in part it is being dammed up. Birth rates have been declining but death rates have also been reduced. Population is still growing and will probably continue to increase for some years to come if not indefinitely. With the large numbers per square kilometer in Europe and with its lower living standards there will be continued outward pressure.

But even a restoration of the emigration stream to its old size might not keep the population to its present numbers, to say nothing of reducing it. And as long as people are as numerous in western Europe as they are now they must be dependent on the maintenance of commercial relations with each other and with the rest of the world.

One or two illustrations of this dependence will make the situation vivid. First, we may notice the foreign trade of Belgium and of Germany for two years, 1913 and 1927. In this tabulation of imports and exports there are revealed four important forms of dependence on other countries.

First is the dependence on outside sources for food supply. In 1913 Belgium imported articles of food and drink valued at 1,034,822,000 francs while exporting food and drink worth only 327,663,000 francs. Germany's food and drink imports in the same year amounted to 2,807,829,000 marks as contrasted with similar exports

Foreign Trade of Belgium and Germany 1913 and 1927, by Classes
(000 Omitted)

Classes	Belgium, francs		Germany, marks	
	1913	1927	1913	1927
Imports:				
Live animals...................	65,273	96,317	289,697	177,205
Articles of food and drink......	1,034,822	7,192,365	2,807,829	4,350,425
Materials: raw or partly manufactured.....................	2,667,035	15,125,011	6,279,949	7,148,956
Manufactured articles.........	869,478	6,595,005	1,392,211	2,466,575
Gold and silver: specie and unmanufactured................	413,251	170,839	436,394	238,271
Total imports..............	5,049,859	29,179,537	11,206,080	14,381,432
Exports:				
Live animals...................	44,413	151,434	7,444	11,045
Articles of food and drink.......	327,663	2,114,756	1,069,522	418,843
Materials: raw or partly manufactured.....................	1,826,078	8,973,303	2,274,087	2,239,294
Manufactured articles..........	1,436,430	15,311,472	6,746,181	7,549,528
Gold and silver: specie and unmanufactured................	81,230	69,773	101,372	21,866
Total exports..............	3,715,814	26,620,738	10,198,606	10,240,576

worth only 1,069,522,000 marks. In each case these values are in addition to the trade in live animals where also the value of the imports was greater than that of the exports for each country. For 1927 the same general situation holds with Belgium's excess of imported foods (even after allowance is made for the lowered value of the Belgian franc). Germany's excess of imported foods is somewhat less in the later year but is still heavy.

These figures show a definite dependence on outside sources for food and to an extent greater than the difference between imports and exports, since some of the exported foods are an excess above needs for particular articles and some of the imported articles could not be produced at home at all, or at least not in adequate amounts. Also, they are of such nature that a cessation of their importation would cause real hardship. An illustration is Germany's importation of fats.

Second to be observed is the heavy importation of raw or partly manufactured materials. For Belgium these values were 2,667,035,000 francs in 1913 and 15,125,011,000 francs in 1927. For Germany the corresponding figures are 6,279,949,000 and 7,148,956,000 marks. Again the dependence on outside sources of supply is heavy and again the exports of similar articles do not show any possibility of lessening this dependence, since the exported raw materials are chiefly an excess in certain lines of domestic output. An illustration is coal which is produced in large quantities in both countries.

Third is the heavy reliance of both countries on foreign markets for manufactured products. The figures in the table show vividly the necessity of selling abroad the articles manufactured in part from domestic raw materials but also from imported raw materials. In 1913 the Belgian exports of manufactured goods were worth 1,436,430,000 francs and in 1927 they were valued at 15,311,472,000 francs. For Germany the values were 6,746,181,000 and 7,549,528,000 marks. Imports of this class of goods were large, though smaller than exports, but to a considerable extent are of goods not readily manufactured in the importing country.

Fourth and last to be noted is that for each country the total of imports exceeds the total of exports in each year. Belgium's import excesses were 1,334,045,000 and 2,558,-799,000 francs, while Germany's were 1,007,474,000 and 4,140,856,000 marks. Each year these differences must be met in some manner and are, of course, offset by what are called "invisible items." Among them are the expenditures of foreign tourists in the countries, the earnings of merchant vessels, and interest on the foreign investments of citizens. In case the aggregates of both visibles and invisibles are to the advantage of the country, its creditor position is strengthened. If the balance is the other way, it is an indication of an added indebtedness to the rest of the world.

At this stage of our discussion the point to be emphasized is that the livelihood of 7,932,000 people in Belgium and 63,440,000 in Germany is dependent on the free movement of both visible commodities and the various invisibles. Food, raw materials, and finished products must come and go. But so must tourists whose expenditures are now so important. Merchant vessels must earn freight charges for carrying goods. Bankers and insurance companies must continue in their business of collecting commissions and premiums. Interest payments on foreign investments must be made regularly. And if there is at any time a balance in one direction or the other (and there always is), the difference must be readily met by an extension of credit in some form. If there is friction in any of these intricate business transactions, suffering is sure to occur.

Chapter IV

CLIMATE AND OTHER NATURAL RESOURCES

BEFORE taking the next step, which is to examine the distribution of important natural resources, it may be pointed out that thus far no reference has been made to capitalism or imperialism or socialism or communism or any other ism. In so far as possible, the isms will be avoided, at least in the earlier stages of our analysis. International economic problems, or at least the most important ones, are not due entirely or even basically to the special economic structure which prevails in the twentieth century. The type of economic organization that has been dominant in the last hundred years has had an influence on certain details of form, but many of the leading facts would exist under socialism as under capitalism. Millions of people in the state of dependency we have described would presumably struggle to maintain or to raise their standards even though some other political or economic organization prevailed.

Also, we have not intended to emphasize unduly present national boundaries or even the existence of states. Reference has been made to England, France, Japan, and others but this has been largely as a matter of convenience and because economic data are furnished chiefly on this basis. We are intending for the present to emphasize the congestion of population, migration, living standards, and the location of natural resources in some parts of the earth as compared with others, regardless of the position of national boundaries and even of the existence of states.

[45]

A little later the importance of states in the picture will be stressed. Just now much will be gained by ignoring them. An economic problem exists which becomes "international" and has certain phases because western civilization is nationalistic, industrial, and capitalistic. But in some of its broader features it would be with us under any economic organization and even though states as we know them had never come into being.

Attention has already been called to the lack of agreement on standards to be applied in connection with migration from congested to sparsely settled areas. Those who live in densely populated regions claim a "right" to migrate to other parts of the world where living conditions are better. Those who dwell in the sparsely settled regions maintain that immigration is a domestic problem and that they have a right to check the influx from other countries.

It will be noticed that the word right may have more than one meaning. Two are important for our purposes. The first is the legal or political meaning. Has a given state the right, as a matter of legal theory or in international law, to restrict the entrance of newcomers? The issue centers around the question of sovereignty. The meaning of this concept and its actuality are challenged by certain modern writers, among them Harold J. Laski, *e.g.*, in "The Grammar of Politics." Into this discussion we are not competent to enter and shall leave the issue to the political scientists and the international lawyers. But no matter what their conclusions, there prevails among statesmen and among the great mass of humanity a belief that sovereignty does exist as an attribute of the state; that many issues are purely domestic and must be settled by each state for itself. This is thought by them to be true of questions like the tariff, although its significance to other countries than the

[46]

one imposing the duties is becoming increasingly clear. It is thought, also, to be true of immigration. Although the latter issue is a matter of concern to emigrant as well as to immigrant countries, this is not yet conceded. The political "right" to impose restrictions on the movements of population is still insisted upon.

But if we pass from political "right" to moral "right" the difficulties are not lessened. Assume that no political or legal issue is involved. Assume, as suggested a moment ago, that there are no national groupings, no political boundaries. Change the problem to one of ethics. Is it proper, is it morally "right" for groups of people in possession of fertile land to debar others from sharing in its use? Or, conversely, have the outsiders any moral right to demand participation?

The answer is far from easy. We are prone to speak more or less carelessly of right or justice or equity, not only in domestic matters but also in international affairs. Yet only the most casual thought shows that the issue is confused. First, what is the abstract concept of justice or rightness which is to be accepted in the relations of individuals to each other? This problem the students of ethics have always argued and will doubtless continue to argue. Assuming the issue settled and some concept of justice for the guidance of individuals to be agreed upon, there is the further step of deciding whether to apply this same concept in the relations of one group of people to another. Professor William McDougall has forcefully reminded us[1] that the code which we profess to guide the relations between individuals in the same country is a sham when we discuss our relations to people in other countries or regions. The Christian ethic, for example, whose form is nominally and widely accepted throughout the Western world, is soberly

[1] "Ethics and Some Modern World Problems," 1924.

[47]

announced as a code of world-wide application. "All men
are brothers" . . . "Go ye into all the world and preach
the gospel to every creature." Yet this concept of the
brotherhood of man is not practiced. In America, at least,
the use of such terms as "the Hun" in war time and of
Dagoes, Greasers, Chinks, and what not even in peace
time is an indication of what we mean.

But even if we could agree on our concept as an abstrac-
tion, there is still the difficulty of its application to such
concrete questions as migration and control of raw materials
and of markets. A few illustrations are worthwhile.

The industrial life of Canada has been developed with
the aid of coal much of which has been imported from the
United States. In 1925 to 1926 the total coal imported was
16,249,000 metric tons, much of it from the States. To this
steady movement of fuel the economic organization of
Canada is adjusted. If there is a coal shortage or a heavy
demand and a high price for coal in another direction—
say in Italy or in the Argentine or even within the United
States—is it morally incumbent on the coal operators to
continue shipments to Canada? If so, what is the concept
of rightness or justice on which it is based and how is
that concept applied in this particular instance?

The United States furnishes at present some 70 per cent
of the annual production of petroleum yet imports a considerable amount each year from Mexico. Is it legally or
morally proper for the Mexican government by modifying
its constitution or by legislation or otherwise to restrict
the movement of petroleum into the United States whose
economic life is adjusted to that supply?

Have the people living in the area known as Brazil any
moral "right" to finance their coffee crops in such a way
as to raise the price of coffee to consumers in other parts
of the world? Was it "right" for the British government

[48]

to maintain a certain price for rubber in the world's markets through the operation of the Stevenson Plan? Shall we give our approval to the action of American producers of cotton or of copper in restricting the supplies of these commodities and in thus raising their price to consumers throughout the world?

An endless list of illustrations might be given including not only the migrations of peoples and the control of raw materials but also investments and markets. Nor can the matter be disposed of by suggesting that no ethical considerations have been applied in the past. Such an answer, of course, merely means that the one who gives it either disapproves the code that has prevailed and hence designates it as immoral or unethical or perhaps non-moral; or else that he finds different codes applied at different times or, perhaps in the confusion of the problem, finds it difficult to determine what the code has been in particular cases.

In this field of inquiry little has been done. The difficulties and contradictions are of two sorts. First are the moral professions that are advanced. At one time we contend that all men are brothers and should be treated as equals with no discrimination because of race, nationality, or color. On other occasions we avow differences by alleging that charity begins at home or that any tax is a good one if the foreigner pays it.

The second difficulty is to be found in our divergent legislation and practice. In the United States the antitrust law is approved for the protection of the domestic consumer but the Pomerene and Edge acts are passed permitting combinations for export trade. Codes are developing rapidly in all lines of business applying to conduct at home while entirely different practices are approved or condoned in foreign trade.

[49]

Economists often state that there are two primary factors of production—man and the resources of nature. We have spoken of human beings, their expansible desires, their living standards, their migrations, and their dependence. Next is a statement of nature's important resources—not all, for the list is too long. Instead, a few only will be named with a minimum of statistical data and with a certain amount of interpretation.

Perhaps the most important is climate. It is significant, first, because it sets limits of many kinds on nature's supplies. Thus, wheat will not grow in all parts of the world. Soil constituents are not suitable in many regions and in many there are not those combinations of heat, cold, moisture, and dryness that are needed. So with cotton, bananas, reindeer, and other articles. To some of the leading products we shall give attention later. For the moment it is the direct effect of climate upon human beings that will be considered.

Professor Ellsworth Huntington is the writer who has given this question its most modern expression.[1] He is cautious in drawing sweeping conclusions about the significance of his findings, but for our purposes we need not go even so far as he does. In an attempt to determine the relations between climate and what is called "civilization," he conducted three separate though related lines of inquiry. First he studied the effect of climatic conditions upon physical and mental activity. He examined the productive output of 550 factory workers in Connecticut and 3,000 or 4,000 workers in certain southern cities of the United States and noted carefully the relation between the fluctuations in this productivity and the changes in the weather. This enabled him to reach certain conclusions

[1] For his views see, *inter alia*, "Civilization and Climate" and "World Power and Evolution."

[50]

regarding the relationship between weather and the physical activity of workers. By a similar analysis of the school work of over 1,700 students at the Annapolis Naval Academy and at West Point Military Academy he discovered a closely comparable set of facts.

The results of these investigations are summed up in the following conclusions:[1]

> A mean temperature of 64 (Fahrenheit), a mean humidity of about 80 per cent and frequent changes of temperature are the most desirable conditions for purely physical health . . . In factory work where physical effort is the chief item, but where mental activity takes a certain share, the best conditions seem to be the same [with certain exceptions] . . . For purely mental work the conditions of humidity and variability should apparently be about the same . . . but the mean temperature should be much lower, perhaps 40.

Professor Huntington next ascertained those parts of the earth's surface where climatic conditions agree closely with the ones he had concluded were most conducive to mental and physical vigor as just summarized. The necessary data for this inquiry were available in weather reports and his findings are presented on a map which is reproduced herewith.[2]

It will at once be noticed that those areas in which, according to his findings, climate is most stimulating include all or most of western and northwestern Europe and an important fraction of the United States.

His third inquiry was of a very different sort. By correspondence with a large number of individuals who might be called "wise men" living in all parts of the world, he secured their judgment regarding those areas of the earth's surface in which the highest degree of civilization now exists. He received 138 answers of which 54 were in such

[1] "World Power and Evolution," p. 8.
[2] By permission of the publishers, Yale University Press.

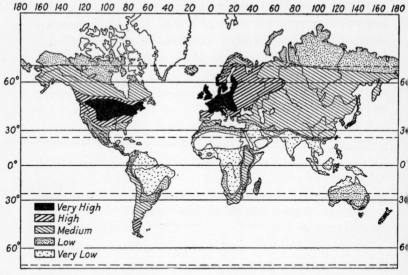

FIG. 2*a*.—The distribution of human energy on the basis of climate.

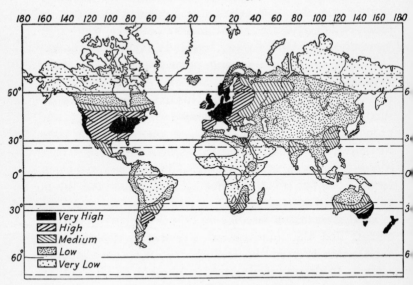

FIG. 2*b*.—The distribution of civilization.

[52]

form as to be usable. Combining these replies he constructed a second map which is also reproduced. If the two maps are compared, their similarity is observed to be very striking. For the most part, the highest degree of modern civilization is found in those regions where Professor Huntington's inductive studies show that climate is most conducive to physical and mental activity.

It is not immediately germane but perhaps we should point out that Professor Huntington does not overlook the fact that in past centuries the centers of civilization have been in other areas than the ones where they are found today. It is his belief that there have been important changes in climate and he presents at length his reasons for thinking so.

We are concerned here, however, with another inference that can be drawn from his studies. It is very striking that the countries in which he finds the most invigorating climate and the ones where the highest civilization is observed are also the countries that are the leaders in international affairs today. England, France, Germany, Italy, the United States, and Japan are the large ones. Belgium, Holland, Denmark, and Switzerland are among the others with invigorating climates but their size is small and for this and other reasons their influence is less pronounced than that of the larger countries. From time to time Russia looms large in the news but thus far her rôle is at least a secondary one. China is at present in ferment but her effective influence in international life is yet to be demonstrated.

There is no reason for alleging that this relation between climate and the international struggle furnishes a sole explanation or even the leading one. We need not even attempt to determine its relative importance. Instead, it can be listed merely as one of the highly significant factors

[53]

with the reminder that it is permanent not temporary, permanent at least to the extent that no significant changes in climate are apt to occur through decades or perhaps through centuries. Political organizations may be modified, certain other natural resources may rise or decline in importance, but as long as climate remains what it is, the people of certain regions will be handicapped in the contest while others will be favored.

Food is properly next on the list. Even the Far East with its low standards of living imports some of its food. But the Occident depends heavily on outside sources of supply. The tables of foreign trade figures presented in the preceding chapter for Belgium and for Germany are a reminder of the fact that modern industrialization depends closely on the ability to import both food and raw materials. Only because of this has it been possible to maintain so many human beings at a standard so high. The $243 prewar per capita income in Great Britain, $185 in France, $146 in Germany, and $112 in Italy seem low compared to the $335 in the United States but they are high compared with only $29 in Japan and the unestimated but probably far lower incomes of China and India. If those are correct who feel that former sources of food supply may not be relied upon for an indefinite number of years to come, there are serious contingencies to be faced by later generations. Our concern is with the present and the more immediate future.

The leading article of food of international significance is wheat. Other forms may be as nourishing but it is one of the most conveniently transported and it furnishes a large amount of nutrition in small bulk. For this and for other reasons it is the outstanding food in many parts of the world. During the war it was a stand-by and in days of peace it dominates its field in foreign trade. A shortage of its crop and a rise in its price mean more troubles for statesmen than similar difficulties with any other article.

Notice, then, the countries that import and export wheat. In the five-year period 1909–1910 to 1913–1914 (both inclusive) the exporting countries were, in order of the numbers of quintals exported, Russia, the United States, Canada, Argentine, Roumania, Australia, British India, Hungary, and Bulgaria, the combined amounts being 176,310,000 quintals. In this same period 148,110,000 quintals were imported by 12 European countries, most of it by 6 of them. The 6 in order were the United Kingdom, Germany and Luxemburg, Italy, Austria, Belgium, and France.[1]

If one examines the data for the other cereals he discovers much the same situation. The newer areas—Canada, the United States, the Argentine, Australia, Roumania, Russia, and the rest—were furnishing western Europe not only with its wheat but also with its rye, maize, barley, and oats. What was true of cereals was true of meats. It was true of food in general. There are changes in the lists of importing and exporting countries if corn or some other food is used, but the lesson remains the same. Certain areas depended on certain other areas and a number of the countries in western Europe relied on outside sources for an important fraction of their total food.

Nor have conditions changed in the postwar years. Population has grown. The foreign trade of some countries has diminished but more food is needed because there are more mouths to feed and also because food is so important that necessary economies will be practiced first in other directions.

[1] *Report to the League of Nations on Certain Aspects of the Raw Materials Problem* by Professor Gini, vol. II, p. 7, December, 1921.

The accompanying table indicates this for a number of different foodstuffs.[1] Only a glance shows the interdependence. To name all the countries separately would be confusing, so they are grouped by continents. There are 12 different foodstuffs in the list. The sign + indicates an importation of a designated number of thousands of quintals and the sign − an exportation.

In each year from 1909 to 1913 Europe (excluding Russia) imported net the indicated amounts of each item. From 1921 to 1925 the same situation was continued with two exceptions. One is a small exportation of potatoes and a very small amount of rye flour. The other is a very appreciable increase in the importation of wheat, wheat flour, rye, maize, sugar, and tea. There were a few small decreases but the gains were appreciable and were in the more important items of human food.

Next it will be noticed that Russia which was in prewar days a source of food supply has sharply declined in importance, her exports of wheat, barley, oats, and maize having nearly disappeared. Reductions in the supplies of wheat and sugar from Asia are also to be noticed. Asian exports of sugar have grown but are being thrown on a highly demoralized sugar market.

North America and South America are the other two continents of importance and their exports of food have greatly expanded while North America's imports of sugar have gained. Central America and the Antilles show a large increase in exports of sugar.

The picture is a convincing one. Certain areas are more dependent than ever before on outside sources of food supply and those sources are, in turn, increasingly dependent on markets abroad. As time passes changes will occur.

[1] Compiled from data in Agricultural Problems in Their International Aspect, a document prepared for The International Economic Conference, Geneva, 1926.

Trade in Certain Foodstuffs

(Annual Averages in Thousands of Quintals. Surplus of Imports (+) or Exports (−))

Products	Europe excluding Russia		Russia		Other countries of Asia		Africa	
	1909–13	1921–25	1909–13	1921–25	1909–13	1921–25	1909–13	1921–25
1. Wheat....	+115,625	+132,430	−41,174	−1,225	−13,701	+952	−570	+125
2. Wheat flour.....	+5,748	+11,784	−1,188	+1,513	+2,073	+3,433	+2,849	+2,817
3. Rye.....	+4,944	+12,848	−5,341	−3,194	+1	0	0	−12
4. Rye flour	+1,342	−71	−1,146	−17	0	0	+2	+2
5. Barley...	+42,786	+15,302	−36,999	−1,811	−2,602	−2,096	−2,184	−2,297
6. Oats.....	+19,398	+11,292	−10,683	−284	+27	+11	−1,047	−734
7. Maize...	+45,322	+51,784	−7,544	−545	−1,374	−1,218	−853	−5,033
8. Rice.....	+10,676	+7,857	+1,172	+383	−20,926	−13,317	+2,682	+1,725
9. Potatoes.	+582	−1,476	−1,705	+31	+238	+297	+460	+399
10. Tea......	+1,522	+2,122	+711	+55	−3,258	−3,199	+80	+152
11. Coffee...	+5,880	+5,450	+118	+6	−309	−494	+185	+177
12. Sugar....	+2,701	+17,549	−2,626	+630	−3,853	−6,687	−685	−1,542

Products	North America		Central America and Antilles		South America		Oceania	
	1909–13	1921–25	1909–13	1921–25	1909–13	1921–25	1909–13	1921–25
1. Wheat..	−34,452	−94,589	+563	+497	−20,848	−28,636	−11,641	−19,771
2. Wheat flour....	−12,826	−22,232	+2,736	+3,540	+1,126	+999	−1,256	−3,503
3. Rye....	−164	−10,459	0	0	−76	−407	−1	0
4. Rye flour....	0	−98	+3	+5	+43	0		
5. Barley..	−2,811	−8,956	−45	+90	−370	−1,288	+182	−352
6. Oats....	−2,401	−6,529	+377	+360	−6,437	−4,874	−214	−9
7. Maize...	−7,628	−15,772	+1,973	+1,372	−29,316	−32,000	+128	+116
8. Rice....	−83	−1,867	+2,282	+3,138	+1,329	+1,075	+343	+476
9. Potatoes	+604	−1,498	+661	+1,374	+694	+138	+27	+56
10. Tea.....	+611	+599	+5	+5	+46	+46	+187	+227
11. Coffee...	+3,959	+5,952	−1,600	−1,599	−8,410	−9,620	−7	−7
12. Sugar...	+29,387	+45,714	−24,232	−48,859	−1,515	−4,720	−4,443	−5,912

For example, Russian exports may grow. But there is no reason to suggest any coming decline in this state of dependence. There will instead be an increase.

In the United Kingdom 191 persons per square kilometer, in Belgium 257, in France 74, in Germany 132 live at their present standards because of this steady supply of nourishment from abroad. In postwar years the reduction of grain exports from Russia, just noted, meant reduced rations for the Occident unless the amount from other areas could be enlarged, which it was. As the numbers of people in Australia, the Argentine, Canada, and the United States increase, new sources of supply must be found at home or abroad or productivity in the New World must be vastly improved to care for local needs and at the same time to feed the growing numbers in the Old World.

A larger volume of agricultural output in Europe is not easy. For the present it can be raised in most cases only at a much higher cost per unit than in newer lands. If the price of imported food rises sufficiently, then the home-grown crops can compete, but the price must be high to make this possible, unless, of course, improved methods of cultivation can be found and applied to lower the costs. Much, too, can be done and has been done by the substitution of one kind of food for another—as of pork for beef or of potatoes for wheat.

That this difficulty exists is illustrated by the efforts of the English during the World War to supplement food supplies by home-grown produce. Because of the urgency of the situation and the high price of food, and under the stimulus of war enthusiasm, something was accomplished. But as soon as the psychology of peace was restored and unrestricted imports of food were resumed, this approach to the food question was found ineffective. Wheat from

Australia, Canada, and the Argentine, fruit from South Africa, and dairy products from Holland and Denmark can be imported more cheaply than similar products can be raised in Great Britain. British agriculture is again in distress.

In Italy efforts are being made to stimulate the home production of food. The avowed reason is to lessen Italian dependence on the outside world and to relieve the pressure on the lira, since all imports must be paid for by the purchase of foreign exchange. It is too soon for a final judgment on the experiment but we may point out the difficulties. Italy has a limited amount of fertile soil. In most of the country, unit costs of agricultural production are high as compared with costs in more fertile regions. Such food as is raised must compete with imported crops unless the imports are debarred. If they are debarred the Italians will presumably be using their capital and labor in a less effective manner and, we might add, there will be no long-run relief to the foreign exchanges. Or, if such relief really comes, it will be at the price of a reduction in the standard of living much in excess of any gains received.

It must not be forgotten that imported food must be paid for. Payment is being made in western Europe and elsewhere by importing raw materials, manufacturing them, and selling the finished product abroad. But this means further dependence—for raw materials and for markets. Another predicament is thus created. Supplies of raw materials must be assured and markets must be kept open. As the newer countries industrialize, using a larger amount of their own raw materials, supplying their own domestic markets, and perhaps even entering into competition with the Old World in foreign markets, the complications are increased. This is just what England

[59]

is facing today, notably in cotton textiles. Formerly she led, but now China, Japan, India, the United States, France, Italy, and others have entered the field, forcing England to readjust her industrial life on a large scale. Can it be wondered that friction results, that problems difficult of settlement arise, that even wars occur? Such forces are powerful. Formal declarations of goodwill, renunciations of offensive warfare, "peace by incantation," as some have called it, though valuable, will be inadequate.

But let us turn next to the two important fuels, first coal and then oil. Industrialization calls for power and these are the two leading sources, supplemented by water power. In time, the tides or the winds or atomic energy or some other force may be harnessed for human use but at present coal, oil, and water power must be our chief reliance.

Coal is produced in nearly every country of the world but in widely different amounts. In 1925 the total world output was 1,187,803,000 metric tons, but of this amount 911,572,000 tons or 76.7 per cent came from the mines of the United States, the United Kingdom, and Germany.[1] Some countries, *e.g.*, Italy, produce little coal but use much. As an indication of the uneven distribution it may be noticed that in 1925 among the leading countries the United States, Czechoslovakia, Germany, Poland, Russia, the United Kingdom, China, Japan, the Union of South Africa, and Australia met their needs from their own production. Others were compelled to import. The Argentine and Switzerland imported 100 per cent of their consumption of coal, coke, briquettes, and lignite, Sweden 94 per cent, Italy over 87 per cent, Brazil over 86 per cent, Canada over 62 per cent. Chile, France, Belgium, Hungary,

---

[1] *Memorandum on Coal*, vol. I, p. 43, League of Nations, Documentation for the International Economic Conference of May, 1927.

the Netherlands, Spain, and New Zealand also imported heavily.[1]

Demand for coal, like the demand for many other articles, is very complex. Man uses it for heating, but he also uses it as a fuel for locomotives and for steamships and thus it aids in transportation. He uses it in his factories, as a fuel in most of his manufacturing processes. But it is a very heavy article, and for the most part factories using coal must be located near the sources of supply, while coal used for domestic fuel costs far more at a distance from the mines than near them.

This high cost of transporting coal means that there is a strong tendency for factories to locate where coal is easily accessible. Many other influences operate, but this is an important one and has meant the concentration especially of iron and steel plants but also of many others in such places as Gary, Pittsburgh, and Birmingham in the United States, in the Ruhr area of Germany, and in England. Raw materials tend to move toward the coal since they are lighter and hence more easily transported. This is true even of a substance as heavy as iron ore, and it is significant to notice the location of its deposits. The important ones are in certain clearly marked areas in the United States, France, Sweden, Luxemburg, Spain, Germany, Algeria, Czechoslovakia, and Austria.

A little reflection on the location of these deposits illuminates this aspect of world strain. The deposits may be divided into two groups. One includes what may be called the outlying areas—Cuba, Spain, Sweden, etc. From these countries ore can be shipped and is shipped to the countries where coal is available. In 1925 England imported 4,472,000 long tons of iron ore and scrap. Even the United States imported 2,191,000 tons, principally

[1] *Ibid.*, p. 12.

from Cuba and from Chili. The second group includes the areas that are located in the countries where the coal - supplies are found. There are large reserves of iron ore in the United States and in England. Before the World War the Lorraine deposits were in Germany but now they are in France.

Since the ore tends to move toward the coal where the factories are apt to concentrate it is important for the industrial interests operating factories in the coal areas to safeguard their supplies of ore. When this ore is in the same country as the coal, for example that of the Lake Superior region, there may be problems but they are not international. When the ore is in more distant regions, as in Spain or Cuba and in another country than the coal, the international element may cause complications, although the seriousness will depend much upon the richness of the ores in question as compared with the abundance and quality of the ore that is nearer and perhaps also in the same country as the coal.

Thus far, really acute strain has developed in only one place—the Ruhr-Lorraine region. Before the late war both the coal and the iron were in Germany and a complex relationship had been established between the two regions. Now the best of the ore is in France while the Ruhr coal areas are still German, a situation that has created one of the most awkward of our international questions.[1] Minor, though significant, problems have arisen because of the need for Cuban ore in the United States and in a few other connections, but the Franco-German situation is the outstanding one.

It will not have escaped attention that there are three important world centers of significance in this connection.

[1] See GREER, GUY, "The Ruhr-Lorraine Industrial Problem," for the best description of this.

One is the Ruhr-Lorraine area just referred to, presenting one of the most difficult of our international questions. Another is the United States, a country of such vast extent that a large fraction of what it uses is found within its own borders. There is no occasion, except in rare emergencies, for the United States to import any coal, and its own supplies of iron ore are largely adequate. The third center is Great Britain which has huge deposits of coal and considerable iron ore but now finds it more economical to import much of its ore from other sources— notably from Spain and Sweden. At present there is, therefore, only one of the three regions that may cause serious international friction.[1]

In recent years oil has been one of the outstanding topics of international discussion. Current news items are constantly informing readers of new discoveries; of concessions granted in South America, in Turkey and elsewhere; of trade wars between the large oil companies; of agreements and disagreements; of threats, compromises, and what not. Book after book has appeared each with a startling title: "Oil Imperialism" and "We Fight For Oil" and "The World Struggle for Oil." Diplomatic correspondence deals with oil, governments aid their nationals in securing concessions, in demanding equal rights, and in protecting them in rights already secured.

There is one peculiarity about it all. One of the points most strongly emphasized is the contention that there is a scarcity of supply, one estimate being that, at the present rate of consumption, the known reserves will be exhausted before many years have passed. This may be true. If so it seems particularly foolish to become so involved in

[1] Readers are referred to a valuable article by C. K. Leith entitled The World Iron and Steel Situation in Its Bearing on the French Occupation of the Ruhr in *Foreign Affairs* (N. Y.) of June, 1923.

dangerous international strain over supplies which will last so short a time. It would seem better to spend the same energy in an effort to develop other sources of power if this one is so meager. If the supplies are not so scanty there would seem to be no reason for such intense excitement accompanied by so much danger.

One way of presenting the situation is by tabulating current production by countries as is done for 1928 in the accompanying table.[1]

World's Production of Petroleum in 1928

Country	Barrels of 42 U. S. gallons	Percentage of total by volume
United States..........	902,000,000	68.2
Venezuela.............	106,000,000	8.0
Russia...............	87,800,000	6.7
Mexico..............	50,150,000	3.8
Persia...............	42,080,000	3.2
Roumania............	30,600,000	2.3
Netherland East Indies..	28,500,000	2.2
Colombia.............	19,900,000	1.5
All others.............	55,866,000	4.1
Total............	1,322,896,000	100.0

Of a world production of 1,322,896,000 barrels in 1928 the United States furnished 902,000,000 barrels or more than 68 per cent of the total. The other sources in order of importance were Venezuela, Russia, Mexico, Persia, Roumania, the Netherland East Indies, and Colombia. And it is from these other countries that the supplies of the future are presumably to come. Of the leading world powers only the United States is at the present time producing a large amount and its reserves are said to be limited.

[1] Condensed from a table in "Petroleum Facts and Figures," p. 4, (published by the American Petroleum Institute).

The international struggle for oil has been traced by a score of writers and each year others are throwing additional light on it. We need do nothing more than to observe briefly that industrial activity in the last 25 years has become more dependent than before on oil as a fuel. The internal-combustion engine with its many adaptations has revolutionized numerous phases of business and social life. Oil is used for driving automobiles and battleships, as power in many factories, and as fuel in many homes. Life as we know it depends as never before on petroleum and its products. Though the reserves may be adequate for only a few years, the struggle for their control will be keen and dangerous.

The perils of the international contest for oil are unquestionably real but at times one is tempted to wonder whether they are not entirely disproportionate to its real importance. Reference has already been made to the belief of many that the world supply will last only a few years more at the present rate of consumption. There should be added to this a reminder that even the huge current consumption is far less than that of coal.[1] The danger comes from the complete dependence on oil of one phase of modern life, the use of the automobile; and on the great superiority of oil over coal in the operation of ships. This latter advantage of oil is of most concern in time of war, since war vessels can so much more readily be operated with the liquid fuel. The oft quoted saying of Lord Curzon that the allies in the late war were floated to victory on a sea of oil is a vivid expression of the significance of petroleum in modern warfare.

[1] It is estimated that in 1926 in the United States 6 per cent of power production was from water power, 6 per cent from gas, 21 per cent from oil, and 67 per cent from coal. And this is in a country which is producing 70 per cent of the annual world output of petroleum.

In the minds of some, water power or "white coal" is a solution of many difficulties. There are countries like Switzerland, Scotland, and Italy where this form of energy presents tremendous possibilities. A word or two regarding this source of power is appropriate, since many enthusiasts see in it a relief from foreign dependence on coal or oil. Its advantages are clear. It is clean, a given source of supply is inexhaustible, electric current generated from it may be transmitted great distances with but slight loss. Its merits seem overwhelming.

Yet there are certain limitations that must not be overlooked. Not all countries and sections are favored to an equal degree with this source of power. Many of the countries in which it is available for development are not in a position to exploit it without the aid of outside capital and these external loans, of course, place on each hydroelectric enterprise and on the country as a whole a burden of carrying charges. This leads to emphasis on a point frequently forgotten. Water power is a natural resource and hence seems cheap. But so are coal and oil natural resources. Coal is expensive because it must be mined and transported a longer or shorter distance to the place where it is to be consumed. Oil is expensive because it is costly to drill wells, transport the crude oil, refine it, market it, etc. Neither can be used where it is or as it is under the soil. Nor can water power be so used. It must be harnessed, be brought under control. The actual cost of operating a hydroelectric plant after construction is moderate but the cost of construction and the fixed charges imposed on the plant by these construction costs are very great. Not always is the unit cost of water power lower than that of power derived from coal. General comparisons between the two are futile. Particular cases must be cited and broad generalizations may well be avoided. Yet it was interesting a short time ago to notice the press reports that the enthusiasm for hydroelectric development in certain parts of Europe was subsiding because of the realization that the carrying charges are so heavy a burden. In many instances coal is cheaper than water power.

To this may be added the observation that industrial demands are growing. Italy has increased her use of hydroelectric power, yet in 1927 she imported 14,059,000 metric tons of coal as compared with only 10,834,000 in 1913. Switzerland imported 439,000 tons in 1913 and 470,000 tons in 1925.

This summary of fact regarding a few and only a few of the important natural resources shows certain areas in a condition of extreme dependence on others for food and raw materials. It must be remembered, also, that although countries importing these articles are dependent on the sources of supply, the exporting countries are likewise dependent on the first group for markets. In 1927 the United States exported cotton valued at $826,000,000. This was 60.6 per cent of its production of cotton. In the same year it exported $486,000,000 worth of petroleum and its products and $325,000,000 worth of wheat (including flour). The dependence is mutual. At the outbreak of the war the cotton-growing areas of the United States were temporarily prostrated by the curtailed European demand for cotton. In fact the United States as a whole is more dependent than is often realized, a fact made clear for the economic field by W. C. Redfield in his little volume "Dependent America." Chili has long relied heavily on natural nitrates as an article of export and as a base for her system of taxation. The production of artificial nitrates in Germany and elsewhere is a serious matter for her.

The question is one of maintaining a free flow of the food and raw materials on which existing economic life so

[67]

closely depends. A few dreamers have talked of abandoning modern industrialism, of returning to medieval ways of living—which means, of course, the elimination of railways, the telephone, the telegraph, bath tubs, and what not. Time need not be spent in comment on this way out of the difficulty.

Another approach is to attempt increased production of food and of raw materials in the industrialized areas. This is, of course, entirely impossible for some articles. England, for example, cannot produce cotton, oil, and gold; Italy cannot mine coal, nor Germany copper. If these articles are used they must be imported. But there are other articles whose local production is possible. Wheat may be raised in England and in Italy. England might avoid entirely the importation of iron ore at least for some time by utilizing only her own deposits; Italy might, conceivably, reduce her imports of coal, relying much more fully, perhaps largely, on water power. Germany might depend entirely on enlarged domestic production of fats. But this effort at increased local production must face the fact that it can be accomplished only by the use of larger amounts of labor and capital than are required in other parts of the world to secure the same results. The annoying law of diminishing returns is the *bête noire* that must be reckoned with. Continued dependence must be accepted. Better use of available scientific knowledge will help, but, in the long run attention must be directed to maintaining the free movement of trade.

The traditional way is to rely on the free operation of so-called "natural laws," on the guidance of what Adam Smith called the "invisible hand." Allow each party concerned to follow his own self-interest. If more coal is needed in Italy the offer there of a higher price will stimulate its production in England or in the Ruhr and

[68]

its export to Italy. So with other articles. Price will be the determinant of production and of transportation. Unfortunately there are reasons for distrusting the operation of natural laws even in a *laissez faire* world. But as J. M. Keynes has pointed out in his admirable monograph "The End of Laissez Faire," the modern world is of a very different sort. In the international field there are tariffs, subsidies, export and import prohibitions and restrictions.[1]

If *laissez faire* cannot be trusted, national control may be better. But the base of the problem is broader than the area of any country. National direction cannot secure coffee and tea for England and coal for Italy or cotton for Germany. Even empire control is inadequate. Great Britain argues it and from time to time attempts it. But some of her needed supplies must come long distances and from dominions and dependencies which often drive as hard bargains as do areas that are entirely non-British.

Neither "natural law" nor nationalism is adequate. The problem is a world-wide one—international, not national. Some form of international adjustment must be found if strain is to be lessened. Such adjustments are not easy and those that may be adopted will doubtless create new difficulties. Yet only by world-wide effort can real progress be made.

[1] For an orderly arrangement by an able writer who believes in them see "Economic Protectionism" by Josef Grunzel. For a good recent study of political influence over such matters see "The Economic Foreign Policy of the United States" by B. H. Williams.

Chapter V

THE INFLUENCE OF LARGE-SCALE PRODUCTION

Up to this point we have spoken of human beings and of natural resources. We have dwelt on growing numbers, congested areas, difficulties in securing food, raw materials, and markets; on attempts to maintain or to raise standards of living by migration and on the recent checks to such movements; on the necessity of maintaining the free movement of business. In the last chapter emphasis was placed on the significance of climate and on the location of certain leading national resources upon which modern life peculiarly depends.

We have discussed the two primary factors in production—human beings (or labor) and natural resources. If the traditional analysis of economic study is maintained, it is possible next to examine the leading secondary factors—capital and the form of business organization. These, too, it will be found, are of a sort to accentuate strain. Large and growing numbers of people who are living in areas whose climate is stimulating and who have become greatly dependent are sure to have a conflict of interests and to become economic rivals. As already pointed out, this would be true under any form of economic organization and even though nothing closely comparable to the modern state existed.

But to these facts must now be added the further ones, *i.e.*, that the growth of capital, the nature of the modern monetary system, the price economy, the corporate form of organization, the existence of huge business combinations known variously as cartels, trusts, combines, mergers, etc., increase the difficulties. In the next few chapters these will be considered.

First is large-scale production. The term is a relative one but there is, of course, no doubt of the general trend among many lines of business. There is in many directions a growth in the size of plants though there are other lines where there is little or no sign of such a movement. We are concerned only with those lines of business in which the tendency appears. The fact that there are others in which it is not to be noticed is immaterial since we do not argue the existence of a general trend. There are many fields in which large-scale production is increasing and it is these that create the problem. Prior to 1775 manufacturing was chiefly by hand processes and was necessarily conducted on a small scale. Investments in particular establishments and in the aggregate were not large. No plant was of any great size nor could it turn out very many units of product.

This has been greatly changed, not in all industries but in many. In some lines small-scale production still prevails and has decided advantages. In others, as in steel, the size of the manufacturing unit grows and may perhaps continue to grow because of the nature of the industries. A few illustrations will make this change vivid.

England furnishes an abundance of them. The Committee of Industry and Trade, commonly known as the "Balfour Committee" from the name of its chairman, Sir Arthur Balfour, has furnished us with the needed data. This committee finds from the *Census of Production Reports* of 1907 and 1924 the number of persons employed, the horsepower available, and the value of the output for the different groups of industries. In the clothing industry the average number of persons employed per establishment increased 13 per cent, the horsepower per person employed gained 162 per cent, and the net output per person employed gained 144 per cent. In textile manufacturing the average number of persons employed decreased 1.7 per cent, the horsepower per person gained 39 per cent, and the output per person gained 128 per cent. In skins and leather the gains were 2 per cent in persons employed, 217 per cent in horsepower per person, and 143 per cent in net output per head.

If we turn to the United States we find that in the manufacture of cotton goods in 1850 there were 1,094 establishments averaging only 84 employees each, with an average capital of $68,000 and an average product of $55,500; by 1910 the number of establishments had grown to only 1,324 but the average number of workers to 286, the average capital to $621,000, and the average product to $475,000. The change in iron and steel was even more striking. In this same period the number of establishments had increased from 468 to 654, the average number of employees from 53 to 426, the average capital from $46,700 to $2,282,000, and the average product from $43,600 to $2,119,000. That these are not isolated instances but represent a general tendency is shown by the fact that in all the manufacturing industries from 1850 to 1914 the average number of employees grew from 7.7 to 25.5, the average capital from $4,330 to $82,602, and the average product from $8,280 to $87,916.

From 1914 to 1919 the number of manufacturing establishments in all the industries of the United States increased only 21 per cent, and the number of employees only 31 per cent. But in this same period invested capital gained 94 per cent and the value of the products 156 per cent.

Illustrations need not be multiplied. The same tendency is observable in all countries. Large-scale production with its heavy investment of capital is on the increase—not in all industries, we may repeat, but in many. We may then attempt an appraisal of the significance of these changes in connection with our general inquiry.

These facts mean that there is a heavy pressure on a large industry to maintain continuous operation. This is not always the case but is true "in the long run"—an expression upon which the economist may frequently and confidently rely. There may be particular occasions when shutting down for a short time appears advantageous— for example when it seems possible thereby to weaken or destroy a labor union—but ordinarily this is not the case.

There are two main reasons why it is a serious matter to shut down a factory or to curtail its operations. One is the difficult situation which it creates with labor. To workers a period of dull business is a hardship. Usually their savings are meager and insufficient to help them through a time of unemployment. Whether organized or not, their resentment may show itself in restlessness or even violence. Perhaps property will be destroyed or lives lost. A still stronger influence in the minds of some employers is the fact that during the period of inactivity a working force becomes scattered. Skilled workers often find employment elsewhere and when operations are resumed new men must be secured. Where unskilled workers are less numerous this consideration is not so significant but to offset it is the growing realization among employers that a high labor turnover is extremely wasteful.

This is the labor side of the problem and the considerations mentioned are often powerful enough to prevent a shutdown. It is significant in small plants as well as in large but is more important in the latter because so many employees are in close contact with each other. Under such conditions radical influences can more easily arouse unemployed and discontented workers to violence.

[73]

Nevertheless this is probably a less powerful reason for maintaining uninterrupted operations than the second one— the influence of "overhead" expense. Volume of overhead, proper distribution of overhead, and how to reduce overhead are among the urgent problems with which modern scientific management and accounting must wrestle. Yet even these experts in their perplexity are concerned with only the minor aspects of a most harassing question. Overhead is one of the most baffling forces not merely within a given plant or in the operations of a given corporation but for the country as a whole and in international affairs.

Such a statement calls for explanation which must be prefaced by a definition or description of overhead. Those costs that persist irrespective of the volume of business done are overhead costs or constant costs, while those that fluctuate with the volume of business done are direct or variable. Any enterprise, even a small one, has some overhead expense. A cobbler has an investment in his shop and tools and if he keeps books at all must remember that interest on the investment should be charged regularly whether business is active or dull. If a week or a month should pass during which he makes or repairs no shoes that fact will not lessen this item in his expense account. He will use less leather and thread but rent on a leased shop or interest on his investment in a shop must still be considered.

While this item may be unimportant and worth little space when one is discussing primitive economic life or even many lines of business in a modern civilized community, it is highly important in others. The railroads will do for an illustration. They do not always maintain exactly the same relationship between the two forms of expense but one calculation indicates their constant charges as 61 per cent of the total and the variable ones at 39 per cent. This exact relationship is not to be understood as a permanent one but we may use it to make our point clear.

Even when little or no traffic is being carried, rolling stock, rails, and other equipment are rusting, becoming obsolescent, or otherwise deteriorating in value. In time they must be replaced and a fund must regularly be set aside for the purpose. Interest on borrowed money, insurance, salaries of many officials and other employees who cannot be discharged during a temporary traffic slump are other items that may be mentioned as of the same sort. If one should add to the list of overhead items the payment of dividends on stock (and for some purposes this might be proper), the percentage would be still higher than 61, for the dividends have not been included in the calculation.

This affects railroad policy in many ways. Suppose a representative of road A is soliciting traffic from a shipper and that a "fair" freight rate for the shipment is $1 per 100 pounds. Of each dollar received 61 cents will be used for the overhead costs above mentioned and 39 cents for the costs connected with the particular shipment, such expenses as loading and unloading, extra fuel and oil consumed, etc.

If the shipper has the choice of two roads he might conceivably take advantage of that fact to play off A, whom we have mentioned, against B, the representative of another road. Let us suppose that he can do this and persuade them to cut rates. How low can he drive them? It is clear that the one securing the shipment must charge at least 39 cents per 100 or the receipts will not cover the special outlay involved. Anything above that amount can be devoted to meeting the constant expense, those items of overhead that must be paid whether goods are

[75]

shipped or not. Even 40 cents per 100 would give a small amount for the purpose, while 50 or 60 cents might net a tidy sum well worth having, particularly if the shipment were a large one. And yet if anything less than a dollar per 100 is charged the overhead must be met by an extra-high rate on other shipments or the road will in time face bankruptcy.

The problem of freight rates is far more complex than this illustration suggests but the relationship between the two kinds of expense and the relatively large size of overhead explain many things that characterize modern railroad management. Railroad difficulties in the United States in the seventys were due in no small part to the bitter competition and rate cutting of the times. Overhead—along with other causes—soon wrecked some of the leading lines of the period. The dangers of this sharp competition (as well as the desire for large profits) explain the railroad pools and go far toward justifying them. They explain, also, the fact that competition has so largely disappeared in railroading, rates today being a matter of informal agreement and of approval by the Interstate Commerce Commission.

But this is not all. Let us assume that a given railroad is in satisfactory condition, receipts being adequate to meet all expenditures, including a suitable dividend on stock, say at the rate of 6 per cent. Imagine a decline of 20 per cent in traffic and perhaps a corresponding decline of 20 per cent in receipts. Expenses are reduced but not proportionately, for only the variable ones are affected, the constant ones remaining unaltered. Under such conditions a 20 per cent reduction in business might easily force the passing of dividends and make necessary a default on interest payments. In fact, a 10 per cent reduction, if it persisted for any considerable length of time, might easily change a prosperous railroad to one in acute financial distress. On the other hand, if this same road while in a satisfactory condition should have a 20 per cent increase in traffic or even a 10 per cent increase, its net gains would be very large, since expenses do not grow at a corresponding rate.

This makes it easier to understand why a rate increase or decrease is a matter so important. If the volume of traffic is not seriously altered it may mean the difference between prosperity and adversity, between success and bankruptcy. Even though the percentage change is small, it may be enough, if a decrease, to force the passing of dividends. If it is an increase, it may be sufficient to change a weak road into a prosperous one or to permit a hitherto successful road to double its dividends.

Similarly, a fluctuation in the volume of traffic with rates unchanged is highly important to the road. The significant point is the influence of a slight increase or decrease in the receipts of the road, a change that may come with an alteration either in the rate or in the volume of traffic.

Railroads have been used for an illustration because standardized railroad accounts permit the compilation of more satisfactory figures than in most other fields and because changes in railroad rates necessarily command a larger amount of public attention than do most other price fluctuations. Yet what is true of railroads is similarly true of any industry where production is on a large scale, particularly those in which the investment is great and overhead expenses are heavy.

All of them must use their plants up to a certain capacity or lose money. Several years ago Mr. Farrell, president of the United States Steel Corporation, was quoted as saying that the ordinary steel plant must operate at from 60 to 70 per cent of its capacity or operate at a loss.

[77]

The meaning of this in business is clear. Assume for a moment the existence of entirely free competition, a condition long since gone among the railroads. For any one of the competitors operation at 60 or 70 per cent of capacity is necessary if expenses are to be met and dividends paid. Anything less than that amount of business means loss, perhaps failure. More than that means a large increase in net gain. The penalty for a decline in sales is severe, the reward for an increase is great. What wonder that competition is keen and disastrous or that the temptation to combine and secure a monopoly price is great?

This has important results in the field of foreign trade. If two steel concerns, say an English and a German, are competing in any market the struggle is certain to be bitter. Each desires orders either to prevent failure or to increase net gains by a large amount. Not only will the rivalry be acute but also the rivals will not be checked by any of the legal restraints or ethical standards that may chance to prevail in either home country and that would govern their attitude toward domestic competitors.

There are accordingly two main reasons why a factory operating on a large scale is under pressure not to shut down. One is the attitude of labor which often makes itself felt in a vigorous and effective manner, the other and the more important is the relentless pressure of overhead costs that are persistently forcing the management to maintain operations. But operation can be continued only in case a regular and adequate amount of raw materials can be secured and markets be kept open. We are thus brought again to these two items—raw materials and markets—to which we have so frequently called attention.

Reference must be made later to the significance of the corporate form of organization but it may be pointed out here that much of the actual pressure comes from the owners of securities—bondholders and stockholders—who demand regular payment of interest and dividends and thereby influence strongly the management of the corporation.

Under the conditions described there is no reason for surprise over the intensity of the conflict for raw materials. British manufacturers must import all of their raw cotton. It is no wonder that they are troubled over their dependence on the United States as their most important source of supply. As long ago as the time of the American Civil War the dangers of this dependence were brought home and the last few years have seen important efforts to increase cotton production in many parts of the British Commonwealth on the assumption that these areas would be more reliable in emergencies and that in any case there is greater safety in a diversity of sources. What is true of cotton is likewise true in varying degrees of rubber, of oil, of wool, of iron ore, and of countless other articles, either in the raw form or partly manufactured.

Our frequent references to raw materials make unnecessary any further elaboration of their importance. Their connection with large-scale production is the point immediately at hand and we are warranted in placing the greatest of emphasis on this fact in modern life as one explanation of the intensity of the international struggle. The same may be said of markets. No matter what the abundance of raw materials, the goods must be sold. It is from the proceeds of sales that interest charges, insurance, depreciation, and the countless other items of overhead must be met.

This is perhaps the appropriate place to observe that the problem may be expressed still differently by going back to the fundamental fact of division of labor. Not to individual division of labor or specialization as illustrated by Adam Smith's account of the making of a pin or the greater specialization of today in any large plant. Not even to the local specialization within any one country.

Instead, there is an important amount of specialization or localization in great world areas. The tropics furnish much that the temperate zones cannot produce for themselves and the arctic and antarctic regions must on the whole be relied upon for our supplies of reindeer and polar bears. But this division of labor, this geographical specialization is never perfect and is constantly being readjusted with serious consequences. Specialization may develop within a given area. The capital and labor of that region may become adjusted to a given line of production. If this situation could be maintained there might be a minimum of strain. Thus, the manufacture of plate glass has been an important industry in Belgium but during the World War American manufacturers in the vicinity of Pittsburgh developed their plants and then demanded a tariff to keep out the Belgian product. Similar treatment is accorded to Sicilian lemons whose importation is not welcome to the growers of citrus fruits in Florida or California.

What is true of particular industries may be of tremendous importance to whole areas—to the people of entire countries. Thus, the United Kingdom in the eighteenth and nineteenth centuries forged ahead with great rapidity. An insular position and freedom from invasion permitted political quiet and an industrial development well in advance of that in other countries.

An economist may refer to it by saying that there were two important laws operating to British advantage. One was the law of increasing returns. In previous chapters repeated reference has been made to the law of diminishing returns. The two cannot be sharply dissociated but for the present purpose, which is merely to draw broad distinctions, they may be viewed separately. The law of increasing returns or of decreasing costs is merely the fact that when a given establishment is operated at full capacity the cost per unit of product is less than when it is operated at partial capacity—a fact related closely to the important overhead costs already referred to.

The early appearance of the Industrial Revolution in England gave to her manufacturers an early advantage with this law and they were not slow to take advantage of it. Their gains were large.

The second law has been called by Alfred Marshall[1] "Lardner's law of squares in transport and trade." It is based on the mathematical formula that the area of a circle varies as the square of the radius. Applied to trade this means that if the distance over which a shipment of goods can be carried at a given cost is doubled, the marketing area that can be reached is multiplied by four. With improvements in transportation this becomes increasingly important.

But as the pressure increases with the size of the business and as the marketing area enlarges (which, in turn, encourages a further increase in the size of the manufacturing plant and compels more advertising) every device must be employed to secure and hold markets. The sale of cotton goods in China, in Russia, in South America becomes highly important. Concessions for construction of railroads, bridges, and irrigation projects are eagerly sought because they furnish an outlet for more product. Affiliations are arranged with bankers through whom such matters are financed and with whose aid the contracts can be suitably drawn. Support of the foreign office is solicited and is more and more often secured. In England

[1] "Industry and Trade," p. 27.

[81]

a Board of Trade, in the United States a Bureau of Foreign and Domestic Commerce, and in other countries still different types of state assistance are utilized. Legislation also is adapted to the exigencies of the situation. In Germany trusts and cartels are viewed with approval or even with enthusiasm, but in the United States we have for many years feared "combinations in restraint of trade." Recently we have relented to the extent of approving them in connection with foreign trade, passing the Webb and Edge laws for that purpose.

All this has been true and increasingly true for decades, but it is peculiarly significant at present. During the World War the belligerent countries greatly increased their plant capacity, especially along certain lines. War demanded particular products in very large amounts and as a result shipyards, coal mines, iron and steel plants, textile mills, etc., expanded rapidly. Also, it should be noticed that this expansion was somewhat similar among the different belligerents. England, France, Germany, Italy, the United States, and Japan were industrialized countries before the war and were already manufacturing along similar lines. During the war their needs were much the same and their increases in plant capacity were in the same lines of production.

At the same time many other countries found themselves cut off from their customary sources of supply. The leading belligerents were not able to export the usual amounts of iron, steel, and textiles. Other parts of the world hastened to manufacture for their own needs. Wherever possible, coal mines were opened, steel mills built, textile plants erected. When the war ended in 1918 there was a greatly expanded plant capacity in all parts of the world.

And this expansion was along similar lines. To a high degree each important country had developed its equipment to meet its domestic needs under a period of war pressure. During the war and through the short period of inflation that followed this was not serious. Prices were high and rising. Everywhere manufacturers were seeking raw materials and operating at full capacity, since goods could be readily sold at the advancing prices. It was a sellers' market.

But in 1921 the blow fell. Prices collapsed and ever since there has been a buyer's market. There has not been a problem of raw materials but a problem of selling goods. With huge investments in plant and heavy overhead expenses to meet, troubles have multiplied.

A few illustrations will help, and shipbuilding will be the first. Shipyards had been expanded to a capacity not easy to estimate but expressed roughly by the tonnage launched in peak years in each country. The accompanying table compares the maximum output for a number of countries, the year for each being indicated after the name.

Relation between Capacity and Output in Shipbuilding for Certain Countries

	Maximum output, thousands of tons	1923		1926		1928	
		Output	Percentage of peak year	Output	Percentage of peak year	Output	Percentage of peak year
United Kingdom (1920)....	2,055.6	646	31.4	640	31.1	1,446	70.3
Germany (1922)...........	525.8	345	65.6	180	34.2	376	71.5
Italy (1921).............	164.7	67	40.7	220	133.5	59	35.8
Japan (1919).............	611.9	72	11.7	52	8.4	104	16.9
Netherlands (1921)........	232.4	66	28.4	94	40.0	167	71.8
France (1921)............	210.7	97	46.0	121	57.4	81	38.4
United States (1919)........	3,579.8	173	4.8	151	4.2	91	2.5

The table also gives the tonnage launched in 1923, 1926, and 1928. The first two are given because they were low points for the world in ship construction and the last because it is the latest available at the time of writing. The percentage of the output in each of three years is calculated in terms of the maximum capacity. This is not entirely accurate, since some of the shipyards have deteriorated in capacity or have been permanently abandoned, but it is the only practicable way of presenting the facts and is sufficiently exact for the present purpose.

The years of maximum ship construction for the countries shown in the table were from 1919 to 1922, when they were still operating under the pressure of war stimulus and post-war inflation. Since that time construction has declined, fluctuating from year to year but in no case returning to the maximum. A certain amount of stability might have been expected by 1928 but whether it has come is doubtful. The United Kingdom, Germany, and the Netherlands were constructing at about 70 per cent of their earlier rate but the rest were far below, the United States being lowest, *i.e.*, 2.5 per cent.

Of course, some of the shipyards have been permanently abandoned but there is everywhere a large unused capacity. This is a burden to be carried by investors who are not securing the returns they anticipated and by workers who are unemployed. It is hardly reasonable to expect anything but bitter competition—a struggle for orders, a scramble for government subsidies, and other efforts to lessen strain and reduce losses.

The pressure appears in a different way in the coal industry, due presumably to the fact that coal is not taken from the mines purely on special order as ships are built under contract. Coal is a somewhat uniform product that may be sold in large or in small amounts and may be mined and stored in anticipation of orders. It may be brought to the surface and accumulate until the markets are congested. With a stimulus to demand, new mines are opened which are not promptly shut down when demand falls off. Instead, they continue in full operation, clogging the markets with coal, or perhaps operate on part time, with loss to operators and privations for workers.

British coal output was 24,337,000 tons per month in 1913 and by 1920 was only 19,435,000 tons per month. The strike of 1921 brought the amount down to a monthly average of 13,823,000 tons, encouraging expansion in other countries to fill the gap. In 1923 the invasion of the Ruhr brought a reduction in German output to 5,193,000 tons per month from its average of 11,354,000 tons in 1921. This stimulated output in the United Kingdom, the United States, Poland, and elsewhere, encouraging an expansion of capacity, much of which became idle when the British strike was settled. Again, in 1926 a British coal strike brought that country's average to 10,692,000 tons while production elsewhere was sharply increased. The coal industry is overdeveloped and is now a world problem. Excessive production, clogged markets, dumping, intense competition, and in many cases very dubious business practices exist on a large scale. The League of Nations is attempting to secure some form of cooperative action in the industry. We might add that a similar attempt is being made in the sugar industry where conditions are also serious but for somewhat different reasons.

Textiles are likewise suffering. In most countries spindles have increased in numbers and this has added to productive apacity, while changes in demand due to shifts in style, the appearance of artificial silk, and other influences add to the distress. Iron and steel plants have a capacity far in excess of prewar, in many cases as much as 50 per cent,

[85]

while demand for steel products has not increased to a corresponding extent.

This growth in capacity is common. There is always a temptation to enlarge plant capacity to meet an increase in demand. If the demand remains permanently higher there is no serious harm done but if it is only temporary the greater capacity is a permanent burden. Or if there are ups and downs in demand there are shorter or longer periods in which losses must be borne while plants are idle.

This tends to intensify competition—unless it encourages agreements and consolidations. The rapid growth in modern advertising is phenomenal and some of it is regrettable, but we need not be surprised. When the production of shoes was merely the activity of a village shoemaker, advertising and salesmanship could not develop. But with the manufacture of shoes concentrated in centers such as Boston, St. Louis, and Czechoslovakia the situation is entirely changed. The factories must be kept in operation. Workers must be kept busy. Raw materials must be regularly available and, most vital of all, the shoes must be sold. Markets have to be secured and kept open, and this means advertising and sales campaigns. The more a competitor advertises the worse the pressure, and a vicious circle is established out of which escape is not easy. Geographical specialization and large-scale production in a competitive world are responsible. This increases distribution and transportation costs until they are an important fraction of the total. As a result a new problem has been created. Large-scale production lowers unit costs if a plant can operate at or near capacity. But the distribution costs just mentioned have grown so rapidly that many observers fear they will more than offset the gains that come from mass production.

There are other results. We hear much today of dumping. Usually it is charged against one's competitor, but the practice is common and not confined to any one line of business or to any one country. Simply defined, dumping is the sale of goods at a lower price in one market than in another. A common illustration is the sale abroad at a higher price than in the home market.

But why? Because at times the home market can be protected from outside competition by tariffs or otherwise. If this is done, then domestic prices can be kept high and competition in the foreign market be met by price cutting, the aggregate receipts from the two groups of markets being adequate to pay the overhead costs that must be met in some way.

Brief reference may be made to concessions sought for business in other countries at sharply competitive prices. Every effort must be made to get additional orders, and the struggle is keen. One interesting tendency that often appears is for loans to be made to foreign borrowers only in case the proceeds of the loan are spent in the lending country—the so-called "tying clause." There is no occasion to interpret these practices as due to any one influence, but a factor of importance is unquestionably the development of modern production on a large scale with its accompanying burdens.

One other tendency may be referred to. More and more of the costs of business are becoming overhead. Some plants are now guaranteeing workers a definite number of days of work per year. In other words, a part at least of wage payments in these plants has become an overhead charge. Unemployment has always been a social burden but this change places it squarely on the shoulders of the management. and makes regular operation more important than ever.

Chapter VI

THE GOLD STANDARD AND THE PRICE ECONOMY

THE analysis in previous chapters has stressed facts and forces that have but little to do with the capitalistic organization of society. Large numbers of people eager to maintain or to raise their standards of living by migration or otherwise; unevenly distributed climate, food, and raw materials; large investments of capital in huge establishments with consequent heavy overhead costs—all these are facts that would persist even though socialism, or some other social reorganization, were generally adopted. The governments of socialized states would have some of the same problems as do the present ones.

In this and succeeding chapters we pass to topics which are more closely related to modern industrialism. The gold standard with the price economy under it is one of them. A reorganized society might attempt some other standard but so might our capitalistic society. Some socialists have criticised modern monetary systems as aids in the exploitation of the proletariat by the bourgeoisie, and the present government of Russia at one time undertook to eliminate money entirely.

Nevertheless, the Russians have reconsidered the idea, and some economists who are not socialists, such as J. M. Keynes, have urged the importance of modifying the gold standard, at least as we know it. In any case, it is unimportant to draw this distinction except as doing so will emphasize the fundamental nature of many of the facts and forces with which we are dealing. Only thus

[88]

can we be fully aware of the serious nature of the dilemma and of the difficulty of finding solutions.

Illuminating definitions of the gold standard are not numerous. Probably the best way to construct one is to notice practice in those countries generally referred to as having the gold standard. In prewar days England and perhaps Portugal were the best that could be found, and their practice included three pertinent facts which may be stated as the tests to be applied in determining whether a country was operating on the gold standard. In a gold-standard country in prewar days we found:

1. Free (*i.e.*, unlimited) coinage of gold and of no other metal.

2. Redeemability in gold on demand of all other forms of money.

3. Gold and gold alone recognized as full legal tender.

To the extent that these three conditions were fulfilled a country was designated as having the gold standard. To the extent that they were lacking the gold standard was qualified. Since the World War few countries fully meet this test. Thus, so long as there are restrictions on the export of gold because an export license must be secured, or for any other reason, the second of the tests is not being fully met. Even before the war few countries wholly met all of them.

It is not inaccurate to say that during the nineteenth century the gold standard was generally adopted. Early in the century most western countries were operating under bimetallism, using both silver and gold coined at a fixed ratio that varied from time to time and from country to country, usually between 15:1 and 16:1. Difficulty was experienced in determining a legal coinage ratio that coincided even temporarily with the market ratio between the two metals. Because this coincidence was lacking, the cheaper or "bad" money persisted in driving out of any country the dearer or "good" money. It was thought by many that concerted action by a number of countries would make possible what no one country could do by itself. General agreements, however, proved impossible and the one important formal attempt—the Latin Union in Europe—was not a success. Organized in 1865 it lingered on, maintaining an official existence until only a few years ago when it disappeared.

Through a period beginning about 1870 there was a distinct movement toward gold as a standard. Russia, Germany, the United States, and others took formal action and in practice all the leading countries went over to it in spite of their legal adherence to some other standard. Their law and especially their practice usually fell short of the ideal expressed in the definition above, but to a greater or lesser degree they approximated it.

Three features of importance to our study characterized this gold standard. As a standard, gold was a measure of value, *i.e.*, the value of all other commodities was stated in gold. It was also a standard of deferred payments, *i.e.*, promises to pay at later dates were ordinarily expressed in gold. Because of its legal recognition as a standard, gold became the most important form in which bank reserves could be kept. Finally, it was used to some extent as a medium of circulation, although this use tended to diminish with the passage of time.

For these monetary uses gold was on the whole probably as well suited as any other single commodity, but it had at least one glaring defect. Although used as a measure of value and as a standard through which deferred payments were expressed, gold did not itself have long-run stability of value. Its value, *i.e.*, its purchasing power, has not been steady, as any examination of the changing price level at once shows.

[90]

The Gold Standard and the Price Economy

A second feature is that its general adoption made it the leading medium for international payments. Not the one most used, since the vast majority of business transactions between countries are settled by drafts, but the one finally acceptable when drafts are scarce or when there is a lack of confidence in them. This has meant a constant flow of gold back and forth between countries.

The third feature is that each country adopting the gold standard determined its own unit—the pound, franc, mark, rouble, dollar. While each of these was a designated weight of gold, the amounts in the different units varied—113.0015 grains in the pound, 4.4803 grains in the franc, 5.5313 in the mark, and 23.22 grains in the dollar. The only significant exception was the uniformity in the weight of the French, Belgian, and Swiss francs and the Italian lira, the reason for which need not delay us. Payments by a debtor in one country had to be made to his creditor in another by the purchase of drafts, paid for with the debtor's money, *e.g.*, a lira, but worded in the creditor's money, *e.g.*, a pound. Hence arose foreign exchange quotations, which are not only bewildering to the layman but which also force all payments to creditors in any given country, *e.g.*, France, to go through the "neck of a bottle." The volume of foreign exchange available at any particular time affects seriously the ease with which payments can be made.

These three features are not to be thought of as peculiar to gold. To some extent they would have existed no matter what single commodity had been chosen as a monetary standard though their seriousness would have been greater with some than with others. They are largely inherent in a money economy and in the division of the world into separate governmental units, each with its own economic institutions and machinery.

[91]

From the general adoption of the gold standard after the middle of the nineteenth century certain effects were noticeable. They had appeared in a different form under bimetallism but the general acceptance of gold did not end them. Instead, with growing economic interdependence and with the increase in foreign trade and investments the results were even more serious.

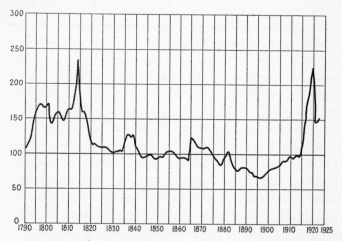

Fig. 3.—Wholesale prices in the United States, 1790 to 1923 (1910 = 100). (*From the Report of the United States Senate Commission of Gold and Silver Inquiry.*)

The accompanying chart showing the fluctuations in the gold prices of commodities in the United States makes clear what occurred, not only in this country but also elsewhere. In all gold-standard countries there was an irregular rise after 1850 for a number of years and then a fall to 1895 or 1896, followed by another rise. These were the long-run or secular price movements as distinct from day-to-day, seasonal, and cyclical changes. The ups and downs produced strain within each country, but with this we are not here concerned. They produced strain also between countries, to some extent between governments but perhaps more between the nationals of one country and those of another.

Notice, first, that gold prices fell for a number of years until 1896. Each gold unit, whether dollar or lira or something else, bought more and more. The value of commodities in terms of gold was falling, or, stating the converse of the same fact, the value of gold in terms of commodities was rising. This created international difficulties of two kinds. The first was between the gold-standard countries and those still using silver, of which there were a few. From the viewpoint of a gold-standard country silver was a commodity like cotton, corn, or coffee. In 1873 silver was worth in gold about $1.30 per ounce but fell until in 1896 it was worth more nearly 65 cents per ounce. In the earlier year an ounce of gold would buy only about 16 ounces of silver, in the latter year it exchanged for twice as many.

This meant trouble for silver-using countries such as India. Their taxes and other internal payments both public and private were made in silver but their external obligations, such as interest on borrowed money, were ordinarily payable in gold. Each year as the gold price of silver fell, it took more units of silver, *e.g.*, silver rupees, to meet the foreign payments. Also, the fluctuations in the gold price of silver introduced an element of irregularity and uncertainty into business dealings between the silver-standard countries and the gold-standard countries. The relation between silver and gold did not remain fixed, and to meet the problem of exchange fluctuations there appeared the device known as the "gold-exchange standard."

It was first adopted by India and later by a number of other countries. One of its important features was the maintenance abroad (particularly in London whose financial importance and even leadership were then unquestioned) of an account upon which drafts could be drawn. The advantages of a large account of this kind were clear and became increasingly important with the growth in the volume and complexity of international business. As the years passed, the central banking institutions of many gold-standard countries also adopted the same practice. Since drafts on London were acceptable everywhere, these accounts were kept chiefly in London. So extensive was the practice that we might describe the situation as one of general drift toward the gold-exchange standard, with London as the only center adhering closely to gold-standard practice.[1]

But the obligations of all debtors increase in severity as prices fall. At this time when the gold price of silver was falling the gold prices of commodities in general were likewise falling. American readers particularly will remember the period as one in which debtor groups in the United States, especially the farmers of the South and West, found it harder and harder to meet their obligations. They received fewer dollars for their corn and wheat but were bound to pay the same number of dollars as before in interest to bankers and to holders of mortgages. Their monetary incomes fell but one group of their expenditures remained the same. Bankruptcies were numerous.

In the international field, of course, the same situation prevailed. Certain countries, such as England and Holland, were creditor countries, *i.e.*, their nationals had purchased the securities of enterprises located in all parts of the world. As prices fell the debtors found payments increasingly difficult, a form of pressure none the less serious because it is not always recognized. Human failure to realize this tendency is due to what Prof. Irving Fisher has called

[1] See KEYNES, J. M., "Indian Currency and Finance," Chap. II.

"the money illusion." When prices alter, that fact is usually thought of as a change in the value of commodities in terms of money. It might just as well be called a change in the value of the money in terms of commodities, and in the judgment of most students the influence making for the secular changes in price levels is more often on the money side than on the commodity side of the price ratio.

While this period of falling prices unquestionably added to the burdens of the debtor countries, it was not something of which they were specifically conscious and does not seem to have contributed to friction. Other aspects of their financial dependence, moreover, to which reference will be later made were probably more significant and were certainly more evident.

After 1896 the price trend was upward, *i.e.*, the value of gold began to fall. Year after year the price level rose until in 1914 it was 98 compared with 67 in 1896 for the United States (according to the index number for wholesale prices published by the U. S. Bureau of Labor Statistics). In England during the same period it rose from 72 to 100 (the *Statist* index number). In so far as an altered price level could do so, this lessened the pressure on the debtor countries and reduced to the same extent the real income received by their creditors. Debts are paid by the sale of goods and as prices mount the debt charges are more easily met.

This statement may give rise to misunderstanding particularly if considered in connection with certain views expressed later. It will be pointed out that as a group the creditors in older countries do not always actually collect the interest due them from abroad. Particular ones do but in the mass they often reinvest much of the interest as it falls due, adding by that much to their total foreign investments. The aggregate thus grows, perhaps for an indefinite number

[95]

of years. It is, of course, to be noted that as the price level changes, particular debtors and particular creditors feel the strain referred to.

More important than this effect, at least outwardly, was that on the banks. It is often argued that the rise in prices was due to the increased output of gold; that this larger supply of the yellow metal accumulated in the vaults of the banks; that interest rates were lowered and borrowing encouraged. The new purchasing power appearing in a competitive market raised the prices of goods. If this reasoning is correct there would have been no competition to secure gold but a competition in lending.

For some reason, however, the period in question witnessed an intense rivalry to secure added supplies of the standard metal. The great open gold market of the world was London to which every seven days came the shipments of gold by steamer from South Africa. At the weekly auctions representatives of the leading central banks bid against each other for the supplies. Orthodox foreign exchange theory leads us to believe that gold would have left London for Berlin or Paris or Vienna or St. Petersburg only where the quotations for drafts in London on each of these centers had reached what is called the export point. Yet an examination of these exchange quotations and the shipments of gold in many cases does not reveal the expected relation but shows gold moving outward, *e.g.*, to Berlin from London, when the rate for drafts in Berlin actually would have dictated a shipment in the other direction.

This may have been due, as suggested by John A. Hobson,[1] to the rapid growth of investments abroad and the accompanying increase in the volume of stocks and bonds that could be offered to the banks as collateral for loans. This expanded their loans and consequently their deposits.

[1] "Gold, Prices and Wages."

As deposit liabilities grew there was need for more and more gold as a reserve against those liabilities. Or, as argued by others, it may have been caused by the desire of the great banks in each country to accumulate gold in anticipation of the coming war. Certainly there was involved the peculiar practice of the European continental banks of enlarging their supplies of gold and then of showing a strange reluctance to pay out the gold on demand.

The contrast between this practice and that of the Bank of England has often been commented upon. Historically the Bank of England has usually viewed its gold reserve as a fund to be paid out as demanded. A reserve was something to be used when called for, not delivered reluctantly to those who had a legal claim against it. On the Continent, however, the practice was different. It has frequently been compared to a curious bit of legislation which is perhaps legendary rather than historical. In a certain city it was observed that often no cabs were available at the cab stands. This was so inconvenient especially on stormy nights that a law was enacted requiring that there must always be at least one cab in waiting at every stand. No matter how much a cab was desired by a prospective patron it could not leave the stand unless and until there was another cab ready to take its place. Thereafter, cabs available for use were scarcer than ever. Bank reserves have often been treated in a similar manner. There must always be an abundance on hand even if they are not to be used.

There is no need to dwell on the war period other than to point out that the difficulties described for the years from 1896 to 1914 were magnified a hundredfold. Monetary systems, business contracts, all financial aspects of economic life in a pecuniary age rested on gold. Gold was secured by every possible means and when secured it was kept by the governments and by the central banks. Against it as a reserve (which could not be used although its amount was widely published) tremendous quantities of paper money were issued. For domestic purposes gold ceased to be used even in the United States whose financial position was the strongest.

Here and there were small countries to which it tended to flow and even become embarassingly abundant. The belligerents, however, safeguarded their holdings. They exported limited amounts only as urgent necessity demanded it. Because of the strong drift of available supplies to the United States the view became common that the amounts in the central banks of Europe were reduced. This seemed especially to be the case when the percentage of gold reserves to note issues was observed. Because of the huge size of the note issues the reserves seemed small. They were small when expressed in percentages of the note liabilities but were actually larger than in prewar days in absolute amounts.

After November, 1918, the money problem for each country was a double one—internal and external. Inflation, the rise of prices, had rapidly reduced the real income of certain groups in the community who were unable to maintain their relative position. All whose wages or salaries were held down by law or by custom or because of weak bargaining power, as well as the *rentier* group whose incomes were fixed by contract in monetary terms, were the losers. Whenever and wherever prices fell the reverse was true. Those with fixed incomes gained while others lost. But rising prices at least meant business activity even though it was feverish and temporary, while falling prices meant for a time business failures, unemployment, and for many no income at all. The gains to certain groups as prices declined were, moreover, by no means an offset to the losses that had been suffered by other groups when

[98]

prices rose. Both movements placed under serious strain the countries where they occurred.

The external problem, which is our special concern, was also serious. It was, moreover, closely related to the internal situation. Prices rose in a given country, say Germany, because of the issue of a large volume of paper money by the Reichsbank. As these issues increased, the probability that they could ever be redeemed in gold at their face value diminished and people in other countries were unwilling to pay for them at their old level, which was 23.8 cents of American money or at the rate of 20.42 marks for a pound of British money. Notes of the Bank of Germany and drafts on German banks could be bought and sold only at a discount. The prices paid varied from time to time and from country to country.

There were two serious consequences of these fluctuations. One was the risk that attended all business transactions. A contract to deliver or receive goods at a specified price in marks or francs or lire was of uncertain value since the worth of the currency was subject to so many changes. There might be gains or losses depending on the direction of the movement. These risks were too great for the ordinary business man to assume and he accordingly was reluctant to trade. An American usually accepted orders for goods only in case he could be assured payment in the only money he thought of as stable, *i.e.*, dollars delivered in New York, perhaps in advance. The consequent friction in business dealings was great.

Another bad effect was "exchange dumping." In a previous chapter dumping, *i.e.*, price discrimination between national markets, has been described. Exchange dumping is not, strictly speaking, to be classed as dumping[1] or, if it is, should certainly be given special treatment.

[1] VINER, JACOB, "Dumping," p. 15.

Inflation, *i.e.*, an extreme rise in prices within any country, *e.g.*, Germany, as explained above, is accompanied by a decline in the external value of that country's currency. But there is a lag. The external depreciation, *i.e.*, the decline in the value of the mark in foreign markets, ordinarily precedes the internal depreciation, *i.e.*, the rise in prices within Germany.

This lag encourages exports and discourages imports. A foreigner can use his money, say dollars, to buy marks at the new low level and then with the marks promptly buy goods in Germany before the prices in Germany can adjust themselves to the new situation. Expressed in dollars the purchaser secures the German goods at a low price, probably lower than that for similar or equivalent goods in the United States. He may, therefore, be able to sell the German goods at lower prices than American manufacturers can afford to meet. Exports from Germany to America are encouraged.

To some extent the same set of facts discourages the importation of goods into Germany. A German manufacturer who must with marks purchase drafts on New York with which to pay for cotton finds the price of dollar drafts high in terms of marks. He will hesitate unless he believes that prices for manufactured cotton goods in Germany will rise materially by the time he can manufacture the raw materials into the finished article.

Enough has been said to show that a depreciating currency encourages exports and discourages imports. If there were a clear gain from such a growth of exports it might seem an advantage to a country to depreciate its currency for the sake of encouraging export trade. But enlarged exports may or may not be wise as a general matter. The issue cannot well be elaborated here but it will probably be agreed that a sudden rush of exports might carry out certain articles that a country would wish to retain, *e.g.*, foodstuffs from Germany in 1922. It must be remembered, moreover, that exports from Germany sold under such conditions, *e.g.*, for fewer dollars than ordinarily, are being sold very low in terms of the other goods that are being imported. The ratio of exchange is a bad one for Germany.

In the country that receives the dumped goods the effect may also be bad. If the dumped goods do not compete with home production there is no harm done. But if the imports compete with a domestic product the results may be harmful. Exchange dumping is temporary, not permanent. The effect may be very demoralizing for the domestic producers and through their distress the country as a whole may suffer more than it gains from the temporarily low prices.

During the early postwar years there was a certain amount of exchange dumping. That it was not large is clear from an examination of the values of the exports from the countries with demoralized currencies. These exports were not swollen. Instead, they were small. In most, if not all, cases they were smaller than before the war. The dumping that occurred was of particular lines of goods, not of goods in general.

It was enough, however, to start an outcry in the importing countries whose manufacturers clamored for protection. In an earlier chapter reference was made to the stories current in America toward the end of the World War that millions of Europeans were planning to emigrate to the States. Similar stories were afloat regarding vast amounts of European manufactured goods, secretly accumulated during the war, that would flood American markets as soon as peace was declared. In spite of the absurdity of such statements they were given some credence and proved helpful as arguments in favor of higher tariffs. In 1921 an emergency tariff law was adopted by the United States, and 1922 saw the passage of the Fordney-McCumber Act generally described as raising American tariff duties higher than any previous legislation. In 1930 many rates were put still higher by the Smoot-Hawley Act.

The United States was, of course, not the only country to raise its tariff barriers. Others were following the same practice, partly as a protection against exchange dumping but for many other reasons as well. Further discussion of tariffs and of other forms of protection is postponed to a later chapter.

There remains to be added here that, at the worst, exchange dumping was a temporary matter. As inflation proceeds, internal depreciation, *i.e.*, the rise in domestic prices, tends to catch up with the external depreciation. In the later stages of such acute inflation as was experienced by Germany the rise in internal prices began to precede the external decline in the value of the mark.

Then, too, inflation could not continue for ever. It has been brought under control in nearly all countries, and in most of them internal prices have become adjusted to those of the world in general. To this France may be an exception, since gold prices in that country still seem to be below world gold prices. Perhaps we should note the current misconception that a "depreciated" currency results in exchange dumping. This is inaccurate. The cause of the dumping is the lag of the internal price adjustments behind the external decline. When stabilization is secured even though it be at a level below the old one and when time permits the necessary adjustments to be made, there is no tendency to this form of dumping. Yet a situation clearly temporary was used as an argument in support of increases in tariff levels. And tariffs are always hard to reduce.

There were two general theories advanced for postwar currency reform. One group wished to abandon the gold standard, at least in the usual sense, and to adopt in its place a managed currency. There is no occasion here to discuss this plan, since there was never much chance of its adoption or even its serious consideration. Its purpose was to provide a system under which the price fluctuations we are describing would have been put under control. Regardless of any merits it may possess, business practice and habits of mind operated against it from the start.

By most expert observers and advisers it was thought better to return first to the gold standard and then to consider ways and means of controlling price movements. This was the advice given by the great international conferences, held at Brussels in 1920 and at Genoa in 1922. Now that the gold standard has been somewhat fully established (1930), thought is being directed to the second question, *i.e.*, price control.

To the countries with demoralized currencies there were three methods of return to the gold standard open, and each of these methods was followed. In some cases the choice was deliberate and in others less so. We need not inquire about motives but merely record events.

One method used was to continue the process of inflation and then repudiate outstanding note issues and other obligations expressed in the old form of money. This procedure was followed more or less fully by Germany, Russia, and Austria, among others. Some of the consequences were tragic and have been fully described by many writers. But it is important not to overlook the gains. In Germany, for example, a great mass of internal obligations, bonds, mortgages, and notes at bank were eliminated, wiped out. Some of the debts were later valorized at moderate rates but the most of the highly complicated network was cleared away. It meant bankruptcies, the loss of savings, and a period of acute unemployment, but as an offset

[103]

there were certain distinct gains. The *rentier* group lost their holdings but there may be set against this the fact that the able-bodied among them had to go to work. At any rate a new money—first the rentenmark and then the reichsmark—was introduced. In a suprisingly short time, in view of the disorganization, monetary order was restored, the new mark being exchanged for the old at the ratio of 1:1,000,000,000,000.

The second method was deflation. This was followed deliberately by England and less thoroughly and less deliberately by certain others. Stated through the English experience it meant a decision that no change should be made in the monetary unit—in name or in metallic content. The pound had been a lump of gold containing 113.00153 grains of the pure metal and was to remain so. As soon as possible, outstanding obligations, public and private, were to be met when due, in gold or in paper money redeemable at face value in gold. This also meant restoring the old relationship or unit par between the pound and the dollar at $4.8665, the quotient found by dividing the amount of pure gold in the pound by the amount in the dollar.

Inflation as just described for Germany meant a rise of prices, the wiping out of many paper values, the sacrifice of the *rentier* group, a short, sharp period of unemployment and bankruptcies. Later economic strain in Germany has been serious but is to be attributed primarily to other influences than the method adopted in returning to monetary normalcy. Deflation meant a gradual lowering of prices, a curtailment of the volume of money and credit, a maintenance of the paper values held by the *rentier* group. It necessarily involved a reduction of export orders, a tendency for imports to rise, an increase in unemployment, and a growth in bankruptcies. It meant aid to the holders of bonds and mortgages and other promissory notes, except in those numerous instances where debtors failed. It meant a heavier burden of taxation and through heavy taxes a serious loss to those propertied classes who had hoped to gain.

Space does not permit an elaboration of all these points, but a word or two of reminder will help. We have noticed that England and later other countries adopted the gold standard, which meant among other things using gold as the standard of deferred payments. Notes, bonds, mortgages —all monetary obligations—were promises to pay a specified number of pounds, *i.e.*, lumps of gold each containing 113 grains of the pure metal. A policy of deflation, of price reduction, was a decision not to let the pound disappear and debts vanish as the German procedure had done with the mark but to bring it back to the old relationship to the dollar. This did not mean reducing prices to their prewar level, since prices in the United States had not fallen that far, but there was a decline from an average of 166 in 1924 to 123 by January, 1930, as expressed by the *Economist* index number.

The policy meant lowering prices but it did not reduce the number of pounds of outstanding government bonds. Taxpayers who were receiving less for each ton of coal or yard of cloth sold had to pay just as many pounds sterling in taxes as before. Their real tax burdens were increased although the nominal amount was the same. Similarly, corporations with outstanding bonds and notes had their real debt burdens increased as did all other debtor groups. Every effort was made to effect economies as the strain grew. Costs of doing business were reduced in every possible way. Wages were attacked, precipitating strikes, particularly in the coal industry, and involving added government aid in a subsidy for coal and through "doles" to the unemployed.

[105]

This account is presented to stress the international problems created by the monetary system. It is not to be assumed that none of the British realized the seriousness of their policy. Some did appreciate it, and a few, among them J. M. Keynes, vigorously protested that the loss through price readjustments was too serious to be undertaken.

But a variety of reasons led to the action. One was the sentimental feeling that the pound should be brought back to its old par with the dollar. Sentiment of this kind is not confined to any one country but is a part of the general national pride that is to be found everywhere. A second influence was the desire of the propertied classes to have the value of their investments enhanced. They owned bonds and mortgages, not only at home but also abroad, whose worth had been lowered by inflation and would be raised by deflation. Hence, they favored it. Third was the belief that deflation was financially virtuous, that it was honorable for all debtors, including the government, to pay their obligations expressed in pounds by delivering pounds of the traditional worth—or at least weight. Americans who applaud the deeds of Hamilton and the redemption of greenbacks at par after the Civil War will agree with this viewpoint. The policy was one of financial virtue and in accordance with the best traditions but here, as at some other points in life, virtue seems to have been its own and its sole reward.

Italy was not able to carry the policy of deflation to the extent that England did. Her inflation had been far more serious. The British pound had once and for a very brief time fallen to $3.18 in American money ($4.8665 being par). This was still nearly 70 per cent of par. But the lira went to nearly 4 cents or only a little more than 20 per cent of par. The task of complete deflation was too great but it was done in part by raising the lira to 5.26 cents where it was set, the policy being thus one of partial deflation and then of devaluation. But even partial deflation added heavily to the burden of all debts payable in lire, discouraged exports, encouraged imports, created unemployment, and caused a general business reaction from which the country has not yet recovered.

The third policy followed in monetary restoration was to devalue the money at the price level prevailing at the time the action was taken. This was neither inflation nor deflation but an endeavor to maintain the *status quo*. With a marked degree of success the plan was put into effect by Finland, Belgium, and, with some qualifications, by France. It meant less domestic strain and less disturbance to foreign trade than either of the other methods. The Belgian franc was held at a new level of approximately 175 to the British pound and the French franc at about 125 to the pound. In each case the prewar ratio had been 25.22 to the pound.

These readjustments of currencies have had a marked bearing on international economic life in these postwar years. The direction of trade has been altered, the real burden of debts has been changed. We have referred primarily to conditions in western Europe, but other countries in other ways have been stabilizing as well. South Africa, many of the countries of Latin America, and now China have attacked the problem, many of them with the expert advice of Prof. E. W. Kemmerer of Princeton University.

As the adjustments are made they bring the world more fully than ever to the gold standard. This step is, or should be, a preliminary one. Gold, the standard of value, is of changing value. As its value declines, *i.e.*, as prices rise, debts payable in gold are more easily met. The debtor finds his task easier and the creditor receives less in real purchasing power. As the value of gold rises, *i.e.*, as prices fall,

[107]

the creditor receives more real purchasing power but the debtor finds the strain growing.

Until recently, only the academic mind has given attention to this. Price movements have been relatively slow, and the volume of debts, both domestic and international, has never been so large as at present. The last few years have directed attention to the issue. In the international field it has two aspects. These are, first, the intergovernment debts of the Western world—reparations and war debts. These have undergone certain reductions but the debtors are quick to point out to the creditors that the debts were contracted when prices were high and are now being paid when prices are lower. When the future movement of prices will be we cannot know but those who, like Professor Cassel, have attempted a judgment believe the trend will be downward. If so, the real burden of the debts will grow except as the effect of falling prices is offset by some other influence.

Another aspect is the attitude of the other parts of the world to the great creditor countries. The growing restlessness in Asia and Latin America will not be soothed by the fact that their governments and peoples are so heavily in debt. No one loves his creditor, and if world gold prices decline still further there will be one more reason for grievance.

There are many economists who feel that the economic and social distress due to price movements are among the most serious questions with which the world has to deal, and increasing attention is being given to them. An organization known as the "Stable Money Association" exists in America for the study of the subject, and the League of Nations is now engaged in an investigation which it is hoped will bring fruitful results.

Three outstanding proposals for price control have been discussed as well as a number of minor ones. Two of the three are based on the belief that the price level is closely related to the amount of gold. The late Professor Lehfeldt of South Africa proposed to control the output of gold by a joint government ownership of the gold mines. Professor Irving Fisher suggests a device which he calls a "compensated dollar." The third proposal, urged by Professor Cassel and others, is that control be exercised by adjustments of the discount rates of central banks.

Most of the discussion in this chapter has been devoted to long-run or secular price movements and their effect on international relations. There is another difficulty. Reference has been made to the scramble for gold in the period from 1896 to 1914. This struggle has again been resumed. For a few years after the close of the World War there were reasons for hoping that an amicable understanding could be arranged under which something perhaps comparable to a general gold-exchange standard could be agreed upon. Unhappily this has not occurred in spite of the recommendations of many experts. Instead, there is the old tendency for many of the central banks to increase as far as possible their supplies of gold.

It appears now in new forms. Since 1914 the pull of gold is with occasional exceptions toward the United States. With occasional reversals the movement has been inward. For a time this was perhaps not unwelcome in Europe for it was assumed that the larger gold supply in America would become a basis for credit expansion there. It was supposed that American prices would rise and that then the gold movement would stop. In the meantime the higher prices would make of the United States an excellent market in which to sell European goods. For reasons that space does not permit elaborating, this result did not follow. It is usually said that the gold was "sterilized." At any rate the general price level did not rise, though there was a wild boom in real estate and later in the stock market.

This pull of the United States on the world's gold has caused great concern. It has been contended that the effect is to create not merely a gold standard but a "dollar" standard; that the location of the world's gold and consequently the trend of gold prices throughout the world are dependent largely on the monetary policy of the United States and particularly on the judgment of the few men who compose the Federal Reserve Board.

Probably this view is an exaggerated one but there is no doubt that the money markets of the world are far from steady. Fluctuations in the official discount rates are an indication of the strain. In 1923 the Bank of England raised its rate from 3 to 4 per cent, and in 1925 to 5 per cent. In 1927 it dropped to 4.5 per cent, where it was held apparently with great difficulty until Jan. 7, 1929, when it rose to 5.5 per cent because of the pull from New York where an active stock market had raised interest rates to an unusually high level. In September, 1929, it was raised to 6.5 per cent. After the stock market collapse in the next month it was lowered and at the time this was written stood at 3 per cent.

The Bank of France rate rose from 5 per cent in 1923 to 6 and then 7 per cent in 1924, fell to 6 per cent in 1925, rose to 6.5 per cent in 1926, dropped to 5 per cent in 1927, and to 3.5 per cent in 1928. For months thereafter the Paris short-time money rate was low and the pull of higher rates in other directions in 1928 and in 1929 was met by diverting, *e.g.*, to Berlin, funds held in London. Also, the Bank of France imported large amounts of gold in spite of its low discount rate and is said to have refrained from carrying the process farther only because of the international strain which such a policy would cause.

This was illustrated in May, 1927, when a large amount was suddenly taken from London. The loss was so serious for England where higher money rates were threatened that a meeting was held in August in New York City attended by the leaders from the banks of England, Germany, and France. Shortly afterward the strain on London was relieved by a reduction in the New York rate from 4 to 3.5 per cent. Soon, however, a speculative movement on the stock market there was followed by a rise in the New York rate to 4 per cent, then to 4.5 per cent in August, 1928, and by August, 1929, to 6 per cent.

Berlin has, of course, been peculiarly at the mercy of international conditions and has kept its rates even where they are only by extensive borrowing abroad. From 90 per cent at the end of 1923 there was a sharp drop to 10 per cent in 1924, to 9 per cent in 1925, and then to 6.5 per cent and finally to 6 per cent in 1926. In the summer of 1927 the rate rose to 7 per cent, where it remained until Jan. 11, 1929, when it was reduced to 6.5 per cent apparently to give a measure of relief to German business. But there was soon a heavy outflow of funds and even a loss of gold which forced an advance to 7.5 per cent in April.

The strain during 1929 is shown by the changes in rates already cited and by many others. The trend was strongly upward until near the end of October, when it was reversed. In the accompanying table the adjustments are shown for the year.

These fluctuations in prices and interest rates, it should be repeated, are not to be blamed entirely on gold. They would doubtless be experienced under any commodity standard, unless it were the so-called "multiple" standard. In part, too, they are related to the far more fundamental question of the scarcity and abundance of capital as distinct from the scarcity and abundance of money. The con-

Foreign Central Bank-rate Changes during 1929

Jan. 7.........	Italy	5.5 to	6.0
Jan. 12........	Germany	7.0 to	6.5
Feb. 7.........	England	4.5 to	5.5
Mar. 15.......	Italy	6.0 to	7.0
Mar. 25.......	Netherlands	4.5 to	5.5
Apr. 20........	Poland	8.0 to	9.0
Apr. 24........	Austria	6.5 to	7.5
Apr. 24........	Hungary	7.0 to	8.0
Apr. 25........	Germany	6.5 to	7.5
Apr. 29........	Danzig	6.0 to	7.0
May 3..........	Roumania	6.0 to	8–9
May 14........	Roumania	8.0 to	9.5
July 2.........	Bulgaria	9.0 to	10.0
July 31........	Belgium	4.0 to	5.0
Sept. 26.......	England	5.5 to	6.5
Sept. 26.......	Denmark	5.0 to	5.5
Sept. 26.......	Norway	5.5 to	6.0
Sept. 26.......	Sweden	4.5 to	5.5
Sept. 27.......	Austria	7.5 to	8.5
Oct. 31........	England	6.5 to	6.0
Nov. 1........	Netherlands	5.5 to	5.0
Nov. 2........	Germany	7.5 to	7.0
Nov. 4........	Hungary	8.0 to	7.5
Nov. 14.......	Belgium	5.0 to	4.5
Nov. 15.......	Poland	9.0 to	8.5
Nov. 16.......	Netherlands	5.0 to	4.5
Nov. 21.......	England	6.0 to	5.5
Nov. 22.......	Norway	6.0 to	5.5
Nov. 23.......	Austria	8.5 to	8.0
Nov. 26.......	Roumania	9.5 to	9.0
Dec. 9.........	Austria	8.0 to	7.5
Dec. 12........	England	5.5 to	5.0
Dec. 13........	Sweden	5.5 to	5.0
Dec. 27........	Denmark	5.5 to	5.0
Dec. 27........	Norway	5.5 to	5.0

sequences, however, are serious and the phenomena we have described add markedly to the economic strain between different parts of the world. To those who know how to interpret them and who understand what they reflect they mean much. Superficially they are only changes in discount rates. But to business men who must borrow from the banks to carry on their operations, even a slight increase in rates may add heavily to costs and cause suspension of operations or even failure. Even if the additions to costs are not too serious to be borne, the high rates are an evidence of a shortage of loanable funds and hence to be dreaded.

Chapter VII

MARKETS IN A MONEY-MAKING ECONOMY

THE modern struggle for markets can be understood only as a corollary of the world economic organization. Hundreds of millions of people are penned up in certain limited areas. They are vigorous and ambitious. They are dependent on other areas for food and for the raw materials used in their factories. But raw materials are useless unless the goods manufactured from them can find a market. Only as they are sold in quantities and at prices high enough to pay for the raw materials and also to yield a profit can the process go on. If there is any hesitation, if markets become clogged, then raw materials are purchased and imported less freely by the industrialized countries. There is a reduction in employment, wages fall, the standard of living declines. If this process goes far, there may even be a shortage of food.

Hence the struggle for markets, a struggle that varies in intensity as conditions change. Notice, for example, the last few years. During the World War and after until the crisis of 1920, the problem was to find raw materials. Prices were rising, goods could readily be sold. But since 1920 attention has shifted. With certain occasional and brief exceptions, such as the supplies and prices of rubber and oil, the problem has not been to get raw materials but to sell the finished products. Statesmen and business men have for some years given their primary attention to markets. Later the pendulum will doubtless swing back.

Markets in a Money-Making Economy

The manufacturer lives in a world organized on the principle of division of labor between individuals, between sections of a given country, between urban and rural areas, between great regions of the earth. He operates a plant in which huge amounts are invested and whose overhead costs are pressing on him mercilessly. He does not carry on business by barter but pays money, *i.e.*, gold or some substitute, for everything that he buys and receives money for all that he sells. His own livelihood and his success in the eyes of his fellows depend on his ability to secure through sale more units of gold than he expends. In other words, he lives in a money economy and therefore must make money. In this particular, as well as in many others, the manufacturer and the banker are exactly like the rest of us.

Markets are imperative. They are a social as well as an individual necessity. They are needed by the Russians as well as by the Italians, any differences that may exist between their needs or between the similar needs of Germans, Belgians, English, French, or Americans being due to the extent of their industrialization or to the degree of their dependence more than to the peculiarities of their political theory or procedure. There are more similarities than contrasts in the foreign economic policies of the British under MacDonald and Baldwin or of the French under Herriot and Poincaré.

That the drive for markets is one which often ignores the interests of the consumer in favor of those of the producer is not surprising. The attitude in any country toward the tariff is an illustration. Assume that in the United States the manufacturers of cotton goods desire a higher tariff for their protection and that the increase would be injurious to consumers. There seems to be every reason why the interested parties should express their views before the

[115]

Congressional committee through which tariff legislation is initiated.

But notice what happens. All who are engaged directly or indirectly in the manufacture of cotton are on the alert. Their chances to make more money through their productive activities are at stake and their interests as producers are concentrated chiefly or perhaps entirely on cotton. Also, their numbers are few and they can readily cooperate. On the other hand, the vast majority of Americans who consume the cotton goods are not easily stirred. Each of these consumers spends only a few dollars a year on cotton— a small fraction of his total expenditures. An increase in the tariff will injure him but only to a moderate degree. Similarly if the proposal is to raise the tariff on iron and steel, on wool, or on anything else. Our interests as consumers are scattered, diffused among hundreds or thousands of articles, while as producers our interests are closely concentrated on a very few items.

Sales efforts will, therefore, be vigorous. Advertising will spread everywhere. Government aid will be sought and ruthless methods will be used. And it is in large part the result of the kind of world in which we live and of the way in which we have organized it. Solutions for any problems created by facts and forces so fundamental, so intricate, and so powerful will not be found quickly or easily.

Markets may be divided into domestic and foreign. No one cares in which of the two he sells his goods. His purpose is to make the largest amount of money possible and this may mean sales at home or abroad or both. Yet the methods used in developing the two are different and they may be examined separately.

Notice, first, the domestic market. A business man, say a manufacturer of steel rails in England, desires to sell as many rails as possible in the British market and of course at a price as high as possible. It is entirely natural for him to limit competition. If his own costs are low he may be able, unaided in any way, to crush domestic competitors and also to keep foreign producers out. But if he does not have any marked advantage he may meet domestic rivals by combining with them, a procedure that does not directly concern us in this chapter. Or, along with his fellows, he will perhaps seek aid from his government. As a result, there has come into existence an elaborate system of devices for shielding the domestic economy from the competition of the world economy. In this system the imposition of protective tariff duties on imported goods is only one element. There are restrictions on the import of human beings and of capital as well as of commodities; and there are restrictions on the export of all three. There are, moreover, methods of encouraging both the import and the export of one or more of them when such seems desirable.[1]

The protective system, defined as an organized attempt, largely through state activity, to protect the domestic economy against the pressure of the world economy, may be defended on social grounds. One of the most serious difficulties faced in modern economic life is the need for stability and the peculiar difficulty of securing it. The need has already been elaborated in our previous discussion of large-scale production with its heavy overhead costs. There might be added, too, the other modern fact that obsolescence is an increasingly serious problem. New inventions are coming with amazing rapidity. No matter what the physical condition of a plant, it may have to be rapidly changed because of some new discovery.[2]

[1] Perhaps the best general picture of this elaborate protective network is to be found in Josef Grunzel's "Economic Protectionism."

[2] See CALKINS, EMEST ELMO, "Business, the Civilizer," especially the chapter entitled Business Has Wings. Also, see FARRELL, HUGH, "What Price Progress." Both express the situation vividly.

Stability is difficult to secure in the foreign markets. They cover a wider area, there are more unpredictable forces that affect them, and to modify or control those forces is not easy. A German manufacturer of dyestuffs cannot readily exercise any influence on what is done in France or in America by his competitors located in those countries.

But stability (which means greater predictability, more certainty regarding the future) may often be furthered in the home market. By judiciously framed immigration laws the supply of labor may be controlled. By adjustments of the discount rates of central banks and in other ways the movement of funds into and out of the country may be guided. Control over gold shipments may affect price levels. There are many forms of direction which may be resorted to within a given country.

Thus, by the use of protective devices, including import duties, the domestic market may be steadied. That such a policy might bring with it certain social gains is clear. Yet it is equally clear that any system of aid to particular industries through import duties or subsidies or in other ways easily comes to be merely an elaborate method of increasing the income of one group in a country at the expense of the other groups.

This is not the occasion to argue the pros and cons of the protective tariff but merely to point out that the forces in its favor are powerful and that there may be social reasons for it as well as the acquisitive desires of particular beneficiaries. A classical statement of the affirmative view is Friedrich List's "The National System of Political Economy," and the best one of later date is Josef Grunzel's volume just referred to. Americans especially will mention the writings of Henry Carey and Simon N. Patten.

But whether the reasoning in support of protectionism is good or bad, the practice of protecting the domestic

[118]

market is more common than is free trade. A survey that includes all protective devices would show protectionism in its many forms everywhere prevalent to a greater or lesser degree, even in so-called "free-trade countries." But though we limit our attention to protective import duties and ignore the many other forms protection may take we find it the frank practice in far more countries than its opposite—free trade. For a time after the repeal of the corn laws by Great Britain there was a free trade drift on the Continent of Europe, but after 1870 Germany and then most of the other countries returned to protection. It is hard to escape the conclusion that the development of modern industrialism made it important to attempt market stability.

Yet free trade is the more orthodox view. Particularly is it accepted by English and American economists, the latter having taken most of their economic theory from British sources to such an extent that one American economist, Professor Fetter of Princeton University, accuses the American writers of modernizing John Stuart Mill instead of modernizing economics. The basic argument for the free movement of goods and of capital and of people is simple. It is based on a sweeping recognition of the principle of the division of labor and the localization of industry where production can be carried on most advantageously. It is also related to the doctrine of *laissez faire* so glowingly described by Adam Smith in his contention that if each individual were allowed to do that which is to his own advantage as he sees it, each will be "led by an invisible hand to promote an end which was no part of his intention."

Some critics have alleged that British writers have advocated freedom of trade only because it is a doctrine peculiarly suited to their own country. This may be a malicious suggestion but the position of Great Britain

[119]

is such that free trade has had distinct advantages for her. Since she gave her attention to manufacturing earlier than other countries the free importation of food became particularly important. The same could be said of raw materials, and since other countries industrialized later there was no serious domestic competition from their manufactured goods until after the opening of the twentieth century. This situation meant that the British manufacturers had little to lose from the freedom of their domestic markets since Great Britain had but few rivals. It also meant a zeal on their part for free markets elsewhere, markets to which British products could be carried in large volume in British ships. For similar, though not identical, reasons a few other countries have kept their tariffs low.

The argument seems simple and some of its proponents defend it with as much vigor as is used by others in arguing for protection. But since 1900 there has been in England a growing movement for a change, defeated once when advocated by Joseph Chamberlin, defeated again decisively when pressed a few years ago by Mr. Baldwin, but apparently gaining ground in these postwar years. The reason is, of course, the peculiar pressure on the British economy. Industrialization has speeded up in other parts of the world and products that compete with the British are appearing in larger and larger quantities not only in her outside markets but also even in England. Irrespective of the merits of either side, the reasons for the current controversy are easy to understand. One may also pause to wonder whether freedom of trade has hitherto been an unqualified gain to Great Britain. It seems to have encouraged industrialization and to have permitted the growth of population to its present 45,000,000. These huge numbers are closely crowded together and under the most favorable conditions are peculiarly dependent. In a dynamic period like the present—and economic life may be increasingly dynamic in the future—stability will be hard to maintain.

But this discussion is concerned with a presentation of the facts and not with advice for the future. Protective devices are usual rather than unusual. From 1870 to 1914 the trend was away from free trade, not toward it. One might perhaps have expected the war to develop a spirit of cooperation in trade, at least among each group of belligerents. To a degree this occurred but the opposite influences were stronger. On the side of the Allies some cooperation was necessary for the conduct of the war but throughout there was difficulty in securing united action, not only in military affairs but also in economics and finance. When the war ended, the machinery for economic cooperation was quickly disorganized.

No matter how disappointing, this was not a proper cause for surprise. All of us must make money. In business the amount of profits received is the main test of success. The drift may be away from *laissez faire*. General world welfare may call for individuals to submerge themselves and cooperate with others far more than in the past. But the traditions are still the other way. In the United States, for example, the general public has listened readily to the allegations of government inefficiency and to the slogan "More business in government and less government in business."

International cooperation was largely abandoned, and where it was retained, as, for example, in the attempts to collect reparations, the results were often tragic. Everywhere governments reduced also their attempts to direct domestic economic life in wise channels. Instead, there was restored the old scramble for private profits, the part played by governments being largely confined to

[121]

raising tariff barriers, providing subsidies, and in other ways assisting private interests to maintain their markets.

It would be a mistake to limit our observations to adverse criticism and to imply that the upward movement in tariffs and the other restrictions on trade in the postwar years were wholly unreasonable and due only to unrestrained private greed. In a previous chapter attention has been called to the huge development of plants in the war period and to the present capacity in excess of the ability of markets to purchase output. Reference has also been made to the extent of exchange dumping during the period of currency depreciation. Under such conditions attempts to protect domestic markets need not surprise us. Especially is this true when we remember that there have been strong reasons for the growth of protection ever since 1870.

Yet this movement proceeded so far and so fast that its effects were harmful even to the interests that had favored it. If the industries of only one country had protected themselves they would have reserved their home markets for their own exploitation and have continued their sales abroad as before—a distinct gain, at least to particular industries. But what was done in one country was done in others and the industries of all found themselves handicapped in their sales abroad. To such an extent was this true that although protection has seemed wise for any one country it was really "collective insanity"—to quote one writer on the subject.

So acute did the situation become that the League of Nations called the World Economic Conference at Geneva in May, 1927. The preliminary committee which had prepared an elaborate documentation pointed out that world population had grown by 5.3 per cent from 1913 to 1925; that production of foodstuffs and raw materials had grown by 16 or 18 per cent. But world trade had grown by only 4.5 per cent, which was less than the gain in population, while in Europe trade in 1924 was only 84.5 per cent of 1913 and in 1925 was only 89.3 per cent of 1913. If Russia is excluded, these two percentages were 88.9 and 93.7. The conference appreciated the gravity of such a situation and succeeded in framing a report that was remarkable for its frank criticism of high tariffs and in its recommendations for reductions. As yet, however, it is not easy to determine what results have followed. Some observers believe that the upward movement has been retarded if not checked. Yet the clamor for higher duties in the United States and the electoral campaign of 1929 in England are reminders that an era of free or even of freer trade has not yet dawned.

As we turn from the problem of domestic markets to that of foreign markets, it is worthwhile first to notice a few interesting facts regarding the destination of exported goods. An analysis of trade statistics is helpful even though it is easy to be misled by them. Close comparisons are impossible because of the different ways in which the figures are compiled and the destination of commodities is uncertain because of reconsignments and other business arrangements. Yet a few comments seem warranted if they are not made too specific.

First let us notice the export trade of the United States. In the five-year period from 1876 to 1880 the value of the annual domestic exports from the United States was only $664,000,000. In 1925 it was $4,819,000,000, in 1927 it was $4,759,000,000, and in 1929 the total was $5,157,000,-000. At the end of the 50 years the amount was between seven and eight times what it was at the beginning. In the latter part of the period the growth has been particularly rapid, increasing from an average of $2,371,000,000

Export Trade of the United States by Economic Classes
(In Millions of Dollars)

Yearly average	Total value	Crude materials		Crude foodstuffs		Manufactured foodstuffs		Semimanufactures		Manufactures	
		Value	Per cent	Value	Per cent	Value	Per cent	Value	Per cent	Value	Per cent
1876–1880	664	214	32.2	159	23.9	162	24.4	30	4.5	99	14.9
1881–1885	775	262	33.8	163	21.0	197	25.5	37	4.8	116	14.9
1886–1890	726	277	38.1	109	15.0	182	25.0	40	5.5	119	16.4
1891–1895	876	295	33.7	151	17.2	239	27.2	55	6.3	136	15.6
1896–1900	1,136	297	26.1	215	18.9	273	24.0	110	9.6	242	21.3
1901–1905	1,427	432	30.3	174	12.2	316	22.2	161	11.3	344	24.1
1906–1910	1,751	555	31.7	136	8.9	317	18.1	249	14.2	474	27.1
1911–1915	2,332	717	30.7	206	8.8	334	14.3	359	15.4	716	30.7
1916–1920	6,417	1,169	18.2	588	9.2	1,133	17.7	487	15.4	2,540	39.6
1921–1925	4,310	1,187	27.5	420	9.7	601	13.9	537	12.5	1,566	36.3
1926	4,712	1,261	26.8	335	7.1	503	10.7	656	13.9	1,957	41.5
1927	4,759	1,193	25.1	421	8.8	463	9.7	700	14.7	1,982	41.6
1928	5,030	1,293	25.7	295	5.9	466	9.3	716	14.2	2,260	44.9
1929	5,157	1,142	22.2	270	5.2	484	9.4	729	14.1	2,532	49.1

in the years 1911 to 1915 to the $5,157,000,000 just given
for 1929. Even if all proper adjustments are made for a
change in the general price level this is a tremendous
gain.

A second feature of American export trade is the constant
change in its composition. A tabulation of these changes
shows highly important alterations. Fifty years ago the
chief exports were raw materials and foodstuffs. The value
of these has continued to grow but they are a diminishing
percentage of the total. In the period 1876 to 1880 crude
materials were about one-third of the total, crude foodstuffs about one-fourth, and manufactured foodstuffs one-
fourth. Together they were over 80 per cent of the total
exports of the country, leaving less than 20 per cent to
semimanufactures and manufacturers. Now crude materials
are only 22 per cent of the total, with crude foodstuffs
about 5 per cent and manufactured foodstuffs about 9 per
cent. In 1929 these three classes combined were only 37 per
cent, while semimanufactures and manufactures combined
had become 63.2 as contrasted with only 19.4 per cent of
the earlier period. Especially have the exports of manufactured goods gained—from $99,000,000 or 14.9 of the
total in the period 1876 to 1880 to $2,532,000,000 or 49.1 per
cent of the total in 1929.

Remembering what has already been said of large-scale
production and of the pressure to operate large plants at
full capacity, we may see a special significance in this
growth in the export of manufactured goods. Year after
year the need for larger foreign markets has grown, and,
as we shall notice later, the same trend is to be observed
in other countries. And a reaction, both curious and serious,
to this tendency is the growth in the costs of advertising
and marketing. Goods must be sold, if bankruptcy is to be
avoided. To be sold they must be advertised and trans-

ported long distances. Expenses mount for salesmen, for publicity, for freight, for storage, and for middlemen until these non-manufacturing outlays threaten to eat up any and all of the gains that arise from large-scale production and the decreasing unit costs that accompany it.[1]

Next of interest is the direction in which those exports go. A tabulation shows that the continent of Europe is the leading export market for the United States and that North America, particularly Canada, is next. Asia comes third with South America fourth. In relative importance Europe has declined in the last 50 years, while the largest gains are being made by Canada and Asia. Europe is still by far the largest market for American exports.

Bringing together these facts, it may be said that the export trade of the United States is rapidly gaining and that the rate of growth is an accelerated one; that manufactured goods are becoming of greater significance as the years pass; and that the most important markets in size are those of Europe, Canada, and Asia. It will be noticed that Europe has a very large population with high standards of living and Asia has a large population though living standards are low. Canada has a smaller population with a high living standard and is near at hand. If one were disposed to indulge in formulæ, he might speak of the size of a foreign market as being determined by the three factors—numbers of people, standards of living, and propinquity.

A second illustration may be taken from the export trade of the United Kingdom. It is usually estimated that only about 10 per cent of the combined domestic and foreign trade of the United States is foreign trade while the corresponding figure for Great Britain is 62 per cent. Also, it

---

[1] See MAZUR, PAUL, "American Prosperity, Its Causes and Consequences"; BORSODI, RALPH, "This Distribution Age"; FILENE, E. A., "The Way Out."

Export Trade of the United States by Continents
(In Millions of Dollars)

Yearly average	North America				South America		Europe		Asia		Oceania		Africa	
	Northern		Southern											
	Value	Per cent	Value	Per cent	Value	Per cent	Value	Per cent	Value	Per cent	Value	Per cent	Value	Per cent
1876–1880	34	5.0	36	5.4	22	3.3	562	83.1	11	1.7	7	1.1	4	0.6
1921–1925	627	14.3	445	10.1	297	6.8	2,318	52.7	499	11.3	141	3.2	70	1.6
1926	748	15.5	429	8.9	444	9.2	2,310	48.4	565	11.7	213	4.4	101	2.1
1927	845	17.4	408	8.4	438	9.0	2,314	47.6	560	11.5	194	4.0	107	2.2
1928	924	18.0	397	7.7	481	9.4	2,375	46.3	655	12.8	180	3.5	117	2.3
1929	962	18.3	434	8.3	539	10.3	2,341	44.7	643	12.3	192	3.7	131	2.5

has been estimated that only 9 per cent of the total American product is exported as contrasted with 25 per cent of the British production exported.[1] These percentages are not to be viewed as accurate but they indicate roughly at least the greater dependence of the United Kingdom on its foreign trade. What has been said of the growing need of the United States for markets abroad is clearly true to a very much greater degree of the United Kingdom. American food and raw materials do not sell themselves but they do so more readily than will manufactured products, which must face much fiercer competition. Besides, more than 80 per cent of British foreign exports are manufactured articles as contrasted with from 50 to 65 per cent of the American.

The United Kingdom illustrates the situation of a country older and more complete in its industrialization, one that is definitely dependent on the flow of a large manufactured output. In recent decades the growth in volume has been great but having had the earlier start it does not, of course, show the percentage gain of the United States. Its composition is from 7 to 8 per cent foodstuffs, about 11 per cent raw materials, and 81 or 82 per cent manufactured goods.

Notice, finally, for the United Kingdom the destination of its exports. A tabulation of the parts of the world to which these exports go is extremely interesting. They may be grouped in many ways, depending on the inquiry one is making. A usual arrangement shows the percentages sent to Empire or Commonwealth markets as contrasted with markets outside, and the accompanying table indicates

[1] The first comparison has been made by Dr. B. M. Anderson, Jr., and the second is taken from Pierre Meynial, *Revue d'Économie Politique* (November, December, 1927), p. 1565, as quoted by Eleanor Lansing Dulles, "The French Franc, 1914–1928," p. 73.

this for the prewar years 1910 to 1913, inclusive. Prewar years are taken only because the changes in distribution during the postwar period may or may not be permanent.

Exports from the United Kingdom, 1910–1913

(In Percentages)

Destination	1910	1911	1912	1913
Europe	34.21	34.73	34.43	34.02
Self-governing dominions	17.74	17.89	18.66	17.54
India	10.69	11.50	11.83	13.38
Colonies, possessions, and protectorates	5.80	5.59	5.86	6.20
South America	11.27	9.85	9.77	9.43
Asia	7.31	8.55	7.73	8.71
Africa	4.27	4.31	4.09	3.84
United States	7.30	6.06	6.17	5.58
Remainder of North America	1.40	1.52	1.49	1.30
Total	100.00	100.00	100.00	100.00

The largest market area in this grouping is the Continent of Europe where over a third of the British exports were sold. Next are the self-governing dominions—Canada, Australia, New Zealand, and the Union of South Africa. Then comes India, followed by the other areas. If we combine the percentages going to the self-governing dominions, India, and the colonies, *e.g.*, for 1913, the total is 36.09 per cent, while for 1910 it is 34.23 per cent—just about the same percentage as goes to Europe.

But most significant for our purposes is another grouping. Bring together those areas where tariffs and other obstacles are most serious. This would certainly include Europe, Asia, the United States, and the rest of North America and South America, excluding Empire areas throughout. For 1913 this includes over 59 per cent of the total. Yet the self-governing dominions are by no means an open market for British goods. There is a considerable amount of Imperial preference but the dominions are developing their own industrial life and to a high degree their tariffs are levied against British as well as non-British goods. The same is true of India. If they are added, the total for 1913 is nearly 90 per cent, leaving only 10 per cent as perhaps strongly under British domination. But the colonies, possessions, and protectorates are only 6.20 per cent of this. Of the small remainder, much of Africa is partly under French, Italian, Belgian, and Portuguese control.

Such an arrangement is in part fanciful but it is serviceable in calling attention to the fact that in spite of the huge size of the British Empire or Commonwealth, most of the British markets are highly competitive and are bound to remain so. There is the somewhat uncertain exception of those parts of the Empire which might participate to a degree in an expanded Imperial preference. But their own interests will apparently prevent this movement giving to the mother country any very great market monopoly.

Germany is also highly industrialized, and France, formerly referred to as not heavily dependent on foreign markets, has become increasingly so since the World War. Germany has no colonies and all of her foreign markets are competitive. France has vast colonial areas but none of them is an important market nor can it become so in the near future.

This summary is altogether too brief but it is convincing. It shows the leading countries more and more industrialized, more and more dependent on foreign markets, and hence driven into a competition that is increasingly bitter. The effect of this on business practice in a highly competitive industry—coal—may be casually illustrated by quoting a statement that recently appeared in the annual report of the Central Committee of French Coalowners.[1] This

[1] Quoted in *The Economist* (London), Apr. 6, 1929, p. 740.

report alleges that in Germany the Rheino-Westphalian Coal Syndicate taxes domestic coal sales 2.20 marks per ton to compensate colliery owners for their losses in competing in foreign markets. It charges that the British are openly applying an export subsidy of 4 to 5s. a ton to the output from the great Midland coal field and are ready to do the same in the Scottish coal field in order to recover lost markets. The report further states that the Poles quote Silesian coal, f.o.b. Dantzig, at prices that practically ignore the cost of transporting it 370 to 400 miles from mine to port.

Other countries than the four specially mentioned—the United States, the United Kingdom, France, and Germany— might be examined, but the same general situation would be observed. In every case, exports have been growing over a period of years. Since the war the United States has continued to gain while the others have been definitely retarded. For all of them manufactured goods are the most important part of the exports. All of them find their largest markets in the temperate regions. For all of them sales seem to be made most easily where there is a large population with high standards of living, located nearby. Markets are smallest in sparsely populated regions that are far away and whose people have small incomes.

This might suggest that the most acute rivalries would occur where the amounts involved are the greatest. And there are such rivalries. Tariff wars between the older countries are frequent; discussions over quotas and most favored nation treatment are common; altercations of many kinds are numerous. At any given time the current news is filled with items that are a reminder of this.

But without minimizing the seriousness of discussions of this type it is to be remembered that they do not readily reach a point where the strain is very acute or where war might occur because of them. This may happen, but the more serious incidents arise from the desire of the exporters of these different countries to exploit the same markets in other regions. Europe took 44.7 per cent of American exports in 1929, while southern North America took only 8.3 per cent, and South America only 10.3 per cent. But concern over Latin-American markets is acute because they are as yet unsettled while western Europe is more stable. Britain's markets in France, Germany, and the United States are more important than her markets in the newer areas yet British attention is directed even more vigorously to the latter than to the former.

Markets in the less settled regions are an object of rivalry because controls can be exercised there that are not possible in the older countries. There is something to struggle for. Then, too, it must not be forgotten that under modern large-scale production even small sales are important. In an earlier chapter stress was placed on the value of each small addition to business, since many expenses cannot be reduced. A large part of the outlays must continue even if sales decline and so the struggle for any small addition to trade will be vigorous. In the newer areas these sales may be relatively small, but, as additions to trade elsewhere, they may mark the difference between success and failure.

Large investments in plant with production under conditions of decreasing costs are only one of several influences that make the modern rivalry intense. Another is the development of transportation and communication that makes possible the quick movement of goods and of news and that has brought closer contacts than could have occurred years ago. The trans-Siberian railway, a direct line from Cairo to the Cape, a Panama Canal—telegraph, telephone, radio, and airplane increase the speed and intensity of these contacts. The clash of French and British at Fashoda 30 years ago has been followed in later years by similar clashes in different parts of the globe. The Russians and the Japanese in Manchuria, the Russians and the English in Persia and Afghanistan, the French and Italians in Northern Africa, the English and the Germans in Turkey, and everybody in China are adequate illustrations. Each group has pushed on until the areas not appropriated by some one of them are few in number. With no significant new countries to quarrel over, England and the United States must perforce argue about Wrangel Island or some apparently unimportant area near the south pole.

Then, too, there is the size and concentration of the interests involved. The struggle is not between isolated individuals whose capital is trivial and influence slight. Instead, we see immense industrial corporations allied with great banking houses, with their direction in the hands of a limited number of individuals able because of their wealth and their affiliations to bring related organizations into line, to influence governments—in short to press the contest on a scale greater and more intense than the world has ever before seen.

During the last 15 years a growing number of writers have described what has occurred. There is revealed an increasing amount of economic penetration and of subsequent political control. Herbert Adams Gibbons in his "New Maps" of Asia, Europe, Africa, and South America and Parker T. Moon in "Imperialism and World Politics" are illustrations. Some writers limit themselves to description, others by their choice of topics or by the language used have shown their abhorrence of the methods followed and of the results attained. In "Red Rubber" and other volumes the late E. D. Morel revealed the horrors of economic exploitation in Africa, and, in part because of

[133]

his efforts, improvements were secured. Leonard Woolf, H. N. Brailsford, and Norman Angell are other English writers of vivid description and protest.

Yet the struggle for economic advantage has persisted with only an occasional softening of method as a result of the publicity given to the worst abuses. It is not at all difficult to find in the scramble for markets one of the causes and perhaps the major cause of the World War. In the peace settlements the same influences revealed themselves, and in the postwar disputes we again find them to the front. Arguments over mandated areas occur because of a desire to control either raw materials or markets; the Polish Corridor was established to give Polish products an outlet to the sea; British friction with Afghanistan is based on an alleged threat to British markets in India; difficulties with China are traceable to the interruption of trade in that country. And all of the strain goes back to the fact that we are human beings and as Mr. Dorsey says we "behave like human beings." We live in a world with a certain distribution of population and natural resources and we have organized our economic lives along certain lines.

There have been many explanations of so-called "imperialism." One has been the need for a population outlet but this certainly cannot be adequate in itself when so few from the densely populated countries actually go to the newer regions. For example, emigration from Germany almost stopped with the growth of industrialization and emigrants from all the older countries have tended to go where they could most improve their own standards. This has meant emigration to Canada, the United States, Brazil, the Argentine rather than to Asia or to Africa. Kipling urged the assumption of the white man's burden; in America for a time there was an appeal to manifest destiny and then to inscrutable destiny. But running through it all as a partial, and perhaps as a major, explanation there has been the desire of particular business interests to safeguard their supplies of raw materials and to control markets. Each business man has been driven by his desire to make money, to secure profits. But his behavior has been in part the method by which the masses behind him have been expressing their needs and desires. In addition to his own impulses, good or bad, there has been the compelling pressure of a social organization of which he has been the instrument.

This is not an attempt to gloss over the horrible occurrences in the Belgian Congo, the tragedies in India, the unfair assumption by the white man of a superiority over the Chinese, or any other gross wrongs of which there have been so many. They have terribly complicated the situation. Instead, we intend merely to observe that even their elimination would leave the major forces unaltered. There would still be the same keen rivalry to market goods. Concessions would still be sought for building railroads, for dredging harbors, for constructing docks, and for exploiting mines. Spheres of influence would be marked out as they have been in the past in Persia, China, and elsewhere and as they are said to have been more recently agreed upon in Albania and in Abyssinia. Protectorates would still be established and colonies acquired if there were left any important areas not yet appropriated.

There is still another phase of the situation to be mentioned now but elaborated later. Goods must be sold and sold as regularly as possible. When England industrialized she thereby increased enormously and suddenly her capacity to produce certain commodities, particularly textiles, iron, and steel. These could not all be sold at home nor could the great flood be sold abroad for cash. Similarly after the World War there was not a cash market for the output of the American factories that had been greatly enlarged to meet war demands. Those to whom the goods were sent could not for the time make payment with their own commodities and services.

This inability to pay outright has been common and the difficulty has been solved by the sale of securities. Stocks, bonds, mortgages, and other obligations have been taken by the people of the industrialized countries. Instead of immediate payment, paper promises to pay later were accepted. There was investment abroad, a process that increased and to a degree steadied the movement of goods to market. This was an aid in the sale of consumption goods, such as textiles, but with the rapid growth of iron and steel during the latter part of the nineteenth century the importance of these sales on long-time credit increased. Steel products are not for the most part directly consumed. They are capital goods and are used to construct railways, to build bridges and factories, and for like purposes. Only with the passage of time will the earnings of railroads and factories be large enough to permit repayment.

This growth of foreign investment will be discussed later. There is one final comment on markets. Developments of the last decade more particularly in Asia, but also in many other parts of the world, have caused great concern both to imperialists and to their opponents. It is said that the people of the exploited areas are chafing, that they will demand more freedom, and that the day of white supremacy is nearly over.

In the political field this seems to be true. Turkey has forced an abandonment of the capitulations. The right of exterritoriality is being modified in China and elsewhere. Protectorates may be softened. One may even imagine colonies and dominions being given complete autonomy.

[136]

But these political changes may or may not be accompanied by economic changes. With a larger degree of political autonomy the government and people of China may protect themselves against many of the abuses that have characterized the past. Tariffs against the importation of particular foreign goods will doubtless be raised. Yet trade has started, the economic organization of these countries has become adjusted to the importation of some commodities and to the exportation of others. These needs will not vanish merely because of a new political structure.

Nor is it clear how seriously higher tariffs and other protective devices will modify the total volume of trade. A protective import duty will, of course, lessen the importation of the particular commodity against which it is levied. Whether it seriously affects the total volume of imports is another matter. Certainly there is little evidence that this result has occurred in the past.[1] Even if an *a priori* argument indicates that such must be its influence, the protective tariff is only one of many factors in economic life and perhaps the others overshadow it in real importance.

[1] See Roorbach, G. B, The Effect of the Tariff on the Import Trade, *Annals of the American Academy of Political and Social Science*, p. 18, January, 1929. Also, Auld, G. P., Does High Protection Hamper the Repayment of Our Loans and Investments Abroad? an article in the same volume.

Chapter VIII

CORPORATE GROWTH AND INVESTMENTS

THE argument thus far developed may be summarized as follows: There are large numbers of people in the world—nearly two thousand million—and these numbers are everywhere increasing even though in a few areas there may be signs of a decline or at least a retardation in the rate of increase. For climatic and other reasons population is concentrated in certain areas and will probably remain so. Emigration has suffered a check and at the best could give only a slight relief.

But food and raw materials are not sufficiently available in the areas where population is most numerous. In part this means that the soil cannot provide an amount per capita adequate for the desires or even for the primary needs of so many persons per square mile. In part it means that some desired foodstuffs cannot be raised at all in the densely populated regions and that nature has located many raw materials far from these areas. Hence a high degree of mutual dependence has developed, a dependence greatly increased because of the growth of manufacturing which demands raw materials and markets and whose profits can be used (1) to pay for foodstuffs and (2) for additions to investment.

And all these millions of people "behave like human beings." Of course they will struggle to secure the bare necessities of life but they struggle even more vigorously to maintain or even to raise whatever standards they have attained. One is tempted to generalize by saying that the

[138]

higher the existing standard the more bitter the effort at maintenance or improvement.

These physical and psychological forces that make for conflict, that would in any case cause rivalry, are intensified because of the forms of modern economic life. Much of our manufacturing and transportation and even many of our marketing activities can be carried on more economically in large units than in small. Hence large-scale production and distribution which are constantly spreading. More and more investment is needed for each plant, and this means a growing burden of overhead costs. If anything, the tendency is in the direction of changing variable costs more and more into overhead costs. But a high percentage of overhead means an intensified struggle for business.

All this has meant division of labor and exchange of products, a process facilitated by the use of money which performs a variety of functions. Barter is not feasible, so as individuals and as groups we produce goods and services which we sell for money. With this money we buy the things we desire, attempting in all our dealings both at home and' abroad to carry on our transactions at a profit. This scramble "to make money" is in itself a cause of strain between individuals, groups, and regions of the earth and is complicated by the choice of gold as the standard. The value of gold constantly changes and so prices move up and down, placing debtor and creditor groups—individuals and often regions—under strain as their gains and losses are altered. The adoption of a money economy rather than barter permits a larger volume of trading and over a wider area. It facilitates the purchase of raw materials in remote places, their importation to manufacturing centers, and the exportation of finished products to distant markets.

This is an involved physical world filled, or nearly so, with human beings whose desires and motives are complex

[139]

and who carry on their affairs in an intricate manner. Compelled by their state of dependence and lured by the desire as well as by the necessity of making money, they compete not only in their purchases but also in their sales. What is bought or manufactured must be sold, and selling is done only in markets. Larger quantities of goods can be sold at higher prices and hence for greater gains if competitors in these markets are reduced in numbers or eliminated. Markets must, if possible, be brought under control and stabilized. There follows the construction of elaborate systems for protecting the domestic markets and bitter competition abroad for contracts, for concessions, for spheres of influence, and often for protectorates and for colonies. And in the effort to maintain a steady flow of products to foreign markets, sales on credit are resorted to by taking bonds and stocks from debtor areas, *i.e.*, by foreign investments to which more attention will be given a little later in this chapter.

Another factor enters—the corporate form of business organization. The customary list of its advantages and disadvantages, its benefits and its evils, is well known but calls for emphasis and elaboration in the international setting. The corporation is a device that permits its members to function in many matters as a single individual. Separate supplies of capital may be combined and larger amounts assembled by a corporation than any one person possesses or could acquire. Many can thus contribute to a joint corporate organization, contributors who could not or would not engage in active business for themselves. Under legal limitations of liability, moreover, the amount that any one security holder may lose is definitely restricted, usually to the amount that he has actually invested.

Corporations are of interest to us in this volume from two standpoints—that of the creditor and that of the debtor. First, it is to be noticed that the people in certain parts of the world have been able because of their earlier economic development, their basic natural resources, and for other reasons to embark first on the process of capital accumulation. This beginning is difficult and slow. Economists tell us that capital originates in saving and that saving means sacrifice. This is undoubtedly true, at least in the earlier stages when small amounts are painstakingly assembled. Production, moreover, with the aid of capital—the "roundabout" or "indirect" process, as it has been called—seems slow. But once started its economies are enormous and with the appearance of new inventions the gains are enhanced. Out of the enlarged product new savings can be made at less sacrifice than for the original ones. The rate of accumulation is thus not merely maintained but constantly accelerated by the two facts—the additions that come from the larger annual product and the constant adoption of new and more productive forms of capital which make the annual output larger.

This acceleration gives those who have the early start a pronounced advantage. They assemble their savings, construct railways, factories, roads, bridges, and steamships which after a time tremendously enhance output. These gains are in part reinvested in the properties from which they have been earned, *i.e.*, they are "ploughed back" as reinvested earnings, thus making possible a still larger output. Or in so far as they are distributed to bondholders and stockholders in the form of interest and dividends, these earnings are, in part at least, invested in other corporations whose productivity is thereby enchanced. There is developed a class of security holders whose wealth rapidly increases, a class that may be a small percentage of the community or a larger one. In some countries—"older" ones, so called—such as Holland and England,

[141]

the volume loaned and of securities thus acquired has been huge as contrasted with the amounts owned elsewhere, for example by the people of Asia and of Africa.

These investments are, almost by definition, largest among the people who carry on production with the aid of tools and machinery, *i.e.*, with capital. And the greater their use of capital the more the savings and the larger the investments. Let these facts—the corporate organization of business with its security issues and the growth of investment—be combined with another one previously developed, *i.e.*, large-scale production and the consequent necessity for continuous operation, available markets, and supplies of raw materials. Factories will be constructed as fast as investors, under the persuasion of promoters and security salesmen, furnish funds; or the process will be guided by boards of directors who may, within wide limits, decide to reinvest earnings and to expand the business rather than to distribute dividends to stockholders. Investments thus made may be in enterprises at home or abroad; and they may be in plants at home for the manufacture of goods to be sold at home or abroad or both. There may be some preeminently wise distribution among these various ways in which funds can be used but no one has yet found a formula to which there is general agreement and in practice no definite balance between them is to be ascertained.

Certainly one fact emerges. So much is invested in some kinds of domestic plants that not all of their product can be sold in the home markets or, if it could be sold, not at prices high enough to cover the costs of production. Hence sales abroad and all the efforts that are made to expand and to control markets. It must not be forgotten, too, that any diminution in the volume of sales is serious. If for any reason demand increases, plants are apt to be enlarged. But

[142]

whatever the size of the plant, a steady flow of orders for its product must, if possible, be secured. The investment in the business cannot be easily withdrawn, since capital is not sufficiently mobile. If the plant is enlarged, even to meet a temporary growth of demand, the new and larger factories must be kept going at a large fraction of capacity or bankruptcy may follow.

An illustration may be of help, and manufacturing in England will do. With the invention 150 or 200 years ago of new mechanical processes for textile manufacturing there came a rapid growth in the output of British goods. Even at the lowered cost not all of these goods could be sold to advantage at home, and foreign markets were expanded. Their capacity was often overestimated and losses were frequent and heavy, but their development was continued in spite of occasional congestion. After all, textile products are consumption goods. Ordinarily they were sold for cash or on short-time credit and a business reaction in the market while undoubtedly serious did not leave the British with an accumulated mass of unpaid long-time obligations on their hands. There were, however, many losses through the inability of the foreign markets to pay regularly for all of the goods furnished them. Also, the sale even of these consumption goods was in part maintained by the willingness of the British investing public to buy the stocks and bonds of enterprises in other regions.

A little later the development of the iron and steel industry further complicated the problem. Iron and steel products are chiefly capital goods. Orthodox financial theory would say that outlays by a railroad for steel rails, for structural steel, or for locomotives may properly be charged to capital account rather than to income. Long-time bonds or stock certificates may, therefore, be sold

[143]

to get funds for their purchase. In fact the necessary cost for such products is so great that they can be paid for only over a series of years. The issue of long-time promises is not only possible but also necessary if the purchases are to be made. Accordingly sales abroad could be maintained only if investors somewhere would buy these long-term securities. And, of course, these investors were chiefly to be found in the older countries, notably in England itself. As a result British manufactured goods made their way overseas, partly paid for at once in cash but to a large extent exchanged for pieces of paper—bonds and stocks of foreign governments and of foreign private corporations. The British were investing abroad. They became creditors.

This is a statement of the significance of the growth of the corporation from the side of the creditor countries. Large funds were accumulated, huge plants erected, a condition created under which a struggle for markets was necessarily intensified. There should be added a reference to the individual owners of securities. It is often said that the corporation is impersonal, that it lacks a soul, and that corporate behavior shows a disregard for the ethical codes that to some degree restrain natural persons. The anonymity of the corporation is suggested by the French designation *Société anonyme*.

But another way of putting it is better. The officers and directors of corporations are in most regards like the rest of us. Professor Werner Sombart properly attributes to the business leader, the captain of industry, certain distinguishing traits, but it would be an error to imply that these leaders are influenced by less worthy motives than are the rest of us. At any rate we must not overlook one important element in the situation. Their continued control of their respective companies depends primarily on one thing—their ability to earn dividends. A default in interest payments is tragic but the passing of a dividend or even a reduction in the rate is serious.

And the trouble makers are the stockholders and bond-holders—many of them ourselves. Our small savings are invested in the securities of huge corporations about which we know little and usually care less—provided we get our interest and dividends. Some of the responsibility for misconduct in high business places rests on the great body of security holders who are kindly and humane in matters that are immediately before their eyes but thoughtless or indifferent to the behavior of the corporation they own—provided they receive their interest and dividends.

As a protection against this corporate misconduct it is possible to raise safeguards. In the United States, for example, there is a mass of legislation restraining business conduct—antitrust laws, pure food laws, market inspection, and what not. There is an Interstate Commerce Commission to watch over the railroads, a Federal Reserve Board which admonishes and within limits controls the banks, a Federal Trade Commission to encourage or to enforce fair competition in other lines of business. And there are the courts to enforce the laws. Also, ethical codes are developing in all lines of business, and at times where the law fails, public opinion and the views of stockholders show themselves effectively.

Other countries have their own ways of meeting the same problem. But these are domestic matters. In the international field, business codes are different. What is considered wrong in my dealings with a fellow countryman may be highly proper if as an American I am competing with an Englishman, a Frenchman, or a Belgian. That does not mean that there is no code of conduct at all but merely that the code is different. Practices are often

encouraged or condoned that would not be tolerated withi
any of the leading countries. When one adds to this sor
of code the limited body of legislation governing inter
national business and the almost complete lack of sanction
that compel obedience to it, the absence of restraint i
international competition is better understood.

Something should be added regarding the significanc
of the corporation to the newer countries. If there were n
corporations, Englishmen might still invest in the Argen
tine or in China. But the process would be difficult. Th
nationals of one country, say Great Britain, can buy rea
estate in the Argentine but the obstacles are great. Lan
is of varying qualities and parcels offered for sale are no
of uniform size. To find a particular Englishman wh
might be willing to buy a certain area of land adapted t
some specialized use and permanently located in a give
spot is not easy. But if a corporation is organized to acquir
considerable areas of land in the Argentine, its bond
and its stocks find a much readier market. An investo
can buy only such amounts as he desires, the securitie
of any one of the issues are entirely uniform in quality
and he may, to the extent he prefers, distribute his invest
ments among several corporations and by diversificatio
lessen the risk.

The corporate form of organizing business thus partic
ularly facilitates investments at a distance and has bee
a distinct aid in the flow of capital from one part of th
world to another. This capital movement has been furthe
facilitated by the fact that banks could be of greater assist
ance. Real estate and other fixed assets are a poor ban
investment or even security for bank loans. If a corpora
tion is organized to acquire this same property, its stock
and bonds have a certain degree of liquidity. To som
extent these securities, especially the bonds, may actuall

be purchased by banks, and both the stocks and the bonds may be used as collateral for loans.

But corporations are not so simple as this description implies. They may be very large but they may also be very intricate. Small corporations combine in numerous ways. They may have simple agreements to pool orders or earnings or to divide markets. The stockholders of a number of them may place their stock certificates in the hands of a group of trustees for coordinated management, thus forming a trust. There are mergers and consolidations of corporations and there are cartels of many kinds. The arrangements may be permanent or temporary. The forms of combination may be fairly simple or highly intricate, as an examination of the financial structure of any large holding company will indicate. Among the most interesting and most important of the modern forms of corporate development is the investment trust. Its assets are not physical properties but the securities of various enterprises. In fact it exists merely for the purpose of investing the funds of its own stockholders and bondholders in the stocks and bonds of other corporations. By wide diversification the risk is greatly lessened and by frequent purchases and sales, as market conditions warrant, the earnings of the investment trust may be greatly enhanced.

There seems to be almost no limit to the development of the corporation. Horizontal combinations bring together all corporations engaged in some given stage of the process of production. Vertical combinations bring together the corporations engaged in the successive steps of producing some article or group of articles, such as iron and steel products. Steps may be taken to unite all the producers in any given line such as textiles or steel or coal within a given country. Or the idea may be carried further as in the theories of the guild socialists in England or of Walter

Rathenau in Germany, to the point of combining all of these groups under a single leadership. This has gone far in Germany where the influence of this centralized direction is already very great.

Such developments, it will be noticed, tend to coordinate the economic life of a given country in such manner as to unify it perhaps to a high degree and to consolidate it in opposition to the similarly organized economic life of other countries. The significance of this and of certain related facts will be considered in the next chapter. For the moment we merely notice that such a movement is greatly facilitated by the corporate form of organization.

From the standpoint of international affairs the corporation is important. Modern production is often concentrated so fully in some one line, such as textiles, or coal, that all of the output cannot profitably be sold in the domestic market. A part of it must be sold abroad and sales must be at a high level and be held there as firmly as possible. There are in practice wide fluctuations but to an important extent a certain steadiness has been maintained because home investors have bought the securities of enterprises in the importing country.

The reasons why these investments are made by a national of one country in the enterprises of another is that he has funds to invest and the opportunities for a high return may be greater abroad than at home. Because the properties he acquires are at a distance and usually in a less developed part of the world the risks are greater. Many investors do not care to take these risks, so the supply of funds available for foreign investment is smaller. The result is usually a higher rate of yield than on investments at home.

From the standpoint of the borrower the advantages of the arrangement are clear. A long time has elapsed since the money lender was an object of scorn and the taking of inter-

est condemned. Relics of the older view are found today
among those who indiscriminately criticize lending abroad,
apparently assuming that those who borrow are thereby
enslaved. Unfortunately it is possible to find among international investments enough illustrations of extortion to
warrant many of the charges that are made. But reckless
condemnation of all loans from investors in some parts
of the world to borrowers in other areas is not only futile.
It usually overlooks the fact that in its fundamentals the
foreign loan is the same as a domestic loan and possesses
the same general merits.

An investor has funds to lend. This is not because he is
peculiarly virtuous. He may have economized and saved
in a way that benefits not only himself but also society,
or he may be the idle son of a business buccaneer who has
no good qualities and who has never toiled nor spun.
But this is at present a world of private property and of
inheritance and unless we are ready to advocate rather
wholesale and very rapid changes we must accept it as
such. Those in whose hands funds have accumulated will
be willing and eager to lend. At present these are usually
private individuals and corporations, but if the Soviet
government should prosper sufficiently it might invest
its funds as has the British government in the shares of the
Suez Canal or lend them to military associates as did the
government of the United States during the World War.
And as yet there are few signs that creditors, speaking
through their governments, are any more generous than
are private investors.

But the borrower has something to gain. There are many
unfortunate instances of international borrowing under
compulsion but usually funds are loaned to a government
or to a corporation or to an individual who hopes to use
the funds so advantageously that he can pay interest,

repay principal, and have something left over. Extortions are frequent and will be discussed a little later. The general situation, however, is one of ordinary business. The loan of capital, the interest rate charged, and the profits made are to be explained by whatever theories or laws of economics are applicable elsewhere.

The experiences of the United States furnish a suitable illustration. During the period ending about 1873 there was an almost continuous import balance of trade, and doubtless also an import balance of all payments. The total value of the commodities and invisible items imported was greater than the value of the exports. This was possible because the people of Europe were willing to purchase American securities—stocks, bonds, and mortgages. Particular exporters from Europe to the United States were paid in cash while other individuals bought the securities. But viewed in the aggregate, Europeans sent goods to America—chiefly capital goods—taking, in part, American exports which were chiefly foodstuffs and raw materials. For the balance they were not really paid but took instead the securities which were in essence merely written promises to pay at a later date. The states, municipalities, corporations, and private individuals of the United States were becoming indebted to the people of other countries.

If this had not been done, the economic development of America would have proceeded more slowly. Capital could have been accumulated only out of domestic savings, a much slower process than borrowing. Development would have lagged. By borrowing abroad, capital was promptly secured and the productivity of the country was rapidly increased. By 1873 the accumulated debt had become rather large and annual interest payments had increased to a very considerable amount. Foreign borrowing continued but at a declining rate and, aided by other factors, the balance

[150]

of trade was changed to an excess of exports. By 1913 even the balance of payments was probably altered and Americans began to send abroad more than they received, thus shifting from the borrowing stage to the lending stage. Since 1915 this movement has continued and the United States is now very heavily a creditor country.

This trend is not peculiar to the United States but is to be noticed in many other countries. The movement through various debtor and creditor stages has led some observers to summarize the tendency by stating that a country will normally pass through four periods in its economic development. First, the immature debtor stage—one of early borrowing from abroad and of a consequent import balance of trade. Second, the mature debtor stage—one of continued net indebtedness but with a debt so large as to make necessary an export balance in payment of the interest annually due. Third, the immature creditor stage, during which the process of lending abroad is started. This, of course, calls for an excess of exports, since lending abroad means exporting more than is imported and receiving promises to pay the balance later with interest in the interval. Fourth and last is the mature creditor stage. By the time this stage is reached loans abroad have become very considerable and the lending country is in a position to receive large amounts each year as payments of interest and perhaps in repayment of principal. This brings an import balance of trade.

These four stages are interesting but should not be too readily accepted as an accurate interpretation. Like other generalizations they should be tested, and two methods suggest themselves. One is to examine the facts for different countries to see whether they correspond with the suggested explanations. General economic histories are abundant and there are a number of special studies. They seem to make clear in particular cases the existence of the earlier stages—immature debtor, mature debtor, and even, in some cases, the immature creditor. But there is more doubt about the last or mature creditor stage. The idea is clear enough. When investments abroad have reached a high level the lenders are presumably to live at least in part on the annual interest payments. One may compare it with the behavior of an individual who in his old age lives on the income from investments made in his earlier years.

But analogies are treacherous and in this case actual illustrations are hard to find. This is due in the first place to the lack of adequate data for any extended period of time. Trade figures are available but information on the invisible items is very scarce. Only in the last few years have careful efforts been made to estimate all of the items in the balance of payments and this is being well done for only a few countries. Most of the results are still meager. Also, in the last few years a number of the countries that might perhaps have become mature creditors have through the World War suddenly been pushed back into a debtor position. Germany is an illustration.

Often the United Kingdom is mentioned as a clear case of the mature creditor, and the evidence usually given is her excess of imported commodities for many decades. But invisible exports such as the earnings of the British merchant marine; the commissions and other earnings of British bankers and brokers; and the expenditures of foreign tourists in Great Britain must be allowed for, and they are of growing importance. Some observers have argued that they are large enough to cover the import balance of trade and that British foreign investments are actually being added to year by year through the reinvestment of at least a part of the interest due and occasionally by something more. Conclusions should not be hastily drawn on the basis of data covering only a few years, especially since what is available includes chiefly a few postwar years whose occurrences may be out of the ordinary. Judgment must be suspended until more data have been collected.

Another method for testing the theory is by *a priori* reasoning. Why should it be assumed that a mature creditor stage is to be expected, and are there any reasons for assuming the contrary? The assumptions on the affirmative side have been stated. On the negative side it may be pointed out first of all that there must somewhere be a limit to the process. Not all countries can be mature creditors at any given time. It would mean that all would have import balances without any explanation of their origin. Such a situation reminds one of the community where all the people made a handsome living by taking in each other's washing.

Nevertheless the process might continue until a considerable number of countries—say the leading ones of the Western world—became creditors while a number of others, *e.g.*, those of Asia, Africa, and Latin America remained for a considerable time debtors, each year sending to the creditor countries an important fraction of their product. How long the debtors may be willing to do this is becoming increasingly doubtful if one is to judge from recent developments in such areas as India, China, and Mexico.

On the creditor side, also, there is a problem. We have dwelt on the fact that investments in recent years have seemed a method by which the huge product of textiles, steel, and other commodities can be sold abroad. With production distributed as it now is some of these goods can be sold only if they are sold on credit, *i.e.*, if securities instead of actual payment can be taken. The momentum of large industry is tremendous and there will be a powerful tendency to continue the process of marketing domestic

[153]

manufactures abroad and of selling the foreign securities at home.

From time to time this practice is criticised. Objections have appeared in the United States to American foreign commercial loans from two groups. The first is those who believe many of these loans to be an expression of imperialism—a word very seldom carefully defined. It is argued that often loans are pressed upon borrowers who desire to borrow much less or not at all; that often the loans are negotiated with sovereigns or finance ministers for their personal gain; that the terms exacted are often onerous or even extortionate; and that the American government is often persuaded to use its influence to secure the payment not only of loans made conservatively and in good faith but also of many whose terms were iniquitous.

Another group object by asserting that the sums lent abroad are huge; that a large exportation of capital means less for domestic industries and at higher rates of interest; that domestic welfare would be enhanced by using more of the funds at home; and that the risk of the loans abroad makes unwise the diversion of such large amounts to foreign sources. In the United States these criticisms have not been voiced so much by serious students as by more superficial observers but in Great Britain at least one economist of repute, J. M. Keynes, has definitely criticized the extent of British loans abroad and urged the diversion of a larger amount of funds to domestic uses, the means employed to be a modification of the trustee acts. In France, too, loans abroad are directed and often discouraged by government control of listings on the Bourse.

These objections do not at present weigh heavily against the forces making for capital export. Temporary obstacles to lending abroad have been employed by some of the larger European countries during their period of domestic reconstruction but these will probably not be permanent. The influences in the other direction are extremely powerful. Large plants with highly specialized output are finding it difficult to sell their product. The heavy and older staple industries are under special pressure—iron and steel, coal, shipbuilding, and textiles being the worst of the sufferers. In all these industries and in some others existing plant capacity is very large. The tendency is to use protective tariffs and other devices to preserve the home market for the home producer and then to permit or perhaps even encourage him to dump a part of his output abroad. This means a discrimination in prices between home and foreign markets and bitter competition with the producers of the same or competing articles in other countries. It is so much true that the general pressure in favor of exports and against imports is very strong.

The situation is a curious one. If one or more countries should have an excess of exports (invisible items included), than others must, of course, have an excess of imports. It is not possible for all countries at a given time to have an excess of either. On any particular day I cannot give you more than you give me while at the same time you give me more than I give you.

The result is interesting. For various reasons a very large number of countries are attempting an excess of exports. Yet some of them who apparently should have such an excess are experiencing the very reverse—an import balance —while others who perhaps should have an import balance are instead maintaining a heavy export balance. I say "apparently" and "perhaps" because it is not easy to decide what ought to be and I have no desire to complicate the discussion with ethical considerations. Even the economic advantages and disadvantages of a balance one way or the other are hard to estimate.

[155]

Germany will serve as an illustration on one side, the United States on the other. Before the World War Germany had an export balance of payments (although she had an import balance of commodity trade) and her nationals had loaned considerable sums abroad, amounting perhaps to 28,000,000,000 marks. As a result of selling many securities during and after the war, of heavy borrowing abroad since 1924 on which annual interest payments are now due, and, above all, of the imposition of reparation claims, her position has become very heavily that of a debtor country. This involves external payments unless outside parties are willing to accept indefinitely further promises to pay in lieu of actual payments of principal and interest. The acceptance of these further promises to cover both principal and interest means, of course, the piling up, the "snow-balling" of the amounts by compound interest. This may continue indefinitely, but presumably there must come a time when external payments will really begin. When they start there will, of course, be an export balance, *i.e.*, Germany will export an aggregate of goods and services in excess of her importation of goods and services.

But to date the situation is quite different. This excess of exports has not appeared. Instead, there is (with occasional brief exceptions) an excess of imports. At times it is a very heavy one and is possible only because the Reich, states, communes, municipalities, and corporations have been borrowing, *i.e.*, selling their securities abroad. The external debt seems to be growing, not diminishing. Instead of taking from Germany, the rest of the world is lending more and more to Germany. To date, the attempt to collect from Germany does not seem to have succeeded. Prior to 1924 the amounts actually paid by the German government that could be credited to reparation account were not large. Since 1924 the amounts due have been punctually remitted but only from the proceeds of the loans just mentioned.

For this there are just two conceivable outcomes. One is for actual payments to begin by a growth of German exports. But in an economic world of the kind we have been describing this will not be welcome. Speaking broadly, an expansion of the trade of one country does not injure others. But it may be pointed out that through the growth of exports from any one country particular interests in other countries may be injured and conspicuously so. Their protests are apt to be so effective that trade barriers will be interposed. German exports will continue to encounter many obstacles.

The second possible outcome is to scale down German obligations, and this process is going on. In the fall of 1918 during the excitement of victory, Germany was to pay the total cost of the war to all belligerents—the first theory of reparations. In May, 1919, in the peace treaty the theory was modified. Payments were to cover all damages to civilians, plus pensions—a second theory. The impossibility of paying these amounts was dimly felt and sought expression in the peculiar settlement of May, 1921, in which A, B, and C bonds were demanded, the A and B bonds totaling 50,000,000,000 marks—apparently being an attempt to approximate capacity to pay—while the C bonds amounting to 82,000,000,000 marks were added as a camouflage for the public and for later trading purposes. There later appeared the capacity-to-pay theory, which found clear expression in the Dawes Plan of 1924.

As time has passed Germany's creditors have seen the necessity of further reductions and there has emerged a fourth theory—that of demanding from Germany only the amount needed by her government creditors to meet their external political debts plus for some of them a sum to

[157]

cover actual outlays on reconstruction. This theory was pressed in Paris in 1929 and the outcome appeared in the Young Plan. It remains to be seen how much will in the end be actually collected by the outside world from the German economy. Thus far Germany has had an import rather than an export balance.

The next illustration is the United States which is now strongly a creditor country. This creditor position is a rapid development of the last 15 years but seems now to be clearly established. Estimates of American total investments abroad vary and, of course, the amounts constantly change, the trend being upward over a number of years past. Today the private as distinct from the political debts are by some estimated at nearly or quite $15,000,000,000.

The Department of Commerce estimates the total private long-term American investments abroad on Jan. 1, 1930, at from $13,366,000,000 to $15,366,000,000. The sums due from foreign governments, ascertained by capitalizing the debt settlements at some assumed rate of interest, are $5,000,000,000 or $6,000,000,000. From these combined amounts which total from $18,366,000,000 to $21,366,000,-000 should be deducted the amounts invested in the United States by foreigners. This is placed by the Department of Commerce at $4,700,000,000.

But no matter what the principal sums, the more important thing is the annual payments due. On the public or political debt this was $212,000,000 in 1929 and was estimated by the Department of Commerce at $976,000,000 on private investments for the same year. These total about $1,188,000,000,000 annually due on these capital accounts and suggest to some that the United States is reaching a "mature creditor" position and will soon begin to collect by means of an import balance of payments.

As yet, however, collections have not begun. Notice the possible methods. One is by an excess of merchandise imports over exports, but the export balance in 1928 was $1,037,000,000 and in 1929 was $841,000,000. Except for several years during the war imports have been growing but exports have increased more rapidly. Another method is through the remittances of immigrants who send appreciable sums home but our immigration laws have affected this and the estimated net amounts from this source have declined from $700,000,000 in 1920 and $500,000,000 in 1921 to only $250,000,000 for 1928 and $247,000,000 for 1929. Foreigners might and do pay in part by carrying our goods in their vessels but we object and their estimated net earnings have been declining with the development of the United States merchant marine and were only $80,000,000 in 1928 and $115,000,000 in 1929. One after the other, foreign methods of remitting tend to decline in net amount and there is no clear indication yet of any change in American policy. Immigration laws are more strict. Tariff levels are apparently being raised, assistance is already being given the merchant marine and more is demanded. As yet there is no clearly visible tendency for the United States to develop an import balance of payments. This is not a prophecy that it will not occur. It is merely a record of what has happened and of present tendencies and a recital of the influences that must be overcome if the reversal appears.

Let us summarize these influences as they may be found in varying degrees in the great industrialized countries, including western Europe, the United States, and Japan: Large and still growing populations dependent on a continuance of manufacturing and commerce, producing in huge plants which represent large investments with heavy overhead costs; specialized production in lines which frequently must compete directly or indirectly with the same or similar or substitute articles from other countries. An economic organization in which man's interests as a producer are specialized and concentrated while his interests as a consumer are widely diffused; in which he must make money by safeguarding his supplies of raw materials but still more by vigorously marketing his goods at home or abroad or both; in which, if need be, investments abroad must be made to keep the goods moving freely to market while protection is sought to keep foreign goods out of the home market. A world in which industrial and even agricultural production and the extractive industries are under strong inducements to make money to satisfy bondholders and stockholders; in which money can be made only by producing on a large scale in order to get the low unit costs that permit low prices; in which this can be done only by vigorous sales methods which often become ruthless and destructive.

It is these influences that operate against cooperative arrangements and which must in some way be overcome or offset if tension is to be relieved. How, under such circumstances, can the strain be lessened? How can any given country be brought to receive the desirable volume of imports? Will creditor countries be willing to collect not merely on public and political debts but on private investments? Or, can the present trend continue indefinitely?

One possibility is, of course, to take large losses on foreign investments, to submit to defaults rather than to continue the present process. This would then presumably be followed after a time by new investments. One intelligent newspaper correspondent in the United States who has been writing in favor of higher tariffs clearly accepts this alternative at least in private conversation, preferring to see investors suffer losses rather than to have textile mills demoralized by large imports.

In any case this suggestion may be hazarded. The world economic machine is huge and intricate and has an enormous momentum. To stop it means a crash. Even to slow it down causes suffering and loss to all engaged in its operation. To change it by reverting to the organization and structure of several hundred years ago is impossible. It is imperative that we maintain its functioning as smoothly and evenly as possible.

Chapter IX

THE ECONOMIC ACTIVITIES OF GOVERNMENTS

U P to this point only occasional reference has been made to the part played in world economics by governments and by nationalism. Illustrative materials and statistical data have been given by countries, because there is no other satisfactory source of information. Here and there, also, particular countries have been mentioned as a convenient way of describing certain areas. But this has been largely incidental and as a matter of convenience. We have attempted to keep to the front the fact that the fundamentals of the world economic struggle would exist no matter what the form of organization. The passengers on this "Good Ship Earth" (again quoting the late Herbert Quick) would compete with each other in some manner, perhaps even fighting for a division of the available supply of the good things of life, no matter what the political structure of the world. Unless and until profound modifications occur in the way men behave, it is improbable that any of us will readily permit our fellow men in other parts of the globe to take all they desire of the economic product which we have helped create. Nor will they without protest allow us to help ourselves to unlimited amounts. Groups of some sort are sure to be formed in opposition to other groups.

The economic world is too intricate for the contest to be carried on between individuals. Possibly those are right who speak of a gregarious instinct or of some kind of fundamental urge for cooperation. Perhaps Professor Giddings has solved the problem by telling us of a "consciousness of kind," or Professor Carver may be correct when he speaks of "self-centered appreciation" as the clew to much of our behavior. It may be that for some ineradicable reason we persist in viewing those who are near us in space, in time and in relationship as more important and hence to be aided more carefully than those who are remote from us in these particulars. Or perhaps we coldly calculate the personal gain for each that comes from cooperating with his fellows or realize that only through some harmony of action is it possible to survive.

But whatever the causes assigned by anthropologists, psychologists, sociologists, and philosophers, men do organize. They cooperate in religion, in art, and in recreation. They play together and they work together. And, of course, chaos of the worst sort would follow if they did not. Only through a high degree of mutual adjustment by division of labor can a machine so large, intricate, and unwieldy as that of the world economy be kept functioning at all. Because of its complexities and its momentum, a crash, with suffering and probable death for a large percentage of the human race, would promptly occur, if cooperation were suddenly to end.

We must rely on scientists in other fields to answer many of the questions which this raises. Psychologists must decide whether there are human tendencies to be called instincts and indicate what ones of our actions are instinctive, what ones are rational, and what ones are habitual. Anthropologists will trace the origins of our conduct. Political philosophers will doubtless settle the nature of the State and such issues as sovereignty. As economists we are compelled to accept their findings whenever there is a measure of agreement among them. Pending such agreement we must consider as best we can what appear to be the important facts with which we must deal.

[163]

One of these facts is the modern state and the extent to which much of the economic strain in the world is manifesting itself through political channels. It is this that create the dilemma. To argue as we have done from time to time that the world is an economic unit is to elaborate the obvious. World economic unity is quite generally appreciated All of us realize that in this interdependent world there is an appalling amount of friction due to what is styled "economic nationalism." Governments, we say, act for selfish reasons. Tariffs and other restrictive devices are used to influence the movements of human beings, of commodities, and of capital from one region to another. Each government endeavors to protect its nationals or at least some of them against the nationals of other countries Economic penetration and control are common. The friction thus created is not hard to see and the economic losses caused can readily be presented.

Under the circumstances it is not difficult to forget that government officials are merely persons much like the rest of us and that they are largely engaged in doing just those things that we want them to do or that some of us at least want them to do. They act largely and necessarily in ways they suppose to be acceptable to the electorate or at least to those persons who are able to influence the electorate and return officials to their positions at the next election. To suggest that these public officials are influenced by such considerations is not to condemn them. If a man enters upon a political career he cannot be entirely indifferent to his own future. There is much to be said, moreover, in support of the view that the holder of a public office should carry out the wishes of his constituents even if his judgment is not always in accord with theirs.

To decry the behavior of governments in economic matters is accordingly not difficult. Nothing is easier than to denounce nationalism, to point to alleged absurdities to abuses of power, to the losses the world suffers from its excesses. We may plead for internationalism as an ideal, we may even characterize nationalism as a myth that should be discarded in the face of the economic reality of an interdependent world.

But to rush rapidly from the admitted weaknesses of present procedure to the other extreme may raise new difficulties. Certainly the obstacles being encountered by internationalism suggest that there may be strong reasons for caution. It may be that the persistence of nationalism is more than the wicked attempts of the hosts of evil to defend themselves against the angels of light.

If the prevalence or even the necessity for economic organization over wide areas be admitted, this organization might be effected in many ways. The advantages of cooperation might be secured by combinations that have nothing to do with national boundary lines. Instead of an organization of the producers of steel or textiles or aluminum or sulphur or paper that includes all manufacturers within a given country and only those in that country, why should not the grouping include the various units in a given industry regardless of national boundaries? For example, there is the lumber industry of western Canada and the northwestern part of the United States. Yet the lumber manufacturers of the entire United States have their own organization. Coal operators in central Europe would seem to have much in common yet they organize first of all along national lines. The steel organization is worked out in a similar way. The international combinations when they occur come second. It is usual for their members to combine first by countries and then as national groups to enter an international combination.

If our analysis is correct we are confronted with an awkward dilemma. Economic interdependence is world wide and complete. The physical basis of economic life

[165]

is broad not narrow. Human beings are never satisfied with what they have and never will be. Differences of interest and rivalries in the production and distribution of wealth may be expected. In order to get the maximum results and to minimize friction and waste, cooperation on a world-wide basis should occur and strain be minimized in every way possible. Most important of all, the outbreak of war should be prevented.

Yet economic groupings are worked out along national lines. Rivalries are often between the producers of some commodity in Country A against those in Country B. Even the bankers operate largely in national groups. Where they are actually living near each other as are the bankers of New York and at a distance from those of other countries, *e.g.*, England or Germany, the tendency may be explained by alleging the convenience to each of being near his associates. But London is no farther from New York than is San Francisco.

One may accept these national groupings without question, viewing them merely as "natural" or perhaps as divinely ordained. Or one may decry them, merely pointing out their dangers and declaiming against nationalism and imperialism as a threat to the peace of the world and even to the future of humanity. It is much better, however, to understand them, if possible, before either condemning or undertaking reform. By accepting them without protest we merely drift without attempting to check the forces that so often make for war. By merely deploring nationalism as a danger we follow a policy just as futile. Instead of either of these ineffective methods we may at least record a few of the facts that create and tend to perpetuate economic nationalism.

Let us state a few of the considerations to be kept in mind, trying to avoid those issues that are not the business of the economist. First, it seems to be true that some degree of political organization is necessary. We need it at least for the administration of what is often called "justice." Or, if we hesitate at the word, let us say for the adjustment of disputes among us on matters which we deem important. It also seems clear that as yet human knowledge and experience do not permit this political organization on a world-wide basis. Not only are tradition and prejudice against a world state. The mere size and intricacy of the task are formidable. As time passes, gratifying progress is being made but it is coming slowly. For the present we must accept the division of the world into areas separately organized for political purposes. We must even admit a strong decentralizing tendency in many directions, the appearance of more states, and an increased independence of action. In recent years many new states have been organized, especially in Europe. The British Empire is now styled the British Commonwealth of Nations and the autonomy of its parts is growing. In the United States there is a strong body of opinion against the unlimited extension of federal control even in economic matters. "Self-determination of peoples" was one of the most important slogans of the World War and today the claim for the "rights of minorities" is one of the strongest that can be addressed to the public opinion of the world.

Nor can the issue be settled by drawing a distinction between political as distinct from economic functions and suggesting that governments should limit their activities to the former and avoid the latter. More than ever before, political activities concern themselves with economic matters—not solely but largely. Tariffs, it is said, should be taken out of politics. But how and why? The administration of general policies may perhaps be delegated to a body of experts who ignore or at least profess to ignore political considerations, but the policies must be determined by the general public acting, of course, through their representatives. This is political procedure. And so with immigration, with protection of foreign investments, with the autonomy of the Philippines, with fishing rights, and more or less directly with disarmament and a host of other questions. No dividing line can or should be drawn.

It must be remembered, moreover, that the necessity for government direction and control of our lives is increasing, not diminishing. There was for a time a reaction against mercantilism and a period during which physiocracy and *laissez faire* were dominant. But with the growth of population and its concentration, with the development of capitalism and the increasing intricacy of life, the changes from an unrestricted *laissez faire* regime were more and more evident. Only a short time ago one of the British papers found delight in attacking a member of a British conservative Cabinet for uttering what should be a commonplace when he pointed out that the time has passed when independence of conduct is possible. The fact that political capital was made out of the incident and that it was interpreted as a determination of a benighted group of Tories to continue the enslavement of the public through the maintenance of the "Dora" regulations need not obscure for us the fundamental truth of his assertion. President Hoover promptly recognized the same principle in his order that facts regarding income tax refunds above a low minimum should be made public. He recognized it again when the stock market crashed in November, 1929. He called one group after another of the business men of the country into conference to plan under his leadership the next forward steps in industry. In the market place the old principle of *caveat emptor* is rapidly being displaced by the multiplication of protections for the purchaser who cannot in modern society adequately protect himself.

Illustrations could be continued endlessly but the few that have been given are adequate. Only a cursory examination of developments in any modern country should convince the most skeptical. The trend is roughly the same in Soviet Russia and in Fascist Italy. In England government assistance has been on the increase through unemployment relief, by means of coal subsidies, and through the Trade Facilities Act, the safeguarding of industry, and otherwise. In the United States a "return to normalcy" along the lines intended by President Harding has been quite impossible. More business may have gone into the conduct of government but there are few signs that government has refused to go to the aid of business. Those who want the scholar's broad, conclusive analysis are referred to J. M. Keynes' "The End of *Laissez Faire*."

Notice the obligations resting on any government, *e.g.*, that of Czechoslovakia or France or Abyssinia or Denmark or X. Let us assume some new country, perhaps one of those brought into existence by the Treaty of Versailles. Assume further that you are entrusted with the task of organizing and directing the new political unit. Assume still further that there are none of the harassing problems that often face a newly organized state, such as the necessity of shouldering the debt burdens of a previous regime, redeeming its paper money, rebuilding a region devastated by war, etc. For the sake of simplicity our new state faces a minimum of problems and you, as its dictator, will have a more simple task than statesmen usually face.

In just what order problems would appear we cannot be sure but certainly one of the first thoughts of a dictator would be that of raising funds to run the government, *i.e.*, of imposing taxes. This means levying burdens of some

[169]

kind upon the individuals and corporations in the country
with a recognition of the complexities of their organization, the nature of their business, and the kind of taxes
which they have paid in the past. It involves a certain
degree of fiscal organization and unification for the country.
The taxes will doubtless be both direct and indirect. There
may be income taxes and inheritance taxes. Almost certainly there will be excise duties and perhaps a sales tax.
In all probability there will be duties on commodities
passing in or out of the country or both. These import and
export duties may be levied "for revenue only" but there
are very few such duties that do not afford some degree of
protection to internal business.

Thus the raising of the necessary revenues immediately
compels a degree of special organization of the country's
economic life along lines that mark it off from surrounding
countries. To some extent this may create feeling, because
the imposition of any tax that retards the free movement
of any article is viewed with concern by those whose
business is thereby affected. The people of England injure
Brazil or even India by imposing import duties on tea and
coffee although no British industry is given protection. Even
within a given country, like the United States, ill will
may be created when a given state such as Pennsylvania
adds to its revenues by taxing anthracite coal, thus making
it more expensive to users in New England who accordingly
resent the tax.

Then there must be a monetary system in our new
state. Perhaps we shall conform to world tendencies by
adopting the gold standard and by organizing a banking
system with a central bank, all along modern lines. But
this consolidates the country still more by giving it a
currency unit probably of a different weight and name
from those used in surrounding countries. Although the

metallic coins, *i.e.*, gold, and at times even silver, pass back and forth across boundary lines, they form only a small fraction of the total circulating medium which is chiefly paper money and deposit currency. Redeemability of these substitutes seems feasible for the present only within the country where they are issued, by the issuing institution and in accordance with local legislation which it may be difficult to bring quickly if ever into line with that of other countries.

But the supply of money used in any country and, even more important, the fluctuations in that supply have much to do with the welfare of its people. We may believe in the quantity theory of money, in which case we say that the volume of circulating medium and the price level are closely related to the amount of gold. It seems to many, therefore, that control over the import and export of gold should be exercised and if so this may easily irritate the people of other countries whose welfare is at once affected and whose interests at any given time do not always coincide with ours. The importation of gold into France from London may injure and irritate the English. Even the raising or lowering of interest rates in one country affects the others and may bring reprisals.

Only the most meager and most necessary financial institutions have been described but they show the tendency toward the economic unification of each country and to a degree its opposition to other countries. But let us pass on to other matters, *e.g.*, the supervision of production, ignoring the necessity for such things as a separately organized police force and a separate system of courts for the administration of justice. May you, as dictator, allow production to be carried on in your country without interference or guidance? A policy of unqualified *laissez faire* has never prevailed and this is particularly true in

[171]

the twentieth century. Notice the necessity for such fundamental matters as the establishment and protection of
property rights, many of which must exist even in a social-
ist state. Then there must be copyright and patent laws,
provision for proper drafting and recording of legal docu-
ments, etc., all of which means a body of complicated
statutes with court interpretations and precedents.

Some lines of production are hazardous and workers must
be aided by protective legislation perhaps going so far as to
limit hours of work and set minimum wages, or provide
health insurance, unemployment insurance, and old age
pensions. Some products may be injurious to the health
of the consumer unless the materials used and the processes
employed in their manufacture are carefully watched—
hence pure food laws and factory inspection. Some productive work cannot be satisfactorily carried on by private
enterprise—hence public ownership and operation of at
least the post office and mint, perhaps also a long list of
other activities.

These controls are chiefly over internal or domestic
forces. But would you stop there? Would your proper and
essential duties be performed if you failed to notice certain
outside forces that might be just as harmful as any of these
internal ones? One of your domestic industries is steel
manufacturing which is also carried on in neighboring
countries. From time to time the output of these foreign
plants accumulates and perhaps is dumped in your markets
in such way as to demoralize your local steel mills. What
policy will you as dictator adopt? Will you do nothing
or will you enact antidumping legislation? And in view of
the circumstances and of the practices of foreigners will
you not perhaps encourage dumping abroad by your own
steel plants?

Then there is the question of health. Quarantines against
plagues should, of course, be established. But tuberculin-

tainted meat ought not to enter your country, nor any form of plant and animal life, parasitic or otherwise, that might harm your flora or fauna. Stringent regulations carefully administered must be arranged even though at times the people of other countries are irritated.

Perhaps you will go still farther. What kind of economic and social life should be developed? Should everything be left to the free play of what are called "natural" laws or forces or should guidance of some sort be attempted? And if there is to be guidance who is to do the guiding unless it be undertaken along national lines? For example, there may be such a thing as a proper number of persons per square mile and if so immigration should either be encouraged or discouraged. There may be a proper relationship between the rural and urban groups or between agriculture and manufacturing. If so, how are these adjustments in numbers and occupation to be effected if not by state action? Since fear of war has not altogether disappeared, there may be some "essential" industries to be maintained by some form of assistance, perhaps tariff duties or subsidies. Then, too, in view of the practices of others, it may not be possible to leave our commerce to be carried in the ships of other nations. It may be wise instead to maintain a national merchant marine by the aid of subventions.

This is only a brief list of the problems with which a dictator would be confronted and seems to warrant a few conclusions:

1. Some degree of political organization comparable to that of existing states is imperative.

2. The number of separate states is growing, not diminishing.

3. Within each state the *laissez faire* principle is rapidly yielding ground under the pressure of modern life.

4. This compels the assumption of more and more duties by the state, whose activities are growing, both intensively and extensively.

5. These activities are tending to make each country more and more of a unit whose economy is organized both for offense and defense against the similarly organized economies of other countries.

Probably no one will object to some of this organization along national lines. Economic life cannot be left without any guidance and the state as we know it seems to be the natural and in some matters the only available guide. Just how far it may go in its supervision is the point on which we are not agreed. For example, a corporation has a right to exist only because of some act of legislation. It receives its charter from the state. The state prescribes the nature and extent of its activities and grants to it a degree of protection. The state orders it to refrain from activities not authorized by its charter, demands that its plant submit to inspection, requires certain standards of working conditions, and perhaps limits the hours of work that may be performed by its employees.

On the other hand, the government furnishes police protection and fire protection. To all persons, both natural and legal, the courts are available and through them attempts are made to secure a just settlement of disputes. If an individual citizen or a corporation suffers from any type of injury he may seek redress through these courts. Infringement of copyrights and patents and any other illegal activities that may cause monetary loss may become matters for consideration and decision by these agencies of the state.

But how far may this protection extend? Is it to be granted only within the country and in disputes with fellow nationals or may it extend beyond national boundaries?

[174]

Viewing the world as it is and not as we might like to have it, are we to say that our own nationals, whether individuals or corporations, are to defend themselves unsupported before the courts of another country? For example, are citizens of the United States in a position to receive the same consideration in Mexican courts as Mexicans receive, or will Mexicans receive in American courts the same treatment as Americans? Would there be no discrimination against British in China or Chinese in England, Italians in France, or French in Italy? And since there is at least a possibility of inequality of treatment should the various governments attempt to assist their nationals in defending themselves abroad?

The extent and the nature of this assistance abroad are varied and we shall attempt no careful listing of methods employed. Most observers concede that there are valid reasons for some of them but that excesses are common. If it is admitted that a reasonable amount of aid should be granted, the camel has his head in the tent. What seems reasonable to one person seems to another quite inadequate. The party seeking the assistance of his government is not contented with the amount of help an outsider might think proper. An unscrupulous national will demand all the assistance he can get with little or no thought of what may be right or even of what may be legal. A large corporation with correspondingly great influence, and perhaps with a record of contribution to campaign funds, may exercise very heavy pressure and secure more help than a less conspicuous or wealthy national.

There is no clear border line between a moderate measure of protection which would be acceptable to all and abuses so excessive that they are generally condemned. But the reasons why any aid is granted and the forces behind it must be clear. The people living on certain islands known

[175]

as the United Kingdom must import from other regions much of their food and can do so only if trade moves freely. Raw materials must be secured and markets be opened and kept open. With the living standards of 45,000,000 people at stake may we reasonably expect a timid or apologetic attitude from the government representing them? British industries are large and directed by intelligent leaders who must make money to survive; some of their raw materials are purchased and many of their products are marketed in regions whose people are less prosperous, whose standards of conduct are different, whose legal code is not the same, and who perhaps view the British with distrust. Under such conditions, with both individual profits and the general standard of living involved, the British government will, of course, give aid. From what other source can even a modicum of legitimate help be secured?

Probably an American may with more propriety describe the tendency shown by the activities of his own government and his own fellow citizens than dwell on the behavior of others. Then, too, the United States is a good illustration because only a few years ago the people of America were prone to criticise the alleged imperialism of others. Today it is said by many Europeans and Latin Americans and even by large numbers of United States citizens that the United States has become a great imperialistic power.

Whether the charge of imperialism is correct depends almost entirely upon the definition of the term. Critics frequently allege it but from time to time defenders of the federal administration then in power deny it. Certainly it is true that during the century and a half of its existence the area of the United States has grown by frequent additions, most of them contiguous but a few of them at a distance. Although there have been no annexations by purchase or otherwise for a number of years, the economic influence of the United States, particularly in Latin America, has been rapidly increasing. Trade has expanded and foreign investments of American nationals have grown and with this expansion the extent to which the government has used its influence has increased. How and where this has occurred is related at length by many writers.[1]

It is easy to recite the incidents as these writers have done and to denounce much that has occurred. We may even employ the term used by Helen Hunt Jackson in describing the treatment given to the American Indian and call it a "century of dishonor." It is more important, however, to observe one or two facts about the procedure of the American government and American nationals. Having done so, we may criticize just as caustically as before, but our criticism will be more intelligent and perhaps more fruitful.

First to be noticed is that what the United States has done and is doing or perhaps is about to do is remarkably like what has been done over and over again for many centuries. Methods differ and motives are not always quite the same, but Greeks and Romans, Dutch and Spanish, French, English, Italians, and Germans have behaved alike. America is doing in the twentieth century what others have done before. In new ways and in different directions, adapting their methods to modern conditions and to the real or fancied needs of the America of today, the process is remarkably similar to that employed by other groups at other times and in other places. Certain

[1] Among them notice especially Benjamin H. Williams, "The Economic Foreign Policy of the United States"; Parker T. Moon, "Imperialism and World Politics"; Nearing and Freeman, "Dollar Diplomacy"; Samuel W. Dunn, "American Foreign Investments." Special studies of more limited scope are Leland H. Jenks, "Our Cuban Colony"; Margaret Marsh, "Bankers in Bolivia"; and Melvin M. Kinght, "Americans in Santo Domingo."

refinements have been introduced that seem to be a distinct improvement over the procedure of the fifteenth and sixteenth centuries but the general outline is much the same. It is not easy to distinguish between Kipling's proposal to "take up the white man's burden" and the later American appeal to "manifest destiny" and the somewhat franker expression "dollar diplomacy."

This persistence suggests that the forces making for imperialistic policies are found nearly everywhere, are persistent through long periods of time and under various forms of government, and, if we believe them objectionable, that they cannot be offset by mere denunciation. At the same time the movement in itself may not be wholly bad. Perhaps its advantages can be retained and its evils eliminated or at least modified.

Second to be noted is that these practices are exactly what may be expected in a world whose economic organization is of the sort we have been describing. The rapidly expanding desires of a numerous population dependent on each other for food, clothing, and shelter will seek satisfaction. Often the methods employed are brutal. This is the more true because an economic organization has been developed that adds to the pressure and at the same time conceals from the agent in a harmful act the injury done to his victim.

Third it should be added that on the whole the abuses complained of in the treatment of the people in the less developed areas, a treatment usually referred to as "exploitation," is not peculiar to foreign affairs. It is found in domestic economics as well. Slavery of the negro within the United States is one illustration. Read almost any modern history of British industry in the nineteenth century for a description of conditions that are not so bad as those of the Congo a few years ago but horrible enough

[178]

to suggest that there is cruelty at home as well as in Africa. The problem is one of finding a better adjustment of our economic relations both in domestic and in foreign fields.

Finally, it should be repeated that in domestic business economic conflict is softened by controlling legislation and by codes of conduct. In the international field these restraining influences are largely lacking. Some contend that there is no ethical code in international affairs. It is far better to say that a code exists but that it is a harsher one. Certain standards prevail but under them there is discrimination against the individual or the corporation of another nationality. This means friction and ill will. It brings economic strain and may be a cause of war.

There are offsetting influences, some of them highly important, which will be referred to in the last chapter of this volume. They are making headway but must do so in the face of such forces as we have thus far analyzed. Before describing them it is worthwhile to explain the way in which the influences presented in these earlier chapters are operating in each of a number of countries.

Chapter X

GREAT BRITAIN'S PREDICAMENT

Having examined one after the other a series of economic influences that make for strain in the modern world and having noted the reasons why there is so strong a tendency for them to operate along national lines rather than in some other way, we take the next step, which is to show more specifically how they appear in several of the leading countries. The countries chosen are those that are most dominant in international affairs, the ones that have progressed farthest in their economic development. They are the industrialized countries, the ones in which capitalism exists to a high degree. They are countries dependent to a greater or lesser extent on outside sources for food, for raw materials, and for markets.

A brief survey of any one of them is difficult and may be misleading. It is difficult because the mass of factual material is so huge that its analysis and interpretation call for a knowledge more extensive and an intellect more penetrating than any of us possesses. It may easily be misleading because broad generalizations must be presented. All generalizations are perilous and they are especially so since they seldom convey the same meaning to all who hear them. Yet only by indicating at least roughly the status of several countries is it possible to appreciate the forces described in preceding chapters, to understand the problems facing each of the countries, and to interpret the policies they are pursuing in the economic and political field.

First in the list is Great Britain, placed there because she is the most developed in many particulars and because her problems are perhaps more acute than those of any other country that we shall examine.

The physical bases of British life need only a brief summary. The area of the United Kingdom—England, Scotland, Wales, and all of Ireland—is 110,874 square miles. This group of islands is just at the western edge of the Continent of Europe, a location admirably suited to a certain type of development, especially when some of its resources are noted. In an earlier chapter attention has been called to its large reserves of coal, its considerable deposits of iron ore and of other minerals, its stimulating climate, and its other natural advantages. Emphasis should also be placed on its isolated position. A little later there will be occasion to comment on the fact that so-called "strategic frontiers" are uncommon, but the English Channel has been one of them, cutting off Great Britain from the Continent, safeguarding her from military attack, and permitting to her a comparatively quiet political and economic growth. Whether or not there can be this same isolation with the development of such modern weapons as the airplane and the submarine is a problem of the near future. For the moment we are speaking of the past.

As trade developed on the Continent and was carried from the Continent to other parts of the world and back by sea, it encountered Great Britain. As a stopping place on the way the British Isles were convenient. Participation by the English in this commerce was natural, and, as the commerce grew, vessels were needed in which to carry it and then a navy was required to protect the trade. Here and there throughout the world, trading posts were established under the British flag. With the passage of time these small areas grew. The amount of territory each controlled was never quite adequate. The trading posts expanded in size and the Empire developed. This stimulated shipbuilding and encouraged more trade.

The isolation already referred to permitted the development of the Industrial Revolution more rapidly in England than elsewhere, which meant a specialization in manufacturing. This demanded control of sources of raw materials and food as well as of markets, which was interpreted to mean a need for still more colonies, *i.e.*, a larger Empire. At the same time it permitted a greater population per square mile, since more people can be supported at a given standard in this manner than by specialization in agriculture and in the extractive industries. This, at least, seems to have been true in the past. Much depends, of course, on the terms of exchange that exist between the industrialized country and its markets—the amount of manufactured goods that must be given in exchange for raw materials and for food.

Under these conditions British population (including England, Scotland, and Wales) grew from 10,500,000 in 1801 to 44,240,000 in 1927. A chart of its growth shows a steady, persistent rise that still continues although the rate of increase is diminishing. It will be remembered that Dr. Kuczynski, whom we have already quoted, points out that the birth rate is now at a level that will mean soon an actual decrease in population and conceivably its ultimate disappearance. Needless to say there is no way of knowing whether the present birth rate will continue. It may decrease further or it may increase. But in any case the population density for Great Britain was 496.8 per square mile in 1927, and for England and Wales it was 674.5 per square mile in the same year. This is one of the highest in the world.

[182]

The British, as well as the people of other countries, are prone to explain much of the development of the economic life of their country by reference to certain characteristics of the people. An admirable recital of these is to be found in Alfred Marshall's "Industry and Trade," and his chapters on Britain's Industrial Leadership are strongly recommended. But no matter how accurate his characterization it is well to remember that the people of no country are pure racial stock and that the ethnologists, anthropologists, and psychologists now deny the existence of fundamental and ineradicable mental differences between national groups or even between races.

Be that as it may, the whole trend of British economic life was upward until about 1870; population increased, the volume of trade grew, the standard of living was on the whole raised, and there was a heavy accumulation of investments abroad. In these things Great Britain led the world. From 1870 to the outbreak of the World War this industrial leadership was challenged by rapid developments elsewhere, notably in Germany and in the United States. The decline that occurred in this period was, however, relative not absolute. Since the war, a new situation has developed and a number of serious problems must be faced and solved unless there is to be an absolute decline and to a most serious degree.

During the last 150 years of British growth certain leading tendencies have appeared some of which may be segregated and emphasized, following roughly the order in which we have been presenting the fundamental economic forces for the world as a whole. First is the growth of population and its economic consequences. An excess of births over deaths and a larger number of persons per square mile makes possible up to a certain point a larger output per capita from the soil. Beyond this point the additional application of efforts, even though aided by enlarged amounts of capital, brings a smaller per capita return. In other words, the law of diminishing returns, always present, may become a disconcerting fact as time passes.

From its consequences relief may of course be found as western Europe, including Great Britain, found it. To some extent emigration may be helpful. From 1853 to 1903 the outward movement of population from the United Kingdom was large, exceeding "13,000,000 of whom 9,500,000 were British subjects."[1] Yet the numbers at home increased, the figures we have given being for the population that remained after these large numbers had emigrated.

A second form of relief is to be found in improved methods of cultivating the soil, and these have, of course, been utilized. Yet this was inadequate and the imports of food from abroad have steadily grown. Unfortunately the trade statistics do not segregate the imports of food from total imports until 1890 but there is every reason to suppose that they were gaining steadily over many decades. From 1890 to 1894 the annual average value of imports of "food, drink, and tobacco" was £169,985,000, and for 1910 to 1913 the annual average was £263,104,000. From 1900 to 1913, after allowance for the changed price level, the imports of food, drink, and tobacco gained 11 per cent. Dependence on the outside world for food was increasing and necessarily so.

At any time, of course, more food could have been produced at home. Large tracts of land were uncultivated but the attempt during the war to add to home production seems to confirm the view that it could be done only at a higher cost for the extra output than it is necessary during more normal times to pay for imported foodstuffs.

[1] Ogg, F. A., "Economic Development of Modern Europe," p. 357.

Another form of relief is to devote home effort to manufacturing and from its profits purchase the food. This was
the main solution for Great Britain and for many years
was particularly easy. As already observed, her economic
life was free to develop in advance of that in other countries
and this permitted her to utilize to the full certain advantages that may be stated in the form of economic laws or
principles.

One is the principle of increasing returns or decreasing
costs. Once having an equipment of a given size with
its heavy carrying charges, a small output from the plant
has a very high unit cost, but a larger number of units of
output may be produced at a smaller cost per unit. There is
consequently a serious financial burden to be carried if the
plant is not operated at or near capacity, a point which
we have already stressed in the earlier chapter on large-
scale production. On the other hand, the rapid reduction
of unit costs as production is carried on at full capacity or
near it means large profits. Aggregate costs rise but not
so rapidly as output nor as receipts, unless prices fall.

From the standpoint of the individual plant the gains
are clear. If sales can be kept up and without a too great
reduction in the selling price, the profits may be huge.
But the same was true for England as a whole. It was in
England that the mechanical discoveries were first applied
on a large scale. It was in England that factories were
built and industrialism developed in advance of that in
other countries. Her manufacturers as a group were in a
position to secure the advantages of large-scale production
and the principle of increasing returns before those of other
countries. Since competition from abroad was for many
years very slight and since the demand for her products
rapidly grew, British exports increased and British profits
were large. Errors of judgment of course occurred, the

markets were at times congested, and numerous losses were suffered. But the general trend was strongly upward and Great Britain gained both relatively and absolutely.

A second principle that aided has been called "Lardner's law of squares" in transport and trade.[1] This is a special application of the principle of increasing returns or decreasing costs. A business cost whose importance increases with the geographical division of labor is the cost of transportation. The more complete this division, the farther goods must be carried from mine and field to factory and then from factory to market, the more significant are freight rates by land and by sea, especially when supplemented by such accompanying extras as insurance, commissions, cost of loading and unloading, and interest on capital invested in the goods during the period of transit. As a total these bulk large and any reduction in transportation costs is an aid.

But there is a peculiar feature of importance. If goods are being sold throughout a given area whose size is definitely influenced by the cost of their transportation, and this cost is lowered, the market area is, of course, widened. But its increase is more than proportional to the reduction in cost. Assume a lowering in these costs that will double the distance through which goods can be transported for a given outlay. The diameter of the effective marketing area, the irregular circle in which goods are sold, is thereby doubled.

But the area of a circle varies as the square of its radius. Therefore improvements in the mechanism or the organization of transport, which increase the distance over which trade in certain goods can be carried at a given expense, are *prima facie* likely to increase in the square of that ratio the area over which the trade can be conducted profitably.[2]

[1] See MARSHALL, ALFRED, "Industry and Trade," 3d ed., pp. 27–28.
[2] *Idem.*

Great Britain's Predicament

This principle also aided Great Britain. Her merchant marine had developed early and with the introduction of iron and steel in ship construction and the prompt decline of American shipbuilding and ship operation, her advantage increased. Lowered transportation costs rapidly and vastly widened her market area, giving her still greater advantages over other countries.

As profits accrued from the growth of trade, British investments abroad gained in volume. The rate of capital accumulation, as we have noted before, is accelerated as time passes. Early savings are slow and perhaps painful. Later ones are made more and more from profits which are either reinvested in plant without being distributed or, if distributed to stockholders, are usually invested by them in other enterprises. If the investments are made abroad and if entirely new accumulations are added, the total increases at an almost amazing rate.

Thus there were favorable conditions for the gains in British trade, for the earnings of her merchant fleet, and for the growth of her foreign investments, interest on which became an important annual addition to the national income. This was closely linked with the development of the gold standard which was adopted by England earlier and more completely than by any other important country. Of course, loans abroad by British nationals were to a large extent payable, both interest and principal, in gold. As gold prices rose (and they did from 1850 to 1873) profits of British manufacturers increased and investments grew. As gold prices later declined from 1873 to 1896, the real income on these investments was, of course, enlarged. Then, too, some of the investments were made in silver-using countries like India and after 1873 the gold value of silver declined. This meant that more and more silver was needed to meet obligations payable in gold and a growing

[187]

strain on the debtors to the advantage of the British creditors.

Thus for many years the British gained from their early industrialization and some critics (including many within Great Britain) contend that they became careless and gave too little thought to the future. In any case we may notice that the retention of the early advantages was largely dependent on a lack of competition. Large-scale production means low unit costs but profits are made not merely from low costs but also from the difference between costs and selling price. If competition lowers market prices then the margin disappears unless costs can also be lowered. And as competition grows it becomes a question of relative ability to lower costs of production, unless, of course, the entire market is so stimulated that selling prices can be maintained at a high level.

It is customary to indicate 1870 as the high point of British supremacy although it is not to be supposed that any exact point in time can be chosen as the one before which a movement so complex was clearly upward and after which it was entirely on the down grade. The change was of course gradual. But it should be carefully observed that there was a real change and a growing pressure on British economic life prior to the World War. A serious error has been committed by those who have attributed to that war all of the difficulties since 1920 and have urged remedial measures based wholly upon that assumption. The war interrupted many processes, hastened many changes that were already going on, and introduced new forces. But many of the present difficulties of the country have been clearly apparent for a number of decades.

It could not be expected that industrialization would be limited to one country. As time passed it was bound to spread, especially to those places which had the physical basis for it. In the late nineteenth and early twentieth centuries this meant Germany and the United States. The most important of the basic natural resources in an industrial age are coal and iron and it will be remembered that there are just two main areas outside England where these are found in large amounts and fairly close together. One is the United States, where the distances between the deposits is great but where this economic disadvantage is more than offset by the fact that the entire area is under a single political control and that there are no customs barriers or other important impediments to the free movement of goods. The other area is the Ruhr-Lorraine region, and after 1870 its combined resources of coal and iron ore were under German control.

As the United States and Germany developed, the effect on England was serious. Her reserves of coal are huge but their economic value in competition with the coal of other regions is dependent first on the cost of mining. In this the British disadvantages are serious because of the depth of the mines, the small size of the holdings, the lack of cooperation among the operators, and other causes that have been emphasized by the Sankey and Samuels coal commissions in recent years. The value of coal depends also on the accessibility of the ore and other raw materials. Coal is heavy and in general the other materials are brought to the coal. Because cargoes inbound to Great Britain are largely bulky food and raw materials and outbound vessels have plenty of available space, British coal exports are enormous. Nevertheless they now meet severe competition and we are all aware of the present demoralization in the world's coal markets.

A second influence on the economic value of the coal is the availability of the raw materials with which it is to be used. One of these is iron ore. The introduction of the

[189]

Bessemer process was for a time a great advantage to England because of the plentiful supply of ore suited to this method. But with the passage of time these supplies diminished and importation of a considerable amount of ore became necessary. Also, there was the introduction of other processes to which the Lorraine, Luxemburg, and French ores were better adapted. The effect appeared in a huge expansion of the German and American steel industries as compared with the much slower growth of the British.

Other illustrations might be added. Cotton for British mills must be imported and has come chiefly from the United States where in recent years there has been a rapid increase in spindleage. The fact that the growth of cotton manufacturing in the southern United States has created difficulties for New England mills does not alter the fact that they have meant an increased competition for Lancashire both for the available raw cotton and for markets. Wool for British mills is found in part within the United Kingdom but much comes from Australia and from the Argentine. One after another the various raw materials and food items could be added to the list. British dependence on the outside world has been increasing not diminishing, and the fact that many sources of supply are within the Empire is not a denial of that dependence. It is merely a qualification, whose significance rests on the extent to which supplies from the dominions and colonies can be quickly and safely secured and on the extent to which their markets can be kept open to the mother country by preferential tariffs or otherwise.

British population has been increasing. In the spring of 1929 it was reported that the latest returns showed an excess of deaths over births but this may have been due to the fatalities from influenza and in any case the change may not persist. But the country is population conscious as is shown by the definite effort to stimulate emigration, an effort the results of which to date have not been fruitful. The numbers leaving the country have not offset the natural growth arising from an excess of births over deaths. Even if emigration should increase moderately and the birth rate decline until numbers remain steady with no gain from year to year there is still the task of maintaining an extremely large population, on a limited area of land. And even though emigration should gain somewhat in the face of all the obstacles and though the birth rate should fall and the death rate rise enough to reduce appreciably the population density this change can come but slowly and will make itself really felt only after the passage of many years.

Perhaps it is permissible to summarize the situation by saying that for Great Britain the population density is so great as to make the principle of diminishing returns as applied to agriculture a very real thing. Food cannot be produced at home cheaply enough to compete with the imported supplies and probably one-half to two-thirds of the needed food will continue to come from other parts of the world. At the same time the advantage gained in the past years from the early start in manufacturing and hence from the principle of increasing returns is lessened and has disappeared or been reduced in a number of lines. It is perhaps rash to name them, but they seem at present to include coal, iron and steel, cotton textiles, and possibly shipbuilding and woolen textiles. This reduction in advantage has come, first, from the gradual growth of industrialization in many countries; second, from the rapid gains forced everywhere by the conditions prevailing during the World War, and, third, from the general dislocation in trade and the imposition of higher and higher restraints

[191]

on commerce in the postwar years. The situation is peculiarly aggravated by the fact that for the world as a whole
plant capacity in many lines of manufacturing has been
expanded far beyond the present ability of the world's
markets to take the total potential output. This is peculiarly serious for Great Britain whose prosperity depends
so fully on manufacturing and foreign trade.

Also, the advantage in shipping has been sharply reduced.
From a merchant marine of insignificant size before the
World War the United States had on June 30, 1928, a total
of 13,289,080 gross tons. Of this, much was idle or engaged
in coastwise shipping and on the Great Lakes but 3,974,-
663 tons were actively employed in foreign trade. Germany
was compelled to surrender her merchant fleet at the end
of the war but on June 30, 1928, she had 3,284,283 tons of
recently constructed modern vessels. France, Italy, Japan,
and others have more tonnage than before with a resulting
depression of ocean rates.

Again it may be pointed out that the gains that accrue
from large-scale production may be appropriated by any
one concern or group only if it has a certain monopoly
of the field. As competition appears prices are driven down.
The fact that production is on a large scale encourages
larger output to get the benefit of reduced unit costs. This
may, at least for a time, be advantageous for consumers
but it merely encourages similar behavior among competitors. In all directions output is increased and prices
still further lowered. Unless the commodity is one for
which the demand is very elastic and quickly so, the
markets are readily clogged. Unsold stocks accumulate
and business failures appear. Distress may arise from the
so-called "paradox of value," *i.e.*, that a large output sold
at a low price per unit may sell for much less than a smaller
output at a higher price per unit. There are more goods

but less profits and perhaps even losses for producers in particular lines. Crises of longer or shorter duration occur with suffering and losses that are not confined to the particular industries directly affected but that spread throughout the whole community and in these modern times to other countries.

No single index adequately pictures a situation so complex but one of the most helpful for Great Britain is her exports. Raw materials will be imported largely for the manufacture of goods to be sold abroad at profits that permit foreign purchases of food and other articles for British home consumption. Hence, exports indicate roughly the state of present business and the possibilities for the future. It is customary to use 1913 as a basis of comparison and if this is done it is found that British exports in the last half-dozen years have been only from 75 to 80 per cent of prewar if proper allowance is made for the higher price level. There are gains but they are very slow with occasional serious setbacks such as that of 1926 during the coal strike.

Another guide is the estimated balance of payments as published by the Board of Trade. This shows a reduced foreign investment of British funds each year. The balance in one sense of the word remains favorable, *i.e.*, there is a balance out of which British nationals are buying foreign securities, but the amounts thus invested are now less each year than formerly. But it is to be remembered that British nationals have very large investments abroad and that each year a large sum is due as interest. In prewar years a considerable part of this interest was regularly reinvested abroad but now a smaller fraction is so used. The foreign investments of the British are still increasing but at a slower rate. Just how these extra amounts are being used at home is not entirely clear but we may notice that

[193]

some seems to be expended on imports of "food, drink, and tobacco" the amounts of which are some 25 per cent higher than prewar even with adjustments because of higher prices.

There has, of course, been a keen realization of the seriousness of this postwar situation and a long list of surveys with their recommendations. Among them have been the Committee on Commercial and Industrial Policy after the War, the Empire Resources Development Committee, the two committees to survey the coal industry, headed respectively by Justice Sankey and Sir Herbert Samuels, the Committee on Trusts, the Colwyn Committee on Taxation, and, the most pretentious of all in its scope, the Committee on Industry and Trade, appointed in 1924 by Prime Minister MacDonald and headed by Sir Arthur Balfour. These investigations have furnished students and statesmen both in and out of the country with a vast amount of information on which to base conclusions and frame policies.

In a single chapter only brief attention can be given to these reports and to the legislation that grew out of them. Both of the reports on coal have recognized certain fundamental facts about that industry in England and have agreed broadly in their recommendations which have urged a greater measure of public control—in fact so much of a change that the term "nationalization" is usually applied to their proposals. In spite of these recommendations and perhaps because of the influence of the vested interests that would be affected by their adoption, the two reports have until recently been ignored by the government. Even yet nothing of outstanding significance has been done to meet the very real difficulty which the industry is facing. From time to time there have been revivals in the coal trade, as for example in 1923, when the French occupation of the Ruhr was accompanied by a sharp decline in the German coal output, and again in the spring of 1929, when trade was aided by the severe cold weather of the preceding winter.

The acuteness of the situation is shown by the two serious strikes of 1921 and 1926 and by the published data concerning costs, wages, prices, and profits. Specific steps thus far taken by the industry itself have placed the emphasis on reducing costs particularly through reducing wages and increasing hours of work and on maintaining prices at home in order to permit a reduction in prices for export. Such measures, while much like those taken in other countries, do not reach the heart of the difficulty which is now quite generally agreed to be overdevelopment and a capacity for output far beyond the ability of the market to absorb it. Gradually it is being realized that only through international action can the world difficulty be met, but no adequate steps have yet been taken.

In the field of finance the action has been more definite. Taxes have been high and the government budget shows year after year a favorable balance that has permitted a regular reduction in the public debt. The reduction is slow and critics of the government allege that it has not always been so great as it seems. Nevertheless one must pay tribute to the persistence with which taxes have been maintained at a high level in spite of the strain such a policy has imposed on the British economy.

The monetary policy as distinct from the government's fiscal policy has been more debated. It can best be understood by first noting a few facts, then by indicating some of the consequences of the policy, and finally by attempting to explain it. Like other countries Great Britain resorted to inflation during the war and after until the crisis of 1920. It was less extreme than in most of the countries on the

European Continent but involved two features of importance. One was close control over gold payments both within the country and for export, the other was a depreciation of the pound sterling below its old par of $4.8665 for the American dollar. It will be remembered that this par is the amount found by dividing the number of grains of pure gold in the dollar (23.22) into the number of grains of pure gold in the pound (113.00152).

Although prices fell sharply in 1920 they still remained high as compared with prices in the United States and the quotations for the pound in terms of the dollar still remained far below the par $4.8665. Four possibilities were open to the British. One was to inflate the currency again. This would have been done by permitting an increase in note issues and in bank borrowing and would have given an enlarged volume of circulating medium. As prices rose sellers of commodities and services would have received larger incomes and stockholders would have likewise received higher dividends. With these larger receipts all debtors could have more easily met their obligations. Taxpayers would have complained less of their burdens, bonds and mortgages could have been readily paid. But to this solution British opinion was strongly opposed. Some commentators felt that it was favored by Mr. McKenna of the Midland Bank and by certain others but a careful examination of their statements does not warrant such interpretation of their views.

Inflation, if adopted, might have been extreme as in the case of the German mark and been followed by a complete repudiation of all outstanding obligations and the adoption of a new monetary unit. Or it might have been less extreme, stopping at any intermediate level with stabilization there.

A second possibility was to devaluate the pound at some agreed level. For example, a new ratio of $4.50 to the dollar might have been decided upon. This would have been the same as saying that the pound would no longer be 113.00152 grains of gold but that it should be about 104.5 grains of gold. Also, it would have meant a decision to hold the price level within the country at about the level prevailing during 1923 and 1924. In its favor was the fact that it would have maintained the *status quo* and would not have forced on the country the strain that always come from fluctuating price levels.

Both of these proposals meant a return to the gold standard as it is usually understood but by different methods. A third possibility advocated particularly by J. M. Keynes but given very little support was to avoid a return to the gold standard and adopt a "managed currency." In brief, this would have meant ignoring the relationship of the pound to the dollar and also to other foreign moneys. Instead, the volume of circulating medium would have been controlled with a view to keeping the internal price level steady, an obvious advantage offset in part by the probability of extreme fluctuations in foreign exchange. As this proposal was not followed we shall not undertake its elaboration.

The fourth possibility, which was the one adopted, was to return to the gold standard in the traditional sense and also to bring the pound back to its old par with the dollar. This meant bringing the price levels of England and the United States together and could have been accomplished either by a rise in prices in the United States or by a fall in Great Britain. Although gold was flowing into the United States, prices did not rise there as was expected, probably because of a certain amount of conscious control by American authorities. Accordingly it was decided to accept the necessity of lowering prices in England as the only way to attain the result desired. The decision to "return to the gold standard" was announced and put into effect in the spring of 1925.

Time does not permit description of what occurred and why, other than to say that British exports were at once placed at a greater disadvantage in the world's markets. After all that has been said in previous chapters it will be realized that Great Britain's prosperity depends heavily on a maintenance of large exports and that her export trades were suffering from an increasingly severe competition. The return to the gold standard by deflation meant the addition of another unfavorable element. With the pound at or near $4.8665 foreign purchasers of British goods had to pay more of their own currencies to acquire British coal, textiles, and other articles which were priced in pounds. Their buying was therefore discouraged except as British exporters found ways of lowering their prices. While, as always, some of them were making large profits there were many who could not sell profitably at lowered prices unless they could reduce costs either on the whole or by so stimulating output that unit costs were reduced. Every effort was made to bring this about, particularly through pressure on labor to take lower wages or to work longer hours. But workers replied that they could not assent, since their own cost of living was still high. There followed years of struggle and even today the readjustments are not completed.

This recital of facts about deflation and a brief description of its consequences has been introduced not only because it is a necessary part of our account but also because similar problems have faced others of the industrialized countries and also because it serves to illustrate certain difficulties that are inherent in the world struggle. There were several reasons for British deflation. Inflation as an alternative need not delay us but there were strong arguments in favor of returning to the gold standard with the pound devaluated at, say, $4.50. Prices need not have been lowered and much internal strain would have been saved. Other countries—Finland, Belgium, and France—devaluated without deflation and England might have done it.

The reasons for deflation seem to have been three. First was the pride of the British in their currency and their feeling of humiliation that it should be depreciated in terms of any other money. Such an attitude is not peculiar to the British but prevails quite generally. Second was the belief that to bring the pound back to its old level was financially virtuous, a view similar to that in other countries, for example in the United States after the Civil War when bringing the "greenback" to par with gold in 1879 was hailed as proof of national integrity. Third and most important was the strength of the investing classes. Industrialists, manufacturers, and traders had much to lose from deflation, since a fall in prices was disturbing to trade, slowing down orders, compelling unemployment, and forcing bankruptcies. But holders of securities gained through a rise in the value of the pound. In Great Britain this group is large and influential. They own bonds and mortgages payable in pounds to huge amounts purchased at home and also in the most distant parts of the world. In the struggle over monetary policy their views were almost certain to prevail. There was the same issue in Continental countries but the influence of the *rentier* group among them was less powerful.

This struggle of classes where different policies are favored by different groups is another of the difficulties affecting international relations. As illustrated by the action of Great Britain it had several repercussions. First, as just explained, it tended to check her exports. Second, by introducing internal strain and economic distress Great

[199]

Britain was to a degree weakened as a market for many goods from other countries. Third, by raising the value of the pound, the real burden of payments from debtors in other countries to their creditors in Great Britain has been appreciably raised.

Only brief reference can be made to the meager results secured from the efforts to encourage emigration; to the necessity of placing on the Exchequer (which means on the general taxpaying public) much of the burden of unemployment insurance; to the direct financial aid given to the coal industry in 1925; to the persistent efforts to develop foreign trade through the Trade Facilities Act and otherwise; to the emphasis placed on the idea of imperial preference; to the growing pressure for protective tariffs as shown by the use of the Safeguarding of Industries Act; and by the repeated introduction of the issue into successive political campaigns.

It should be possible to summarize the position of Great Britain without being charged with undue optimism or with unwarranted pessimism. About 45,000,000 people are living in a relatively small area. They have developed a high standard of living, ranking second to that of the people of the United States, but its maintenance is dependent on the regular conduct of business with other parts of the world. If population declines the strain is to a degree relieved; if it remains stationary the difficulties are still present; while if numbers grow the problems become harder to solve. Relief through emigration can apparently be only slight.

Heavy investments abroad seem to many a sign of financial and hence of general economic strength upon which the country can rely, but two considerations must not be overlooked. One is that these foreign securities are owned, with a few exceptions, by private individuals and it is not easy for the community as a whole to utilize them in any way or even to know of their existence. There are many ways of concealing them and it is chiefly through the self-interest of their owners that they can become of social advantage. A second fact is that to some extent these foreign investments are an actual handicap. Thus British capital has been utilized in the construction of cotton mills in India yet these mills aid in supplying a market that would otherwise be more open for the mills of Lancashire. Then, too, India has a tariff on the importation of cotton goods that actually helps to keep out the British product.

Past advantages, as we have shown, were based on location, climate, certain natural resources, and an early start. These have all become less significant. The immediate future depends on the maintenance of exports which in turn means freedom of markets and accessibility of raw materials on favorable terms. Apparently the British people have more to gain than those of any other country in the world from freedom of trade. One may speculate, as we did in a previous chapter, on whether free trade in the past has aided Britain since it has encouraged the growth of a population so large and created so much dependence on the rest of the world, but it is very hard to see how the adoption of a protective policy now would give any long-run relief. Antidumping laws that will prevent short-run raids on the domestic market are, of course, necessary but any policy that will restrict the free flow of trade will be harmful. This is true for Great Britain no matter what policy other countries may follow.

If an outsider may venture another suggestion it is that a more even distribution of the national income is highly important. Wide differences in wealth and income make for social instability and under present conditions this is peculiarly the case for Great Britain. To some extent the problem is being definitely met by heavy income and death duties which are breaking up many of the larger property holdings. To some observers this means a loss of much they have admired and enjoyed in British institutions but the situation seems to demand the change.

Our analysis has emphasized the great dependence of the British economy on a few large industries—coal, textiles, iron and steel, shipbuilding and shipping. These, however, are just the ones under challenge. In England, as elsewhere, many have been seeking the solution by attempting to lower costs and thus permit lower prices that will regain markets. But with similar difficulties in so many other countries this method is ineffective. What the British can do in this direction others also can do and in some instances they have better natural advantages and may be able to do it more successfully. They, too, can lower prices, and only as the market demand is sufficiently elastic to absorb a larger output if prices are reduced does any competitive advantage accrue. For the time being, certain large industries are suffering from excess capacity. Reduction of prices by one group merely brings reductions elsewhere, perhaps with the assistance of subsidies or other forms of public aid, and the relative position is unchanged. This is particularly serious if there has been no reduction in real costs as distinct from a reduction in money costs or if there is indiscriminate price cutting.

From this predicament two lines of relief seem possible. One is to shift capital and labor from the industries under strain to other lines. If this can be done without concentration in new fields that will in a short time be open to competitive strain that will be as serious as the present one, the gain will be clear. Better still, if there is a distribution among many lines there is a lessened danger of the repetition in new directions of the difficulties now experienced in shipbuilding, iron and steel, textiles, and coal. This shift is taking place and fortunately a large number of small industries are appearing. The movement is, however, slow and does not yet give relief on the scale that the problem requires.

The other type of aid whose importance is becoming increasingly evident is to be secured through some form of international understanding. To this the British tradition responds slowly. In the political field the reaction has been more prompt as is shown by British cooperation in the work of the League of Nations and in many other ways. It is apparent, too, in such politico-economic matters as German reparation payments where the British have realized that for them stability in finance and trade is far more important than the receipt of any sums likely to come from Germany. But in private business, progress is less marked, not only in the domestic field where business mergers, outside of banking, have lagged behind those of several other countries but also in the international field where there has been a reluctance to cooperate in cartels and otherwise.

Unfortunately improvement in England is slow and many of the qualities that the rest of the world most admires in British life and character are the ones which apparently must be modified and adapted to the new world in which we all find ourselves in the twentieth century.

Chapter XI

GERMANY'S ECONOMIC RECOVERY

IN the preceding chapter we discussed Great Britain, noticing the advantages of her early start which enabled her to maintain supremacy until about 1870; her relative decline after that date; the acute struggle through which the country is now going; and the obstacles to be overcome if her general standards are to be maintained. Emphasis was placed on the gains derived from the development of manufacturing and shipping in her early years and on the resulting high standard of living, which is above that of all of the countries on the European Continent. But attention was also drawn to some of the present disadvantages— a very dense population; an extreme dependence on other parts of the world not merely for many comforts and luxuries but also for a large fraction of the necessities of life; and the rapid development of industrialism in other countries which introduces sharp competition and tends to lower profits.

It may be wise to point out that this does not mean that the world's markets are sharply limited in extent and that the gains of one country are necessarily the losses of another. There are, of course, some such limits. Food supplies cannot be increased indefinitely, since the law of diminishing returns is a sharp restriction. Supplies of certain raw materials are not unlimited in amount. Oil wells may be exhausted and many minerals may not be abundant enough to satisfy all human desires. On the other hand some raw materials will not be exhausted for centuries, if ever, and scientific methods of agriculture, reforestation, etc., will permit increases in soil output for a long time to come. Markets, too, are capable of almost indefinite expansion. If there is sufficient diversification of effort, if the people of various countries do not all attempt to make the same commodities or other commodities that are closely competitive, an amazing degree of prosperity is possible for everybody.

This suggests a difficulty which we shall be able in this chapter to illustrate from the growth of Germany. If each country would specialize in the production of those articles in which it has an advantage either absolute or relative, difficulties would exist but they would be moderate. There would still be intense competition at certain times and in particular places with many serious losses. But with appropriate diversification of effort the producers of each country could sell indefinitely large amounts in the markets of the other countries. This seems clear for the relations between countries specializing in agriculture and those others that emphasize manufacturing. There is, however, a strong desire among the people of every country not to become too dependent on other parts of the world but to manufacture for themselves.

This is understandable. Self-sufficiency during war is important, not only for belligerents but also for neutrals, since wars are no longer local but tend to become world wide and since all elements of the population in each country are involved. But even in peace times self-sufficiency has advantages. If one's food and raw materials come from other countries, crop failures, industrial disturbances, business crises, or political revolutions among them may be serious. Western Europe has realized very keenly in the last few years its former close dependence on Russia for wheat, because Russian exports of that grain have been sharply reduced. Similarly, internal difficulties in China, India, and elsewhere have had most damaging effects on the markets for the manufactured products of the Western world.

On the other hand there is an advantage in dependence or at least in having outside supplies accessible. A failure of grain crops in India or China or Italy or France is less tragic now that wheat can be brought readily to those countries from the Argentine, the United States, or Australia. A coal strike in Great Britain is less serious since the curtailed output of the British mines can be offset by shipments from other coal-producing areas. When the people of India found their incomes reduced in the postwar years, there was a distinct advantage to them in being able to purchase cheaper cotton piece goods in Japan than they could get from England. On the whole the advantages are strongly on the side of interdependence.

It would be a mistake, however, not to keep in mind the disadvantages of territorial specialization and of the extreme dependence that results. We cannot yet be sure that wars are effectively outlawed and even in the absence of military conflicts other disturbances may be almost as distressing. An illustration of current interest is the effect of high money rates in New York in 1929 on money rates and on general business conditions in nearly all parts of the world. This may be dismissed as a temporary influence but the world is increasingly dynamic and economic life today is a series of changes that are coming with greater frequency and that are each year more fundamental in their effects. There is a growing need for careful analysis and for systematic control. The advantages of specialization and of free interchange of commodities and of capital should be preserved but if the problems that arise from extreme dependence are not faced and solved the new condition may be worse than the old.

These observations may be applied to the rise of Germany; to the importance of her growing economic power; to her recent economic collapse and its disastrous effects on other countries; to her remarkable postwar recuperation; and to the problems created by her present relations with the rest of the world. The development of no other country furnishes an illustration so good of the possibilities and the limitations of economic forces and of our present world organization.

At the end of the Franco-Prussian War the area of the newly organized German Empire was 541,000 square kilometers and the population numbered 41,010,000, a density of 76 per square kilometer. In 1925 the area was 470,628 square kilometers in which there were 62,592,575 people or about 133 per square kilometer. When this growth is charted the rapidity of the gain is impressive and has in it many elements of interest, especially if it is examined in connection with the record of emigration from the country. For a time this emigration was on a considerable scale, averaging 134,242 annually from 1881 to 1890. As the years passed, this outward movement was checked and from 1911 to 1913 there were only 22,359 per year leaving the country.

The explanation of this reduction is to be found partly in changed political and general social conditions but especially in the economic policy of the Reich. In 1870 the country was placing its emphasis on agriculture and there was also a disposition to follow the free-trade leadership of Great Britain. This was abandoned, however, for a policy of protection with the purpose of balancing German economic life more evenly between agriculture and manufacturing and of thus lessening German dependence on the rest of the world. The results attained are reflected in the fact that by 1925 there were over 40,000,000 people or

[207]

64.4 per cent of the population living in cities; by the production in 1913 of 190,000,000 metric tons of coal, 16,764,000 tons of pig iron, 17,604,000 tons of steel, and a large volume of manufactured products of a great variety. Germany became a great manufacturing country producing many articles for herself that she would otherwise have imported. By so doing she was able to support a larger population per square mile and emigration diminished to an almost insignificant amount.

In this transformation Germany was aided by the possession of huge reserves of coal, particularly in the Ruhr and in Upper Silesia, by the large deposits of high-grade iron ore in Lorraine, by miscellaneous deposits of other minerals, by a fertile agricultural area, and by the industry and frugality of her people. In her industrial development, moreover, she utilized more than any other country the findings of modern science. Alfred Marshall termed it "science in the service of industry." She had, of course, the advantage of industrial youth in her competition with England and she directed her efforts into those lines of manufacturing where (again to quote Marshall) "academic training and laboratory work can be turned to good account."

Judgment on this change will be influenced by the observer's preference for one form of social and economic organization as compared with another. The growing importance of urban life and the increased industrialization of the country may have been losses rather than gains. We shall merely record first that at the end of the period more persons per square mile were being supported than at the beginning and that the estimated per capita income was $146 in 1913. It will be remembered that this compares with $335 for the United States, $185 for France, and $243 for the United Kingdom in the same year. With all allowance for errors in these figures, they show one of the highest living standards in Europe. It is interesting to notice that this per capita figure is quite close to the similar estimate for France whose entire economic and social life was on a very different basis.

But if the leaders of Germany were hoping to make Germany economically independent they must have been bitterly disappointed. There are no detailed estimates of the German balance of payments for this period, but Prof. Charles Rist of the University of Paris presented the following summary as his opinion[1]:

Balance of Payments for Prewar Germany
(Five-year Averages, in Millions of Marks)

Debtor		Creditor	
To purchase of foreign goods...	9,750	By sale of merchandise.........	8,250
To purchase of foreign securities and investments............	1,000	By coupons of foreign securities held by Germans and dividends on German enterprises abroad.....................	1,500
		By freight for sea transport on foreign account..............	500
		By disbursement of foreigners in Germany, insurance premiums paid to German companies, etc.......................	500
Total.....................	10,750	Total.......................	10,750

This shows a country with a large foreign trade amounting to 8,250,000,000 marks of exports and 9,750,000,000 marks of imports. Behind it were farms and factories and markets that were bound to suffer if this trade should be disrupted, as it was for years after 1914. There is also to be noticed an annual income of 500,000,000 marks from the earnings of the merchant marine, and another 500,000,000 marks from interest on foreign investments whose total capital

[1] "Les Finances de la Guerre de l'Allemagne," p. 232.

value in 1914 was estimated by the McKenna Committee (Second Committee of Experts of the Reparation Commission, 1924) as about 28,000,000,000 marks. Any interference with the merchant fleet would, of course, cause a double loss—a curtailment of receipts for carrying goods for the people of other countries and also a disturbance to German trade to the extent that such trade was dependent on the use of German vessels for its transportation rather than on the shipping of other countries. Loss of foreign investments, too, would cut off interest receipts from the outside.

In an earlier chapter attention was called to the classified imports and exports of Germany, and they may be repeated here.

Foreign Trade of Germany, 1913

(In Thousands of Marks)

	Imports	Exports
Live animals.....................	289,697	7,444
Articles of food and drink................	2,807,829	1,069,522
Materials raw or partly manufactured......	6,279,949	2,274,087
Manufactured articles....................	1,392,211	6,746,181
Gold and silver........................	436,394	101,372
Total.............................	11,206,080	10,198,606

A large amount of food was being imported, some estimates putting it as high as 20 per cent of total food needs, in which was included perhaps 50 per cent of the fats consumed. Raw materials imported were worth over 6,000,000,000 marks, while markets abroad were needed for raw materials worth 2,274,000,000 marks. Manufactured articles worth 1,392,000,000 marks were imported, and, most important of all, 6,746,000,000 marks of manufactured goods were sold abroad. In the aggregate Germany was receiving over 11,000,000,000 marks of goods from the rest of the world and selling over 10,000,000,000 marks of goods to the rest of the world. Next to Great Britain she was the most dependent large country on earth. It may be observed also that the dependence was mutual—that the rest of the world was relying heavily on Germany.

This development had not been entirely automatic. It was in part the result of planning and effort. The gold standard was adopted in 1871 in line with the rest of the world. Business cooperation was not discouraged but encouraged, particularly by the formation of cartels which had their highest development in Germany. In the United States "combinations and conspiracies in restraint of trade" were declared illegal and in Great Britain tradition and sentiment favored the independence of each business man. In both these countries there were obstacles to cooperative action in the field of big business but in Germany the reverse was more nearly true and with the government sympathetic or even actively helpful the German economy was closely knit together. While it is easy to exaggerate the extent of this cooperation and to attribute calculated intent on the part of the Reich and of German business leadership where none existed, yet it is not unfair to emphasize the greater unity of action and coordination of effort that was shown by the German economy over that of any other country.

But, to repeat, this meant dependence of Germany on the rest of the world and of the rest of the world on Germany, a fact thoroughly demonstrated by the war. As the blockade tightened and was maintained even after the war, German economic life was weakened. A lack of many raw materials hampered manufacturing. A shortage of petroleum meant limited supplies of gasoline and of lubricants, while curtailed imports of food and particularly of fats slowly undermined the health of the people. Gradually resistance weakened and morale gave way under the terrific pressure.

[211]

At the same time many German products were no longer available to the people of other countries who suffered accordingly. The British suddenly discovered that they had been relying heavily on Germany even for lenses used in their gun sights. Here and there throughout the world the sudden disappearance of German goods from the markets made itself felt. One of the most important shortages was that of dyestuffs. Another was beet sugar. While the producers of these articles elsewhere gained, the general world public were of course the losers.

This growing interdependence of world economic life is one of the modern facts to which lip service has long been rendered but which has had only a slight influence on political and general social behavior. Norman Angell's valuable volume "The Great Illusion," which appeared just before the war, was ignored or else its author was condemned and misinterpreted. War could not be a paying venture under modern conditions. Really to win a war is no easier than to win an earthquake. Everybody must lose, aside from the few who always gain in any disaster.

Yet this lesson so generally obvious during the war was ignored after its close. Some might argue that more important issues than the economic ones were at stake, that considerations of justice and right determined the attitude of the Allies. To this the cynic voices strenuous doubts but we need not debate the issue. If moral ends were served in any way it was clearly with economic sacrifice.

As the war closed there were several economic facts that should have been vividly clear and should have determined the economic attitude of the victors. To say that the world is an economic unit is a commonplace. It is trite almost to the point of boredom. But the real application of the idea is rare. Cooperation may seem socially desirable but the world is organized largely on an acquisitive basis and rivalry is intense. Then, too, as we argued in Chap. IX, economic organization has almost of necessity proceeded along national lines. To this may be added the development of national feeling during the war and the expansion of industrial plants and of agricultural output for war purposes.

It is useful to present a brief contrast. First is what a confirmed internationalist would consider a rational view for the postwar years. Germany had been and could have again become a market for 11,000,000,000 marks of goods from other parts of the world, chiefly from her former enemies. Still better, if the higher price level of postwar years is allowed for, she would soon have been able to purchase some 16,500,000,000 marks of goods and have increased these purchases as the years showed a normal economic expansion. She had a merchant fleet which had been carrying much of her own foreign trade and in addition goods for the people of other countries who paid the owners of the vessels an estimated 500,000,000 marks per year for the service. That it was a service is evidenced *prima facie* by the fact that people of other countries did pay her fleet rather than build more vessels and do it for themselves. Then, too, German goods representing the employment of capital and of human labor could have been received from Germany to a value of about 15,000,000,000 marks at the postwar price level, an amount that would have undergone a normal increase with the passage of time.

These possible contributions from the German economy seem important and not lightly to be ignored. A strong case can be made out for the Allies to have waived reparation payments even on purely selfish grounds. Free resumption of the old economic relationships was highly important and if reparations were to be demanded at all the amounts and the methods of payment should have been carefully adjusted in a way that would not have hampered the German economy in the task and that at the same time would not have disorganized economic life elsewhere.

Such in brief would seem a rational procedure. Against it may be placed in contrast what actually occurred. Nothing is easier than to present it with caustic reference to the "greed of the victors" and to the "selfish interests" of the capitalists in other countries. But such a picture is wrong. What the Allies actually did is, *mutatis mutandis*, what the Central Powers would have done had they won. The situation was highly complex. Remember the analysis of preceding chapters, noting not only the importance of world cooperation but also such other facts as the intricate organization of world economic machinery, the delicate balancing of parts, the momentum of economic life, and the ease with which crises and business failures can be precipitated. Do not overlook the existence of a price economy and of an economic mechanism that is to a very high degree competitive. Keep in mind the fact of large-scale production with its heavy capital investment and the relentless pressure of overhead costs, the immobility of both capital and labor, the difficulty of controlling raw materials and of acquiring and retaining markets.

Add, also, the inflated currencies, the unbalanced government budgets, the crushing tax burdens, the huge inter-government debts. In some countries, as in France, Belgium, and Italy, the *rentier* group had lost their holdings, and even the small peasant savings had melted away while the wages and salaries of many income groups had lagged behind the rise of prices. In other countries, as in Great Britain, where inflation had been checked or even deflation accomplished, the burden of debts had been greatly enhanced. Thus the interest on the public debt of Great

Britain, with proper adjustments for the altered price level, was in 1925 nearly eleven times as great as in prewar days.

Everywhere there was dislocation and disorganization. Perhaps it should be pointed out that the popular view is wrong that the world postponed to later generations the economic burden of the war, this being accomplished by borrowing, by bond issues rather than by taxation. The world as a whole could not borrow from the outside any more than it could carry on the war by using up the accumulated wealth of the past. Month by month during the conflict, guns, ammunition, food, and clothing were needed. Stocks previously manufactured and stored were soon exhausted. Current production carried on month by month during the conflict was the only source of supply. There could be no delay, no waiting for later generations to manufacture the supplies needed. They had to be available at once and no financial device could save the people living and toiling between 1914 and 1918 from the labor and sacrifice involved in furnishing them.

Some tasks were, however, thrown on the people of later years. Much property had been destroyed in the fighting areas. Yet without intending to minimize the tragedies of reconstruction in Belgium, France, Poland, East Prussia, and elsewhere it is highly important to see them in proper perspective. The outlays involved and the public burdens assumed in the work have been crushingly heavy for the people and governments concerned but as a world problem we should remember that the areas involved were small. We should also not forget that much of the replacement would have been necessary in any case after a few years. All property depreciates and within 10, 20, or 30 years all of the railway tracks and equipment and many of the buildings would have disappeared to be replaced by other and for the most part better properties. Seventy-five years ago John Stuart Mill commented on the general public surprise over the promptness of economic recovery in postwar years. It is to be explained by the high productivity of human beings in a world where nature helps lavishly and where much of the annual wear and tear on property must be cared for in any case, war or no war.

Also, there was a great neglect of property even in the areas where no fighting occurred and some years were needed to atone for this deferred depreciation. But the most important burden passed on to the postwar generation was the new debtor-creditor relationship. The world as a whole could not borrow but some individuals and groups could and did borrow from others. Governments borrowed from their citizens by issuing huge quantities of bonds. Banks, often acting for governments, issued their notes. Governments of some countries borrowed from the people and governments of others. And this network of new obligations has placed the world under a heavy strain.

Within Germany these debt burdens became impossibly heavy. Inflation of the currency proceeded slowly during the war and for a short time thereafter but after 1921 gained more rapidly until the volume of outstanding notes of the Reichsbank, of the various obligations of the government, of the bond issues of corporations, and of the promissory notes of citizens in general became too huge for payment in marks of the old weight and value. Repudiation occurred in 1923, followed at a later date by a mild revaluation or valorization of debts by many debtors.

But for the most part the complicated mass of internal debts disappeared. The sufferings of individuals were heavy and often tragic, the social strain immense, and the social losses serious. Yet there was an advantage in clearing the decks of encumbrances, an advantage that has been more than offset by the reparations difficulties, but one which viewed by itself is a clear gain.

Now let us return to the Allies and their attitude toward reparations, noting the defects of their procedure but with full realization of the influences that determined their conduct. If it seems contradictory, irrational, and even destructive, no one need be surprised unless it be those who believe that human beings are of the sort attributed to classical economics—cold, unemotional creatures always wisely calculating how to secure the maximum of advantage or pleasure with a minimum of loss.

First to be noticed is the failure to settle the amount of reparations before May, 1921, thus leaving everybody in a period of uncertainty for several years. For a time the German economy was hampered by the maintenance of a blockade and by the surrender of her entire merchant fleet. This crippled her earning power and hence her ability to pay reparations, while its advantage to the Allies was dubious, since the total of world tonnage was far greater than before the war. Germany was reduced, moreover, in geographical area and in number of people, while the delay in settling the amount of reparation claims discouraged any desire for economic recovery. The greater the evidences of German prosperity and of capacity the greater presumably would be the burden ultimately imposed.

Still under the influence of war psychology and harassed by their own financial difficulties, the Allies in May, 1921, demanded through the Reparation Commission the ultimate payment of 132,000,000,000 marks, annual remittances starting at about 3,000,000,000 marks. These sums were too heavy and in 1924, after the year 1923 had been spent in the occupation of the Ruhr, the Dawes Plan was prepared and put into effect. The amounts demanded of Germany under that arrangement were graded upward from 1,000,-000,000 marks the first year to a minimum of 2,500,000,000 marks in 1928 to 1929, the first standard year. It has been possible with some strain to collect these sums within Germany but their transfer has been more difficult and real payments to the Reparation Commission have been possible only because the Reich, the states, the communes, the municipalities, and private corporations have been borrowing abroad the funds with which the payments have been effected. In financial jargon it is said that the foreign exchange needed for the remittances has come not from exports but from foreign loans. Germany as an economic unit has been borrowing from Peter to pay Paul and even, to some extent, from Paul to pay Paul.

In 1929 the Young Committee met in Paris and drafted a new plan which has been slightly modified by conferences at The Hague. Its final acceptance was postponed until certain preliminaries connected with the proposed Bank for International Settlements had been arranged but it is now in force. For our purposes the most significant features are four.

First, the period through which Germany is to pay reparations is definitely set at 58 years.

Second, the annual payments have been reduced from the Dawes Plan schedule to amounts that average 2,050,-600,000 gold marks during the first 37 years.

Third, of these annual payments only 660,000,000 gold marks are unconditional, the balance being postponable under certain conditions.

Fourth, while the plan is, of course, referred to as final, there is a very widespread belief that it is only another step to a more permanent settlement to be entered upon when political and economic conditions are sufficiently favorable.

This experience with reparations furnishes an admirable illustration of the economic limitations of the modern world and of the peculiar or even contradictory nature of many of its phenomena. For many reasons the Allied governments and peoples attempted to get large payments from Germany. On their own side there were real difficulties in receiving the payments, since ultimately they would have to appear in the form of German goods and services. It will be remembered that Germany's organization, as we have sketched it, is one which permits actual deliveries to be made chiefly in the form of manufactured goods. These, however, must be manufactured chiefly from imported raw materials and a part of the resulting product must go to pay for these same imported materials. To get the requisite export balance of at least 2,050,600,000 marks, the total volume of imports must be very large and the exports still larger, a frequent estimate being that 90 per cent of the exports are needed to pay for the raw materials and other imported articles. If this is so, total exports must rise to 20,506,000,000 marks per annum with imports at 18,455,400,000 marks per annum.

But an examination of German foreign trade shows that these amounts have not been reached and that progress toward them is still slow. The year 1928 has been the best to date, but even then the imports were only 13,995,000,000 marks. Still more important, the exports instead of being greater than the imports were much smaller, amounting to only 11,641,000,000 marks, a deficit of 2,354,000,000 marks, instead of the needed surplus of 2,050,600,000 marks. Nor is the upward movement of exports rapid enough to arouse much hope. The Agent General for Reparation Payments in his report of December, 1928, noted the steady gain of exports for several years past but it should be remembered that the rise to which he referred has been

[219]

from the alarmingly low level of 1924 and that exports are still far below prewar volumes, if allowance is made for the changed price level. Also, to repeat, imports are still in excess of exports.

It may properly be contended that not the balance of trade but the balance of payments is the important thing. This is true but an examination of the latest estimates of this balance shows an even larger deficit. The Agent General in

Balance of Payments of Germany, 1927

	Credit	Debit	Balance
Current items:			
1. Merchandise............................	11,072	13,899	−2,827
2. Bullion, specie, and currency notes........	10	199	− 189
3. Interest and dividends...................	......	430	− 430
4. Other current items....................	719	1,900	−1,181
Total................................	11,801	16,428	−4,627
Capital items:			
1. Known long-term operations.............	−1,510	255	+1,255
2. Known short-term operations...........	1,186	504	+ 682
3. Undefinable capital movements..........	2,690	......	+2,690
Total................................	5,386	759	+4,627

the report just referred to examines the balance for each year since the Dawes Plan went into effect and summarizes the situation as follows:

In the first Annuity year there was a substantial increase in the sum total of German debt owing abroad both at long and short time. In the second Annuity year the increase in the sum total of the German debt was slightly less than the increase in the Reichsbank's stock of gold and devisen. In the third Annuity year the debt was again much increased without substantial increase in the Reichsbank's stock of gold and devisen. In the fourth Annuity year there was again an increase in the sum total of the German debt owing abroad, but with a considerable offset in the shape of further increments to the Reichsbank's stock of gold.

After this statement by the Agent General was written the Reichsbank's stock of gold and foreign exchange was heavily reduced during 1929 by the drain of funds to New York, and the discount rate of the Reichsbank was raised. The supply of gold reserve fell until it was little more than the 40 per cent required by law. The stock market decline in New York in the fall months reversed the gold movement but its effects cannot at present be stated.

It is entirely clear that reparation payments have been made, to date at least, chiefly by foreign borrowing, and yet the requisite amounts have been regularly collected within Germany and deposited in the Reichsbank to the credit of the Agent General for Reparation Payments whose business it is to make the transfers to Paris. A very large number of economists have contended that this might occur; that there is a double task involved—first, that of collection within Germany and, second, that of transfer. A minority, however, among whom may be mentioned R. P. Auld, formerly Accountant-General for the Reparation Commission, Robert Crozier Long, a British newspaper correspondent in Berlin, Prof. Frank D. Graham of Princeton University, and Prof. Jacques Rueff of the University of Paris, argue that there is no transfer problem—that the funds can be transferred if they can be collected. This is not the place for an elaboration of the very technical and theoretical issues involved. Instead, we may merely observe that current developments seem to support the majority rather than the minority view.

An examination of the German economy of today shows a number of highly interesting facts. For years, as the Agent-General says, the external indebtedness of the country has been increasing. Yet internal progress has been considerable. Coal output was for a time reduced because of the loss of mine areas under the terms of the peace treaty and the decision regarding Upper Silesia but is now nearly as great as in 1913, and if lignite output, converted to its coal equivalent, be added, the total is considerably larger than the prewar figure. Pig-iron output, though it has gained since 1923 and 1924, is still considerably less than in 1913 because of the loss of Alsace-Lorraine, the Saar, and Upper Silesia, but the steel output is almost as great as in prewar days. Unfortunately there is no suitable general index of industrial production that permits a comparison with the output of 15 years ago. The one that exists covers 14 commodities and is heavily weighted by iron, steel, and textiles. With the average of July, 1924, to June, 1926, taken as 100 the level was 123.7 for 1927 but declined six or eight points in 1928. While this gain is encouraging it is of course to be interpreted with reference to the low output of 1924 to 1926 which was used as the base. Agricultural output shows gains but, with the exception of potatoes, is not yet back to the prewar level. Car loadings of the railways and bank clearings are decidedly on the advance.[1]

These increases have been made in the face of serious handicaps. Although the major part of the war burden was met during the war in Germany, as in other countries, the postponed burden was greater there than in some of them. East Prussia's devastation, of course, had to be restored. The blockade had cut off many important supplies, which meant that capital equipment as well as human strength had depreciated, while stocks of goods on shelves had been depleted. The disorganization arising from the depreciation of the currency, from the occupation of the Ruhr, and from the passive resistance to that occupation were other demoralizing factors. How these handicaps were met and to a degree overcome is a fascinating and instructive story.

[1] *Note.* Since this was written conditions have changed. In 1930 Germany is suffering from the general world depression.

Germany's Economic Recovery

We have noticed that Great Britain with an early start made great gains from her manufacturing and shipping. This came because of her low unit costs and the absence of competition from other countries. As Germany and the United States entered the field her advantage was reduced. In fact, by the introduction of science into industry the Germans threatened to wrest European leadership from Great Britain in a number of lines. British gains were dependent largely on the absence of competition. The appearance of German and American products in the market was, broadly speaking, a world advantage because more commodities were being produced; but it soon became a disadvantage to Great Britain. In many lines it was increasingly difficult for her to compete. Her capital investments were in plants of an older type, her educational system had not been adjusted to twentieth century industrial needs, the form of her business organization and her habits of thought were still those of the nineteenth century. Capital and labor are to a considerable degree immobile and changes were not forced as in Germany, France, and elsewhere by physical devastation during the war that compelled a reconstruction which might have been on modern lines. Old industrial plants and unfortunately old habits of thought prevailed.

Germany had thus several advantages from which four may be chosen for emphasis. First were those arising from large-scale production. Second were those due to her adoption of scientific methods aided by an educational system adapted to her economic needs. Third, an economic organization in which cooperation was not only permitted but was also even encouraged. Fourth, the necessity of rebuilding and of exerting herself to the utmost because of her weakened condition and because of the persistent economic and political pressure from the outside.

In her recovery since 1924 the most important development has been the adoption of what is called "rationalization." Attempts to define it have brought a diversity of
results. The one appearing in the report of the World
Economic Conference in 1927 is:

. . . the methods of technique and organization designed to secure
the minimum waste of either effort or material. It includes the scientific
organisation of labour, standardisation both of material and products,
simplification of processes, and improvements in the system of transport
and marketing.

Careful reading of this description reveals the comprehensive nature of the movement. It is scientific management in an advanced form, applied not only to mechanical
technique, to speed of machinery, to movements of laborers, to planning departments and the rest but also to all
matters connected with the business—to finance, to organization, to cooperation with labor, with banks, with government, with other lines of business. No one aspect of it
should be emphasized as its essence, but for our purposes
special attention may be given to the elimination of high-
cost plants. This is done with the emphatic reminder
that it is only one phase of a very comprehensive movement
which extends through all aspects of business, financial,
and industrial life whose general purpose and effect are to
eliminate inefficiency and to bring about lower unit costs.

One element in the postwar situation to which we referred in discussing Great Britain is the excess of plant
capacity, especially in the heavier industries. This had
developed even before the war in some lines, notably in
shipbuilding, but was exaggerated by war needs and since
1921 has been a serious handicap. In coal production, for
instance, capacity for output has been far greater than the
readiness of the markets to take the coal at a price high
enough to cover unit costs in the high-cost mines. Lower-

ing of the price has not adequately stimulated demand, since the demand for coal is relatively inelastic, at least in the short run. The easy but short-sighted way to meet the difficulty was to operate on a part-time basis. But this did not lower unit costs, since overhead expenses were maintained for all or most of the plants and when these expenses were spread over the reduced output the average was still high.

One feature of the German rationalization movement has been the closing down of many plants in coal, iron and steel, chemicals, and textiles. This was a difficult step in England where business is carried on largely in independent units which do not readily cooperate. It was easier in Germany where cooperation had for decades been usual and where perhaps also the rigidly scientific approach to economic matters was more common. Under a consolidation of plants it has been possible to shut down many of the higher-cost plants and with the aid of the other features of the rationalization movement to operate the low-cost plants on a much more efficient basis.

In the German coal industry the average output per man per shift (for all workers above and below ground), which was 18.6 hundredweights in 1913, had fallen to 12.3 in 1921 and was only 16.8 in 1924. In January, 1927, the amount was 22.4 hundredweights.[1] Average earnings per shift for all workers, which were 5s. 4d. per day in 1913 and 5s. 5½d. per day in 1924, had become 8s. 2½d. per day in July, 1927.[2]

Other illustrations with their supporting statistics need not be introduced. What has been done in coal has been done in iron and steel, chemicals, and elsewhere. The whole movement, which has been quite fully developed

[1] MEAKIN, WALTER, "The New Industrial Revolution," pp. 36, 63.
[2] *Idem.*, p. 70.

in Germany, is often referred to now as the "New Industrial Revolution." One would readily assume that its advantages will accrue to those countries that can adopt it most promptly and most fully. As it progresses, the result will presumably be a larger and larger output of goods at lowered unit costs—an obvious gain to all of us.

But once more we are faced with the dilemma to which we have so often referred. The rationalization process means among other things the use of larger amounts of capital than ever before. The newest and best machinery must be installed. Out-of-date equipment must be promptly displaced as improvements appear. This means not only heavy original investment but also frequent scrapping of plant, *i.e.*, a larger charge than in the past for obsolescence. Unit costs are bound to be high unless output is near capacity. The pressure will be heavier, therefore, than ever before. Markets must be kept open. Advertising and other selling costs will mount, expenses of distribution will be high, competition to sell goods will be keen. To facilitate exports, assistance will be more necessary than ever. In any given country, say Germany, exports will be encouraged in every possible way, by subsidies, by bounties, by loans at low rates of interest, by discriminating railroad rates, and otherwise. The domestic market will be safeguarded still more rigorously by protective tariffs and other devices that will keep out foreign products. This lessens competition at home and, especially if there is a domestic monopoly, permits a high domestic price the profits of which make possible a low export price or dumping. This invites antidumping legislation and reprisals of various kinds from other countries. In each country the economic organization tends to become more and more unified against the similarly organized and unified economies of other countries.

[226]

In other words, the pressure to collect reparations from Germany intensifies the problem. The Allied countries have felt impelled to collect impossibly large sums. For a time the attempt failed but only with a serious demoralization in Germany and indirectly at heavy cost to her creditors. In so far as recovery has occurred to date it has been with financial aid from the outside to such an extent that it may be said that the people of other countries, especially the United States, have actually been furnishing the funds from which reparation payments have been made. Under the pressure, too, German industry has improved its technique until it is apparently superior to that in the other European countries, particularly her most important rival, Great Britain. To date, Germany as an economic unit has not been making external payments as is shown by her balance of trade and by her balance of payments.

Nor are there yet signs that real payments are about to start. Trade barriers were rapidly rising up to 1927. There was a pause in 1928 but 1929 and 1930 showed another upward movement. In Paris the claims against Germany were reduced, a movement that slightly relieves the strain. Even so, the economic equilibrium has not yet been restored. There must come still further reductions unless the world cares to face the strong probability of defaults, either public or private or both. If the reductions are not made and German defaults are avoided, there must come soon a huge flow of German goods that will cause acute difficulty for her competitors in the world markets.

No clearer case could be found of the need for world cooperation and of the hazards of continuing along present lines. As yet, however, adequate cooperation is lacking and there is much reason to fear that the strain will become worse before effective means for dealing with it can be found and applied.

[227]

Chapter XII

FRENCH ECONOMIC GAINS

NEXT in our list is France, a country whose area in 1927 was 551,000 square kilometers or 212,659 square miles and whose population was 40,743,851. This is a density of 74 per square kilometer or 191.5 per square mile. For some reason there exists a widespread misunderstanding of French population. It is commonly believed that the number of people in the country is decreasing or is stationary. This is inaccurate. In 1801 there were 27,349,003 people in France as contrasted with 39,604,992 in 1917 and 40,743,851 today. A chart of population growth shows a steady increase although a slow one since 1800 with only an occasional year in which there was no actual gain. The increase has been far less rapid than that of other countries but there has been an increase.

Another prevalent misconception in this same connection is that the French birth rate is very low. Actually it has not been strikingly below those of other countries of western Europe and is now about the same as that of several, being even more than for a few of them. The reason for the relatively slow gain in numbers is to be found in the death rate.

A comparison of birth rates and death rates for a number of countries shows that the birth rate for France in 1927, which was 18.1 per 1,000, was higher than those for Sweden, Switzerland, England, and Wales and almost as high as those for Belgium (18.3), Germany (20.6), and Norway (20.0). Even in the United States the rate in 1926 was only

20.6. The death rate in France for the same year, however, was 16.5 which was higher than the corresponding rates for Holland, Italy, Denmark, Czechoslovakia, Norway, Germany, Switzerland, Belgium, Sweden, and England and Wales, most of whose death rates were much below that of France. Thus Italy had a rate of only 15.7, Germany 12.0, Belgium 13.5, Sweden 12.7, and Holland 10.3.

This relatively high death rate, especially in the early years, has given to France a slow increase in numbers but nevertheless there has been an increase. Its adequacy cannot be arbitrarily settled but those who fear an excess of world population will find nothing alarming in the birth rate or in the present number of people per square mile. Apparently there should be concern felt only by megalomaniacs or by those who for some reason object to the slower gain in France than in other countries, an objection presumably based upon a fear that the military strength of the others may exceed that of France. If larger absolute numbers are desirable it would seem better to seek them through a lowering of the death rate. If the concern is over the smaller numbers per square mile in France than elsewhere, the remedy might be found not through an increase in France but if possible through decreases in other countries. This may be what will occur, since birth rates are declining in many parts of the Western world.

For many years France has been an illustration of a fairly stable and a relatively self-contained country, although statistical demonstration of this is difficult or impossible. At times, comparisons have been attempted by noting the total or per capita amount of foreign trade. But this is highly misleading, for much depends on the size of the country, just where its boundaries chance to be drawn, and on other matters. The proper weighting of each factor is difficult and the net result is often not sufficiently helpful to warrant the attempt. Thus a sparsely populated country, exporting a large amount of food and raw materials and importing its manufactured products, may have a very large amount of trade per capita but suffer far less in a crisis than does the manufacturing country. If trade is demoralized, the food-producing country can get along much better without manufactures than the manufacturing country without food.

Among the elements of importance influencing French economic life have been the system of inheritance under which the property of a decedent is divided among his children instead of passing to the eldest son as in England. This has given to the country a multitude of proprietors of the soil, each with a small parcel of land, as contrasted with the great estates of England or even of Germany. It has encouraged the children to remain at home rather than seek their fortunes abroad and has contributed much to the stay-at-home tendencies of the French and consequently to their outlook. There has followed also a frugality and an industry which are imperative when such intensive cultivation of the land is necessary and a thriftiness which is displayed in manifold ways, including the large number of small savings.

For much the same reason, too, the French have not been daring in their investments. They have purchased largely the bonds of their own government or, if they bought abroad, have favored the bonds of other governments as presumably safer than industrial bonds. These tendencies were of great help to the French government in paying the indemnity of five milliards of francs in 1871 but have been less of an asset in recent years. Immediately preceding the World War a large and, as it has proved, a very dangerous amount of French funds had gone into Russian and Balkan government bonds and the losses on them have been heavy.[1] On the other hand the wide distribution of property and the fact that nearly every peasant is to some degree an owner has probably been a stabilizing influence and has operated against radical movements in France. From time to time there are radical agitations in Paris but it is difficult to imagine an upheaval in France like that of 1917 in Russia.

France is by no means poor, as is shown by her estimated per capita income of $185 in prewar days as compared with $243 for England and $146 for Germany and the much smaller $112 for Italy. This is to be attributed to her fertile soil with its important supplies of coal, iron, and other natural resources; to the industry and frugality of her people; and in part also to the fact that the number of people per square mile or kilometer was not so great as in England, Germany, France, or Italy. Thus her income per capita was higher than in any of the others except England, and yet she had avoided the emphasis on industrialism shown by several. Alfred Marshall, whom we have quoted as stressing England's leadership through "massive production" and Germany's strength from utilizing "science in the service of industry," explains French leadership as due to "individuality and refinement in production." He points out that:[2]

The physical features of France have not favored industrial concentration; the political conditions of the seventeenth and eighteenth centuries suppressed the middle class; so that French industry was mainly given to cheap local products, on the one hand; and, on the other, to fine goods, embodying some artistic feeling and individual judgment. The Revolution removed many obstacles to massive production. But the equal division of property made for industrial quietism; and in spite of the exceptional brilliancy of her engineers, France owes relatively little to

[1] See PERQUEL, JULES, "Les Vicissitudes des Placements Franҫais à l'Étranger,' Paris, 1929.

[2] "Industry and Trade," Book I, Chap. VI.

the aid of mechanical power in manufacture. Individuality contends under ever increasing difficulties against the forces of massive organization.

For years the usual interpretation of French economic life has been in line with this characterization by Professor Marshall. But the last sentence of the quotation should not be overlooked. "Individuality contends under ever increasing difficulties against the forces of massive organization." In other words, many French products have found it more and more difficult to compete in the world's markets against the machine-made output of England, Germany, and the United States. Under this pressure France was for a long time changing and the process has been hastened during the last 15 years. The World War made necessary a strong emphasis on rapid, large-scale output of products at times when individuality and artistic effect were of no importance. Next came the acquisition of Alsace-Lorraine and vast deposits of iron ore besides the control of the Saar for at least 15 years. Then reparation payments and the necessity of receiving part of them in the form of coal and other articles that Germany could furnish have added their influence.

France is, in consequence, more industrialized than before the war and the process seems likely to be increased rather than diminished. An examination of production and trade statistics shows many changes. They should not be misinterpreted. It should be remembered that the shifting of a boundary line makes some trade foreign that was formerly domestic and some domestic that had been foreign. Iron ore going from Lorraine to the Ruhr was formerly the domestic trade of Germany while now it is a shipment from France to Germany and appears among both French exports and German imports, swelling both their value and their weight. Nevertheless this area is now a part of the French economy. Its statistics are a direct addition to the economic facts about France, its resources are at the disposal of the French government for purposes of taxation, and indirectly its influence will be imposed on other parts of the country.

The receipt of reparation coal from Germany in addition to the output of French mines, which have rapidly recovered their productivity since 1918, has furnished an abundant supply of cheap fuel at moderate prices. Reconstruction has been largely completed and the new equipment is superior to the old. Perhaps the best statement that can be given is in the words of J. R. Cahill, British Commercial Secretary in Paris:[1]

Economic Power in 1914 and 1928.—The devastated areas possess now an economic capacity far superior to that of 1914. Their coal mines produced, in 1927, 33.32 million tons against 27.39 million in 1913, their coke ovens 3.28 as against 2.46 millions, and in patent fuel 2.42 against 1.80 million tons; in gas, benzol, synthetic ammonia and other by-products the advance has been in a far greater proportion. In equipment, whether as regards permanent plant, electricity installation, mechanical appliances for coal getting and transport, the advance has been immense. The iron mines, which show great advance in methods and equipment, produced in 1927 more ore than in 1913 (when half the mines were in German territory) . . . As the linen, cotton, woolen and jute trades with important branches such as the cotton, lace and embroidery, and the woollen hosiery and the carpet trades, had all their chief centers within the ten counties, it is probably in these trades that the greatest advance has been realised. They comprised 60 per cent of the cotton spindles, 50 per cent of the looms, nearly all the wool combing mills, about 80 per cent of French woollen yarn and cloth capacity, 93 per cent of linen yarn and about 80 per cent of linen weaving capacity. The war robbed them of over one-third (2.8 millions) of their spindles and of 13,000 looms, of 400,000 out of 750,000 wool carding spindles, of two-thirds of the combing spindles, of three-fifths of the woollen looms, and of two-thirds of the 600,000 flax spindles, whilst whole linen weaving centres like Armentières and Bailleul were reduced to utter ruins. All

[1] *Report on Economic Conditions in France in 1928, Department of Overseas Trade,* pp. 50, 51.

[233]

these losses, save to a slight extent numerically speaking (for replacement has often been by larger machine units or by more efficiently organised factory units), have been made good by the newest types of machinery in practically all cases, and when rebuilding was requisite by better planned, better equipped and larger units. In other important branches the same thorough overhauling and modernisation has occurred. In the beet-sugar industry the 145 destroyed or damaged works have been replaced by 50 new works on a larger scale, and the prewar total of 213 (most of them in the ten counties) is now reduced to 107, which possess a superior production capacity than the greater number in 1914. Similar reconstruction and superior capacity is to be observed as regards the very numerous small breweries, brickworks, distilleries, building and other undertakings in these areas. It results from all these transformations that, although the official statement returns the percentage of industrial reconstruction at 88, on the basis of the number of establishments with over 10 persons that have been damaged and reconstructed, yet owing to the nature of the reconstruction one may regard the industrial reconstruction from the point of view of potential production as more than completed, and may even assume an excess margin of, say, 25 to 40 per cent.

These extracts, if read with even a little imagination, picture a change of great significance. France was of course not economically independent before the war. No country could be. But this account of reconstruction is one that shows a rapid growth of large-scale industry with the familiar story of increasing dependence on other regions for food, raw material, and markets. Since 1913 French territory has been enlarged and her industrial power increased. This was done largely at the expense of Germany. But Germany has met the situation by increasing her own efficiency and productivity within her reduced area. Under continuing pressure from without for reparation payments and from within because of the economic forces we have been describing, she is bringing her economic capacity back to prewar and may soon exceed it. With France also adding to her industrialization there is in the aggregate an immense gain in productive capacity in western Europe, a growing stimulus to economic competition, and hence a potential addition to the intense rivalry which causes so much trouble between industrialized countries.

Señor de Madariaga in his recent volume "Disarmament" reminds us that armaments are not so much the cause of wars as they are an instrument of policy used both during war and during peace. It seems certain that this enlarged economic capacity with all it means in a growing need for resources and markets elsewhere will make more important than ever before these military "instruments of policy." Unfortunately the signs of disarmament are not yet very reassuring. If disarmament actually comes it will come in spite of the growing need for military equipment as an aid in the economic struggle. Every aid, military and other, will be needed more than ever. Disarmament under such conditions may be attributable to a changing code or to a dread of the burdens of militarism and of the horrors of warfare. More likely, as we shall argue later, it will be due to the gradual appearance of other forces which may soften the international rivalry and ease the tension between the competing units.

France, then, is a larger area than 15 years ago, with a more numerous population and with an economy more industrialized. She still excels in the production of what Marshall calls "fine goods embodying some artistic feeling and individual judgment," but the gains of the machine process are clear. A combination of developments has given her more coal and iron ore and has increased her emphasis on large-scale output of heavy products. In discussing Germany we saw the emphasis there on the heavy industries—on coal production, on iron and steel, on chemicals, and on shipbuilding. Much of this stress is on the manufacture of capital goods, the making of steel rails, locomotives, building materials, ships—or on the output of coal, much of which must be used in plants which produce iron and steel, etc. Looking back two chapters, we recall that these are the products on which so much of British life depends. And here is France with growing emphasis on the same lines of production. In the coming pages attention will be called to certain similar developments in Italy, Japan, and the United States, and still other countries could be added to the list.

This at once suggests the problem of markets. If the manufacturers of so many countries are trying to sell the same kind of articles, can the market absorb them? The immediate reaction of many is to insist that the market at any given time is limited, that what one group gains another group loses. To this view others reply that this may be true in the short run but that in the long run the world economic organization will become adjusted. If too many articles of a given kind, say steel rails, are being produced, the price will fall and some of the capital and labor employed in making them will after a time be shifted to the making of other articles. In the long run, certain natural economic laws will make themselves felt.

Both views are, of course, correct. Short-run difficulties are constantly apparent, but if economic events are viewed with a little detachment and perspective, adjustments may be seen. If one may dare to generalize at all, he will say that the tendencies making for strain are the stronger at present; that in the last 15 years the pressure has been to invest more capital and labor in much the same heavy industries in all western countries; that modern processes call for more and more capital for each plant; that the inducement to run each of these plants at full capacity is strong; and that the new machinery and the new processes are designed to add to output, not to curtail it.

[236]

From this difficulty two general lines of relief may be visualized. One is to expand the markets in order that all of the huge output may be regularly absorbed. While markets are expanding, the gain is not yet sufficiently rapid to handle the problem. Even German rationalization often tends to permit production at lower unit costs but does not always reduce production. It may merely concentrate it in the most efficient, *i.e.*, the low-cost plants. In France industrial equipment is modernized. Loans have been made to Germany on a huge scale, particularly by American investors. If those are right who justify these loans by saying that they have been utilized productively, we face both in Germany and in France a huge productive capacity, for which it will be difficult to find adequate markets. When, as, and if Germany really begins to pay reparations by some other method than through loans, the struggle will become more intense than ever. Germans will demand a market for their goods; the British have so much at stake that they will not yield without a struggle; and we have noticed the strengthened position of France. To the list of countries may be added Italy, Belgium, Czechoslovakia, Austria, and others. A large and very rapid expansion of markets is needed if the potential supplies of certain goods are to be sold. It is too much to expect that friction can be avoided.

The other line of relief is to be found in a greater diversification of output. If the aggregate of labor and capital in the coal industry is too great, some of that labor and capital may perhaps be used elsewhere. If there are too many coke ovens or steel mills or shipyards, some of them might be abandoned at least temporarily. It will be remembered that this has been done to a degree, especially under rationalization in Germany. But the process is not an easy one to carry out. No one owner or group cares to take the

[237]

lead. No corporation will close voluntarily, accepting the loss of shutting down and dismantling a plant for the sake of the general good. In an early chapter on large-scale production we stressed the tendency for a large plant to continue operating for a long time even at a loss. And even if the organization within each of the countries is thorough there is no reason to expect that any one of the groups thus organized—British, German, French, Belgian, Italian—will shoulder the sacrifice for the sake of the others. The same is true for groups organized along any line if the organization does not include all or a high percentage of the producers. This means that the solution is ultimately to be found in international cooperation on a huge scale—not in one industry but in many.[1]

France has more fully aligned herself with the industrialized countries and her movement comes at a peculiarly difficult time. But we must pass on to other phases of her life, about some of which there is more or less misunderstanding. One is her currency policy. In the chapter on England attention was called to the three different possible solutions of the currency problem—inflation, deflation, and devaluation at the price level of any given date. England deflated until the pound was at the old par with the dollar. Germany inflated further until virtual repudiation was compulsory. But France devaluated the franc, a *de facto* solution from the fall of 1926 that was made legal in June, 1928. The franc is no longer a lump of gold weighing a little more than four grains. It is permanently about one-fifth of that weight. Instead of some 25 francs being the equivalent of a pound sterling, one can exchange at the rate of about 124 francs to the pound. One may acquire about 25 francs with a dollar instead of 5 francs for a dollar as in 1913.

[1] See, for example, J. R. BELLERBY, "Coal Mining: A European Remedy," London, 1928.

Apparently the decision to devaluate the franc at this level was taken only after a long struggle between the rival economic groups concerned. Investors in obligations payable in francs now receive only about one-fifth as much as they would have received if the franc could have been brought back to the prewar parity with the pound and the dollar. These losses seem serious but like many others in life are not so bad when closely examined. We have noticed the strain on the British economy that has been due to falling prices and have pointed out the reasons for it. This strain occurred in spite of the fact that the pound had never fallen below $3.18 and was that low only for a short time. Yet that brief low level represented a loss of only about 35 per cent of its value. The French franc, however, fell much lower. Overlooking the brief period in the summer of 1926 when it was worth less than 2 cents, we may point out that it was for a long period worth only about 20 per cent of its old par, or less than 4 cents. If the owners of obligations payable in francs had been able to carry out a complete deflation policy—one that would have brought the franc back to 5.18 for a dollar and 25.22 for a pound—prices would have been driven down correspondingly. In the face of such a slump, business would have collapsed, unemployment would have become well-nigh universal, and recovery might have been delayed for years. Such a disaster would have been no help to the *rentier* group. As creditors of business and of the government their claims would for the most part have become worthless. Their debtors would not have been able to pay. Even the government would have defaulted.

It is understood that there was a prolonged struggle between those who favored a restoration of the franc to the old par and those who opposed such a move. Fortunately, devaluation, or, to use the more complimentary term, "stabilization," was finally determined upon at approximately the level of 1927, *viz.*, at about 124 to the pound and 25 to the dollar. The shock of *de facto* stabilization proved to be moderate and when *de jure* stabilization occurred its effect on business was not noticeable. Prices are perhaps not yet fully adjusted to the new situation but are apparently becoming more nearly so each month. France was saved the severe social strain that inflation and repudiation placed upon Germany and also the difficulties that the opposite policy—"deflation"—produced in England.

It is premature, at least for one not thoroughly conversant with the details, to speak with much assurance, but one suggestion at least may be hazarded. In spite of the fact that so many of the French have small savings there is not a *rentier* group with the concentrated power that is to be found in England. Nor have the French invested so widely all over the world, owning promises of other people to pay in francs. Their foreign investments were important but were somewhat concentrated and many of them had already become worthless or nearly so. Losses from devaluation were, therefore, comparatively slight. The British have felt that their own procedure was one of financial virtue. But as they have observed the comparative ease with which the French passed through their currency stabilization as contrasted with the British difficulties, some of them have voiced a doubt regarding the wisdom of their decision.

In France the stabilization of currency was long delayed Some observers have argued that it might have come sooner but many such critics seem to be talking of a different world than the one in which we live. If human beings were omniscient and rational, doubtless their behavior would be different. It is at any rate certain that the French government and people faced an extremely difficult task at the end of the war. Prompt reconstruction of the devastated regions was highly important—partly as a matter of relieving human suffering and partly because the economic life of France would be tremendously aided by the recovery of those rich provinces that had been laid waste. Their coal mines and their factories and their agricultural output were needed to help other sections and their resources were likewise important to the government.

How to finance the reconstruction was the problem. An unwise reliance was of course placed on the ultimate receipt of reparation payments from Germany. The economic and other human limitations were not fully appreciated. Yet, in practice, the method followed was probably the only one that was feasible. Even if Germany were to pay, there would of necessity be a long delay and it was important that reconstruction proceed at once. By starting promptly, employment was at once given to labor used directly and indirectly in the process and much friction was avoided. The amounts needed were so huge that taxes adequate for the total involved would have been impossibly heavy. If, moreover, Germany were ultimately to foot the bill, there was no reason to resort to taxes. It was much better to borrow the money and then repay when the funds from Germany were received.

Such, in brief, was the setting. Funds were borrowed in various ways that need not be analyzed here. The salient facts are that (1) the funds were borrowed and the government thereby assumed heavy obligations either direct or through endorsement; (2) under the strain of events much of the borrowing was done on short-time paper, thus creating the problem known as the floating debt; and (3) since many purchasers of these miscellaneous government promises could not or did not pay outright in cash, inflation was resorted to. Much of the money needed was borrowed

[241]

from the banks, many of whom secured it from the Bank of France. The government also borrowed heavily direct from the Bank of France whose real assets were inadequate. Consequently its note issues grew in amount and as they were put into circulation the price level rose. The usual vicious circle was in evidence. Financial strain forced borrowing from the bank, which handed out its notes freely. But these notes when put into business use raised prices, thus forcing business and government to borrow still more.

To record this process seems to many observers an adequate condemnation. Inflation means suffering, social dislocation, loss of savings. In some cases, as in that of Germany in 1923 and even in France something over 100 years ago, it meant ultimate repudiation. But before passing adverse judgment on the French procedure prior to 1926 it is well to notice a few important facts.

One is that France during this period and even since, with the exception of a short time in late 1926 and early 1927, has been remarkably free from unemployment. Everybody has been at work. True, prices rose, but all workers had something even though it was inadequate—a situation better than that in England where there was rigid adherence to orthodox finance, but a huge amount of unemployment.

Next it should be noticed that after a remarkably short time the reconstruction was completed—not fully, for there is still much to do, but largely. By setting to work, homes and factories and railroads and highways were rebuilt. They were new and in many particulars they were modern. The coal mines were restored and the coal output by 1925 exceeded prewar. And so in other lines. France prospered. There was for years an actual shortage of labor and "between the end of 1921 and the spring of 1927 about

[242]

one and a half million foreign workers had to be imported from Poland, Belgium, Italy, Spain, Czechoslovakia, North Africa, and elsewhere." After a slight reaction in 1926 and 1927 the year 1928 saw a new wave of prosperity.

Whatever one may think of the method, the economic gains have been clear. The result is a busy population, a reconstructed country in better economic condition than before the war, a technical equipment probably far better than would have existed had some other method been followed. Inevitably there were errors of judgment, there have doubtless been waste and extravagance, some of the charges of dishonesty may have been true. But France is today economically strong.

In the economic field the main problem is the government debt. In 1913 the total was 34,204,000,000 francs. On Aug. 31, 1927, after *de facto* stabilization had been accomplished, the total was 474,797,000,000. Of this, 294,957,-000,000 was "domestic," or internal, debt payable in francs. The remainder, or 179,840,000,000 francs, was external debt payable chiefly in pounds and dollars but converted into francs at the new stabilized level. A few comments on these two groups of debts will be helpful.

First, it is easy to create a wrong impression regarding such a debt either by minimizing its significance or by exaggerating it. Both views have an element of truth. Those who contend that the burden of an internal debt is not important argue that the money collected by taxes to meet the debt charges is merely taken from the public as taxpayers and handed back to the same general public who are likewise bondholders. The process is merely that of taking money out of one pocket and putting it in another. If one looks merely at the money one can say that no money leaves the country. If instead one refers to the flow of commodities which constitute the real income of the country one can say that by taxation the government acquires a temporary control over a part of that stream but promptly diverts it back to the general public by its payments to bondholders. As long as the processes of farming, mining, manufacturing, and trading are continued there will be an endless stream of the good things of life produced and distributed. If the debt is an internal one these commodities and services are still in the possession of the home population and the only loss is the outlay for the services of the public employees who collect the taxes and disburse the interest.

Like most other arguments seriously advanced in economic discussions this one is partially true and errs chiefly through its omissions. If each individual taxpayer were a bondholder who received each year in interest and repayment of principal an amount exactly equal to the sums paid in taxes for the debt service, then the contention just recited would be true. It would also seem to mean that each bondholder ought to be willing to have his bond destroyed. He would lose the bond but also he would be free from the burden of the corresponding tax.

Needless to say, the burdens are not distributed in this manner. Some taxpayers own no bonds and some bondholders pay only moderate taxes. The real incidence of taxes, moreover, is very difficult to trace. The taxes may be wisely imposed or unwisely. It is highly probable that in most modern communities the result of a heavy public debt and consequent high taxes is to place the public under considerable strain. More is taken from some groups in taxes than is equitable and more is received by groups of bondholders than is best for the country or even for themselves. There may be and often is a very serious social strain if there is a heavy debt. Some individuals and industries bear a larger part of the burden than is wise.

[244]

Yet the funds do not leave the country. The taxes do not drain the country of its wealth or of its income. The burden, if any, is connected with the inequitable distribution of wealth and income within the national borders.

Of course the external debt is different. As long as all people living within a given area call themselves Swiss or Roumanians or Americans or English or French and feel that they are in some peculiar way different from other people, just so long will they resent the idea of having any part of their income drained off to the people of other areas. And they are correct in contending that there is a real loss. It is interesting, however, to notice that the resentment is usually less general and less bitter if the recipients chance to live in the same area and under the same governmental jurisdiction as the taxpayers.

The external debt of the French government on Aug. 31, 1927, was 179,840,000,000 francs, of which 159,638,-000,000 francs was political debt, *i.e.*, debt arising from the war and owing chiefly to the governments of Great Britain and the United States. It is this debt that causes the most discussion, especially the amounts due to the government of the United States, since the British government in the Balfour note of August, 1922, and in later affirmations of it has announced a willingness to take from its debtors, including Germany, only the sums needed to meet its payments to the United States.

It is, of course, hopeless to attempt a statement of the pros and cons of this debt in a few paragraphs. Instead, we shall merely reiterate our regret that the debt still exists and a willingness to use almost any formula to bring about further reduction or cancellation of all the sums due to the United States. Unfortunately there is no probability of such reduction in the near future and in the meantime there is no valid reason for exaggerating the seriousness of the economic burden involved. The political and moral arguments are not to be ignored and perhaps should be decisive.

At present the French government is paying to the British and American governments £8,000,000 and $32,500,000, or a total of about $71,432,000 each year, the amounts reaching a maximum of $193,131,000 per annum by 1957. These payments are being made at the rates called for by the funding agreements negotiated with the creditor governments. The amounts are for the present not large and perhaps it may be added that of the $32,500,000 paid to the United States government $20,000,000 may be thought of as interest on notes given in 1919 as payment for war supplies valued at $400,000,000. This leaves only $12,500,-000 to be paid per annum on the strictly "political" debt. Or if another one per cent or $4,000,000 is viewed as an annual sinking-fund payment on this same war-supplies debt, the total annual amount to be assigned to this obligation is $24,000,000, leaving for the present only $8,500,000 payable on the "political" debt.

If it were not for the non-economic arguments, the amount involved would not be tragic. The present burden of $71,430,000 per annum is clearly within the realm of possibility and is only one-ninth or one-eighth of the 2,500,000,000 marks asked from Germany as a minimum under the Dawes Plan, and it is only between one-seventh and one-sixth of the annual amounts Germany is asked to pay from 1930 to 1966 under the Young Plan.

The amounts are definitely being paid by France and not from borrowed funds. The French balance of commodity trade is at present adverse, although in several recent years it has been slightly favorable. The balance of total payments is one that is greatly strengthened by tourist expenditures in France and readily permits the payments that are being made. The real economic difficulty centers more about the budget. It is an internal question but a serious one and even the somewhat moderate amount due on the political debts is large enough to be appreciable. It is not unfair, however, to point out that these political debts call for only about three and a half per cent of the 54,000,000,000-franc government budget.

But having argued that the political debt burden is not an impossibly heavy one for France, an American ought not to risk being misunderstood. Let us immediately add that as an economic matter the total amounts coming from the 13 debtor governments to the government of the United States are relatively unimportant. They amount to less than $250,000,000 per year and are about one-fourth of one per cent of the aggregate national income of the United States, only a little more than five per cent of the federal budget and five per cent of the imports. If these questions could only be settled on their economic merits, there would be little reason for the government of the United States to press its claim. And no matter what one's judgment may be on the moral arguments, an American cannot but be disturbed over the feeling on the issue that he finds in Europe.

Chapter XIII

ITALY'S HARD TASK

ITALY is one of the best illustrations of the dilemma faced by the modern economic world. Among the countries of western Europe Great Britain has the largest per capita income, has industrialized most fully, and has the highest degree of dependence. Germany has developed rapidly and among the large countries is perhaps second in the extent of her dependence on the rest of the world, although if smaller countries were included in our survey Belgium would probably come second. France, as we have seen, has in the past had a somewhat independent economy but is rapidly adding to her industrialization and is becoming a keen competitor.

Yet Italy differs from the others in our list. First, notice her population. In an area of 119,705 square miles there were on Dec. 31, 1927, a total of 40,910,175 people, which is almost 342 per square mile or about 131 per square kilometer. This is more than for France and for Switzerland, is about the same as for Germany, but is less than for the United Kingdom, Holland, and Belgium. It will be remembered, however, that these are crude figures. Italy is a mountainous country and has few natural resources. Much of her soil is not arable and much is not suited to any form of agriculture, while a considerable amount is in no way productive. As pointed out in Chap. III, it is estimated that there are in Italy 143 persons per square kilometer of productive land, 188 persons per square kilometer of agricultural land, and 307 per square kilometer of arable land.

It will be remembered also that even alike areas of productive or arable or agricultural land are not equal in fertility or in productivity; that river-bottom lands and land on an Italian hillside are not equally productive; that trees are not all of the same height; that mines have ore of varying richness; that one kind of deposit such as oil may be far more valuable than a deposit of, say, sulphur found over the same area. We must not forget, too, that in an industrial age such a resource as coal is peculiarly important and must be imported if it is lacking. And Italy lacks coal, a deficiency which must be met not by doing without the coal but by importing it in huge quantities and at great expense. As we shall notice later, the development of hydroelectric power has gone on rapidly since the war, but more coal than ever is being imported.

It is difficult to find a suitable test that will express Italy's comparative position but we may revert to the one already used—the per capita income of the country. It will be remembered that in the list given (which was taken from the estimates of Sir Josiah Stamp as published in the *Journal of the Royal Statistical Society* of March, 1919, and as adapted by the National Bureau of Economic Research) the per capita income of Italy just before the World War was $112, which was greater than the $29 for Japan, $54 for Spain, and $102 for Austria-Hungary, but below the $146 for Germany, $185 for France, $243 for the United Kingdom, and $335 for the United States. Although low as compared with several other countries, this per capita income is well up among the countries of the world. Yet all such matters are relative and the observer from the more fortunate countries is apt to feel keenly the poverty of Italy. A highly important fact must not, moreover, be overlooked. This living standard that is none too high rests upon a narrow foundation. Italy lacks natural resources, her population is growing rapidly while emigration is restrained, and she must depend on other parts of the world for some of the most important of her economic needs—food, raw materials, and markets.

Notice next the growth of her population. From perhaps 17,000,000 in 1800 there has been a rapid increase to the 40,910,175 at the end of 1927. And the increase continues to be rapid. The death rate which was 15.7 per 1,000 in 1927 is a relatively high one, being greater than the death rates in that same year in Holland (10.3), Denmark (11.3), Norway (11.5), Germany (13.3), Belgium (13.4), Switzerland (12.4), and Sweden (12.0); but it was lower than those for Poland (17.4), Roumania (22.2), Hungary (17.6), and Spain (18.9), and even lower than the 16.5 per 1,000 in France. But the birth rate in 1927 was 26.9, which was exceeded only by Spain and Portugal and Czechoslovakia in western Europe. In 1927 there were 1,121,072 births in Italy while the deaths were 631,897, an excess of births amounting to 489,175.

One needs but slight imagination to realize that a country with so many people and with a standard of living no higher than the one prevailing in Italy might feel the pressure. Perhaps we may quote Mussolini:[1]

We are forty millions squeezed into our narrow but adorable peninsula, with its too many mountains and its soil which cannot nourish so many. There are around Italy countries that have a population smaller than ours and a territory double the size of ours. Hence it is obvious that the problem of Italian expansion in the world is a problem of life and death for the Italian race. I say expansion: expansion in every sense: moral, political, economic, demographical.

There are those who feel that this pressure of population on resources might properly call for a retardation in growth,

[1] As given by SCHNEIDER, H. W., "Making the Fascist State" pp. 35-36.

[250]

for efforts to reduce or at least not to increase numbers. Yet this is not the Italian policy, although the outlets for Italian emigration are reduced and those who cannot go abroad must stay at home. Thus emigration, which averaged 597,000 per annum from 1901 to 1909 and 650,000 per annum from 1910 to 1914, was only 280,000 by 1925 and is still less at present. Figures for repatriation should be subtracted but they are available only since 1902. Repatriation was particularly important during the World War but the movement inward was heavy even after the conflict ended. Yet when this is allowed for, the result is a decline in net emigration from 225,000 per year from 1922 to 1924 to 131,000 in 1925 and 106,974 in 1927. The net annual gain to the numbers in Italy in recent years is about 11 or 12 per 1,000.

This human pressure on a country "with its too many mountains and its soil which cannot nourish so many" does not bring proposals for reduced numbers, however, but the contrary. The official effort is to secure an increase of the population. Bachelors are taxed and attempts are made to check the spread of knowledge about birth control. Although some of the tax measures are for fiscal rather than for social purposes, the official and church influence are in favor of large numbers.

On May 26, 1927, Premier Mussolini delivered an address which was seized upon by many as furnishing a key to some features of Italian policy. At that time he said:[1]

We must be ready at a given moment to mobilize 5,000,000 men and be able to arm them; we must strengthen our navy and also our aviation, in which I believe more and more, and which must be so numerous and so powerful that the roar of its motors can drown out every other noise on the peninsula and the surface of its wings hide the sun from our

[1] Quoted from SCHNEIDER, H. W., *op. cit.*, p. 35, 39.

[251]

land. Then tomorrow, when, between 1935 and 1940, we shall be at a point which I would call crucial for European history, we shall be able to make our voice heard and to see our rights finally recognized.

Some unintelligent persons may say: There are already too many of us. Intelligent persons reply: There are too few of us . . . Let us speak plainly. What are 40,000,000 Italians to 90,000,000 Germans and 200,-000,000 Slavs? Turn westward: What are 40,000,000 Italians to 40,000,000 French plus their 90,000,000 colonial inhabitants, or to 46,000,000 English plus the 450,000,000 in their colonies? Gentlemen, if Italy wants to count for something, it must appear on the threshold of the second half of the century with a population of not less than 60,000,000 inhabitants . . . If we fall off, Gentlemen, we cannot make an empire, we shall become a colony . . .

Every couple should leave behind it its own equivalent plus x, that is at least three or four children.

We might speculate on the political implications of these pronouncements but this is an economic study, not a political one, and it is enough to record the economic facts without seeking for a political or military interpretation. Italy is poor, her population is numerous and rapidly increasing, and, as we shall see, the signs of difficulty are numerous enough. Notice, for example, the amount of unemployment. It was serious in 1921 and 1922 as in all other industrial countries after the business crisis of 1920. Then there was an improvement, but this was followed by another increase to a seriously high level. On Dec. 31, 1927, there were 414,283 totally unemployed through lack of work, 75,807 partially unemployed through working on short time, and 32,157 partially unemployed through working on the alternating-shift system. These total 522,247 and show a condition almost as serious as in 1922. At the end of January, 1930, the corresponding total was 489,416. These are high points but the periods of improvement in the postwar years have been brief and have been during monetary inflation. A considerable amount of difficulty in maintaining regular employment in Italy might be expected but the large numbers in 1927 and in early 1930 which have been lowered since are to be explained in part by the Italian currency policy.

In Chap. IV we noticed a map prepared by Prof. Ellsworth Huntington on which he has indicated those areas in which the climate is most conducive to physical and intellectual activity. It will be remembered that this revealed for northern Italy an invigorating climate but one less satisfactory in the south. In general, natural resources are scarce in Italy. Fuels are especially so and for heating and power, coal must be imported except as water power can be developed. Only low-grade lignite is found locally in quantities. There are extensive quarries of marble, granite, and other minerals but their commercial significance is diminishing rather than increasing. There are only scattered deposits of iron ore of rather poor quality. There are some deposits of nitrates and large ones of sulphur. Agriculture is carried on in a wide variety of products but so intensively that increases in output can be secured only at a high unit cost.

With political unification, Italy undertook also industrial development. Despite a shortage of fuel, meager supplies of iron ore, and but few other basic raw materials, there has been a marked expansion of the so-called "heavy" industries and also of textiles, chemicals, leather, rubber goods, glass, beet sugar, hats, etc. This has been accomplished largely with the aid of a protective tariff, the commercial policy of Italy being frankly protectionist, especially after 1887. From other countries a considerable amount of food is imported each year and huge quantities of cotton, copper, rubber, wool, and other raw materials. Finished products manufactured from these articles can be sold in the Italian market behind tariff walls.

Whether the gains to the Italian public warranted such a policy we cannot now inquire. We may emphasize, however, first, the extent to which this permitted the employment of a larger number of people per square mile, particularly in the industrial regions in the north; second, the increase in the number of Italian-made products available for home use; and, third, the growing dependence of Italy on outside sources for food, raw materials, and markets. This is the same phenomenon we have seen for Great Britain, Germany, and France. But those countries have possessed to a greater or lesser degree a considerable volume of natural resources as a basis for their action and perhaps as a warrant for it. They have become dependent, it is true, but their position is somewhat strengthened because other countries in turn depend on them for so many products. British coal, German coal, French iron ore, and German nitrates will do for illustrations. But Italy is far more dependent on other countries than other countries are on Italy. It is largely (though, of course, not entirely) a one-sided dependence.

Agriculture in Italy can be carried on only at relatively high costs and Italian industry could have developed but little in competition with that of other countries had it not been supported heavily by high protective tariffs. This economic position of Italy has been an important, if not a determining, factor in her past policies and will probably play an important part in the future.

The monetary unit of Italy is the lira, a unit of the same weight in prewar days as the French, Belgian, and Swiss francs. During the World War and in the years immediately following, the paper money of Italy, which was primarily the note issues of four leading banks and a few notes issued by the government, was greatly inflated. At the end of 1913 the amount outstanding was 2,783,000,000 lire. By the end of 1920 the amount was 21,744,000,000 lire. There was then a decline followed by another growth to 21,450,-000,000 lire at the end of 1925. That this was inflation and not merely an increase in the volume of money, that it was an increase greater than the growth in the volume of business to be done with it is shown by the rise in prices. If 1913 is taken as the base and designated by 100, the wholesale price level at the end of 1926 was 603. In July, 1926, the cost of living in Milan was 649 with the period anuary to June, 1914, taken as the base.

This rise in prices had all the effects with which the world is now so familiar. The prices of some articles rose more rapidly than the prices of others. Wages, particularly of unorganized labor, lagged behind prices. Debtors whose obligations were payable in lire found it easy to pay their debts as these lire became more abundant, easier to secure, and less valuable. Creditors, the owners of bonds and mortgages, received the number of lire to which they were entitled but found that prices were so high that their real incomes were reduced, that with their incomes as large as ever in lire they could buy far less than before of the necessities of life.

We are familiar with the way in which the problem was met in other countries. The World Economic Conference held at Genoa in 1922 urged the countries with inflated currencies to return to the gold standard. Germany and several others did so by first continuing with inflation and ultimately repudiating the vast mass of paper obligations. England, as we have found, deflated before stabilizing, thus putting her industries under a heavy and, as some feel, an unwise strain. France did not deflate and was able by strenuous efforts in 1926 to avoid further inflation. She finally effected a stabilization that became legal in June, 1928, and accomplished it without the harmful

[255]

effects of a changed price level that were felt in Germany, in England, and in so many other countries.

Italy followed a plan that has been quite generally criticised. It will be remembered that in 1926 prices were over 600 compared with 100 in 1913. Italian economic life had largely adjusted itself to that level. Not all the adjustments were complete but many had been made. Wages were at least on the way to the new high level of prices. Borrowers who had raised needed funds at banks, by the sale of bonds and otherwise, had adjusted their borrowings to the high price level, *i.e.*, had obligated themselves to pay the number of lire necessary to carry on business at that level. The government, too, had adapted itself to this situation, and by June 30, 1927, its internal debt, *i.e.*, the amount payable in lire as distinct from the amounts payable in dollars, pounds, etc., was 83,675,000,000 lire.

Now it is curious that this situation, *viz.*, one of high prices, had certain very distinct advantages. Unquestionably those who had bought lira bonds when the price level was low had lost. Nevertheless the government and, therefore, the taxpayers had been put into a very favorable position. Although large amounts had been borrowed by the government and the public debt had grown in nominal amount from 15,766,000,000 lire on June 30, 1914, just before the war, to 83,675,000,000 lire on June 30, 1927, the burden of this public debt had actually not increased. Instead, if proper allowance is made for the fact that the general price level had risen as compared with a prewar 100, it is found that the debt in 1925 was really 15.6 per cent less than before the war.

Yet the Italian government carried out a policy of deflation before returning to the gold standard. How extensive a deflation was planned it is not possible to say. Rumor has it that many had hoped to bring the lira back to its old relationships of 25.22 to the pound and 5.18 to the dollar, *i.e.*, to resume redemption of paper lire in gold lire of the old weight of over four grains of pure gold. A measure so extreme was entirely impossible, and, if seriously undertaken, industry would have been prostrated and the government would have been bankrupted. Prices would have fallen from their level of over 600 to, say, 150, *i.e.*, would have been reduced by 75 per cent. All or nearly all borrowers at the high price level would have failed. English readers will remember the strain of a much slighter reduction of prices in Great Britain, and Americans will recall the difficulties brought on by a much smaller decline in 1920.

Stabilization was at last decreed in December, 1927, at 92.46 lire to the pound, which gives to the lira a value of 5.26 cents in American money. But the raising of the value of the lira from 3.30 cents, at which it was quoted in August, 1926, to 5.26 cents meant in effect the addition of a large burden of government debt, and hence a larger amount was placed on the shoulders of taxpayers. Every other debtor whose obligations were payable in lire likewise found his difficulties increased. Wholesale prices fell until in March, 1930, they were about 400. Bankruptcies were multiplied. The numbers of totally unemployed had shrunk to 122,200 on Dec. 31, 1925, but by January 31, 1930, they had become 466,231 in addition to large numbers on short time and on the alternate-shift system. Both exports and imports declined.

We may summarize at this point by saying that Italy is a country of limited natural resources and with a numerous population whose per capita income is low compared with that of the other countries we have examined. The war and the inflation created a burden that was heavy but could have been carried much more easily had there not been a partial deflation. The industrial life of the country has been developed with the aid of high protective tariffs and with raw materials and fuel which are secured almost entirely from outside the country. Like other industrial countries Italy has become very dependent on foreign areas but the dependence is somewhat one-sided. Under such circumstances either the Italians must make a vigorous effort to maintain and to raise their standards or else there will be a reduction.

In her trade with the rest of the world Italy has for nearly 60 years been importing more than she exported. Not since 1871 has there been an excess of exported goods over imported, the amount in that year being 123,000,000 lire. Every year since has shown an excess of imports, now more and now less, but always an excess. The unfavorable balance rose in the eightys and declined in the ninetys to a low point of 64,000,000 lire in 1899, after which it became constantly heavier. In 1912 imports exceeded exports by 1,290,000,000 lire and in 1913 by 1,075,000,000 lire.[1]

During the World War Italy, like the other European belligerents, imported heavily for military needs but even since the war ended the unfavorable balance has been maintained. Expressed in gold lire of the old weight, for the purpose of comparison with prewar figures, the trade deficit was 643,000,000 lire in 1924, 1,071,000,000 in 1925, 939,000,000 in 1926, and 1,259,000,000 lire in 1927.[2]

This is a deficit in commodity trade only and takes no account of invisible items, which are of increasing importance for all countries. When both commodity trade and invisible items are included, the balance of payments is

[1] McGuire, C E., "Italy's International Economic Position," p. 264.

[2] Rawlins, E. C. D., and H. C. A. Carpenter, *Report on the Economic Situation in Italy*, 1928, p. 31.

less against Italy. The excess of imported commodities is in part paid for by foreign tourists traveling in Italy and by home remittances from Italians living abroad. One estimate by Bonaldo Stringher for about 1910 placed each of them at 450,000,000 lire and along with other items reduced the deficit to about 135,000,000 lire.[1]

In his volume "Italy's International Economic Position" C. E. McGuire brings together the available data on the international accounts of Italy and we may state briefly his conclusions. For the period 1901 to 1905 he finds that the invisible items so fully offset the trade deficit as to create an annual average surplus of 320,000,000 lire. From 1906 to 1910 there was an average annual deficit of 125,000,-000 lire and from 1911 to 1914 one of 185,000,000 lire. For 1915 to 1919 the total deficit was 23,150,000,000 gold lire; for 1920, 3,500,000,000 gold lire; for 1921, 885,000,000 gold lire; for 1922, 230,000,000 gold lire; for 1923, there was an approximate balance; for 1924, a slight surplus; and for 1925, a probable deficit the amount of which McGuire does not attempt to state.[2] It is, of course, to be remembered that during these postwar years the huge gold debt due from the Italian government to foreign governments was not being cared for and that unpaid interest on it was accumulating. Later by her debt settlements this burden was materially reduced.

The international economic task for Italy, like that of other countries, is to maintain a flow of goods and services in and out. There is a large annual deficit on commodity trade which will probably persist and the gap must be filled with the invisible items. In fact, it must be more than filled, because there are invisible imports to be offset. Particularly there is the fact that both the Italian govern-

[1] McGuire, C. E., *op. cit.*, p. 270.
[2] *Op. cit.*, pp. 285, 294, 300, 305, 314, 318, 324.

ment and Italian private business have debts abroad on which annual debt payments must be made. The leading invisible exports are the remittances of Italian emigrants living abroad, the expenditures of foreign tourists traveling in Italy, and the earnings of Italian shipping.

Before the World War the remittances of emigrants are thought to have been about 450,000,000 lire per annum. During the war they were perhaps 640,000,000 gold lire per annum, in 1920 they may have been as high as 975,000,-000 gold lire. But since 1920 they have declined. This is to be attributed to the reduced activity of business after that date and also to the restrictions now imposed on immigration, especially into the United States. Fewer Italians are emigrating and those abroad send home smaller amounts as the years pass. For 1924 the estimate was 540,000,000 lire, and for later years the estimates have been considerably less.

Shipping earnings of 115,000,000 lire just before the war were 200,000,000 in 1924 and the amounts per annum since then are not carefully estimated. The Italian merchant fleet must, of course, meet the competition of a volume of world shipping that is greatly expanded and is probably in excess of the needs of world trade. To maintain this item of national income at a level as high as possible, the Italian government, like most others, subsidizes its merchant marine. This is a further illustration of our main thesis. A modern vessel represents a large investment of capital and it can earn a reasonable return only in case it can be kept busy. To be kept in operation at full or nearly full capacity, rates must be low, especially in a field where competition is keen. But rates low enough to attract traffic may be too low to permit profits. The rates must be low to attract this traffic from competing lines struggling to get business. The only way operation can be maintained is with the aid of government subsidies which are, of course, a challenge to other governments to aid their merchant fleets in a similar manner.

Remittances of emigrants are at present a diminishing form of income and competition in ocean traffic holds down the earnings of the fleet. But tourist expenditures in Italy are increasing and presumably will continue to grow. They were estimated at 600,000,000 of the old gold lire for 1923 and at 550,000,000 for 1924.

This assumes that the trade balance is one that can be readily maintained and that the problem is merely one of filling the gap. But this is not the case, as is clearly shown by a brief examination of the items entering into Italian foreign trade. The nature of that trade is shown by the accompanying table which gives the averages for the years 1922 to 1924.

Italy's Imports and Exports by Classes, Annual Average, 1922–1924

	Lire	Per cent
Imports:		
Foodstuffs and live animals...	4,895,000,000	28.1
Raw materials.............	6,903,000,000	39.6
Partly fabricated goods.......	3,112,000,000	17.8
Manufactured goods..........	2,537,000,000	14.5
Total imports.............	17,447,000,000	100.0
Exports:		
Foodstuffs and live animals....	2,885,000,000	24.9
Raw materials.............	1,302,000,000	11.3
Partly fabricated goods.......	3,266,000,000	28.2
Manufactured goods..........	4,116,000,000	35.6
Total exports............	11,569,000,000	100.0

Only a glance at this table is needed to show Italy's trade problem in its broad features. Food and raw materials worth 11,798,000,000 lire per year were imported. Partly fabricated goods and manufactured goods worth 7,382,-

000,000 were exported. The chief foodstuff imported is wheat. Among the raw materials, wool, cotton, and wood lead the list. Wheat may be raised in Italy but the domestic output can be increased only by intensive cultivation, with great effort and at high cost. With the price of wheat declining, effective competition with the huge output of Canada, the United States, and elsewhere is not feasible. Attempts to raise wheat in Italy face the opposition of the law of diminishing returns and it can be marketed, if at all, only with the greatest difficulty. In other words, wheat can at present be produced elsewhere and imported into Italy more cheaply than the domestic supply can be raised.

Coal is the second import in significance. There are no deposits in Italy and thus far the development of hydro-electric power has not lessened the amount bought from abroad. The growth of industry has called for as much coal as ever. One may check the other items—cotton, wool, hemp, and the rest—with much the same results. Importations of food and raw materials cannot easily be reduced with population rapidly increasing.

Italy's exports are the means by which she pays for at least a part of her imports. But they are not easily expanded. Her food exports are faced everywhere with tariffs, for agriculture in all countries is at a disadvantage and is endeavoring to secure protection. Her important manu-factured articles also face keen competition and tariff barriers. Silk, both pure and artificial, cotton textiles, motor cars, and rubber tires and tubes are among the leading items in the list. To name them is enough. In other coun-tries, too, these products are being manufactured. At least for the present, productive capacity exceeds market demand. It is a buyer's market. Italy can sell only if she can compete effectively against a reorganized Germany, a roused

Britain, a recreated France, and an America whose resources are the greatest of all of them.

One is impressed still more with the difficulties if he notices that Italy's leading export market is Germany, a country still under pressure to make heavy reparation payments. The Germans with the aid of foreign capital are speeding up their own production of motor cars, textiles, and other manufactures. Their exigencies may call for more raw materials but not for foreign-manufactured goods, and raw materials cannot be secured from Italy. France, Great Britain, Switzerland, and the United States are next in the list of markets. And all of them are seeking markets, not offering them. Instead, the tendency everywhere has for some years been for higher tariffs.

Attention has been called in previous chapters to the connection between foreign investments and exports. If newer and undeveloped parts of the world borrow in England by selling their bonds, the funds thus raised are spent directly or indirectly in England, thus increasing the sales of British goods. But Italy is not in a position to export capital. Savings are small and instead of lending Italy has been borrowing.

Still another way of stating the situation is to observe that when world trade is active, as in 1919, Italy must pay a high price for the raw materials she needs and has few to sell to others. When the problem is to find markets, as at present, she must meet the competition of rivals who are in many particulars stronger.

To recite these difficulties is not to prophesy disaster of any kind. It is well, however, not to forget limited natural resources; a dense population, growing with great rapidity; and an industrial life dependent on imported fuel and high tariffs. These are the limiting economic factors. Progress by Italy must be made in the face of these obstacles and against bitter competition. No other industrialized country of the western world has more economic reasons for cooperating with the people of other countries than has Italy.

Chapter XIV

JAPAN'S APPEARANCE ON THE SCENE

A n Associated Press dispatch dated Apr. 11, 1930, announced that the Tokio Stock Exchange had suspended trading operations for an hour and later closed for the remainder of the day to stop a selling stampede; that banking officials had been in conference; and that members of the Cabinet declared the difficulties were due to manipulation of the market by the political opposition.

The news was not unexpected to those who have studied at all the Japanese economy through a period of time, nor to those who have been observing such recent incidents as the deflation of currency, the fall of prices, and the growth of unemployment. Japan is experiencing some of the same difficulties we have noticed in other countries and has an additional handicap—that of recent and very rapid development from a different type of national life to a quite advanced state of industrialization. One index of this change is the growth of the country's foreign trade. Combined imports and exports averaged only 38,000,000 yen per annum from 1868 to 1872 but were 4,878,000,000 yen or nearly 129 times as great in 1925.

A few fundamentals will furnish the background. With an area of 147,201 square miles Japan proper had a population of 61,275,000 at the end of 1927 or 417 per square mile. In 1872 there were only 33,111,000 in the country and in 1909 there were only 50,254,000. Thus, in 18 years there has been an increase of nearly 22 per cent, and in 55 years a gain of 85 per cent. Reference to the com-

[265]

parative tables of births and deaths given above in Chap.
II (p. 18) will be a reminder that in 1927 the birth rate
for the country was 35 per 1,000, the highest among the
19 countries named, and that the death rate was 19.8
per 1,000, also the highest with the exceptions of Bulgaria and Roumania. The excess of births over deaths
for that year was 15.2 per 1,000, the highest in the
list given.

It is well to remember, also, one further fact that was
mentioned earlier in this volume. Much of the area of the
country is mountainous and hence is not arable. A large
part of it cannot be utilized for any agricultural purposes
and much is in no sense productive. Expressed in the
number of persons per square kilometer, there were, in
1925, 154 persons per square kilometer of productive land
and 993 per square kilometer of arable land. About 48
per cent of the total area is forest land.

On the agricultural land many crops are raised but a
special document of the League of Nations (1927) entitled
Population and Natural Resources estimates that in 1925
over 50 per cent of the cultivated area was under rice.
Mineral resources are very poor. Coal and copper are the
most important and there are moderate supplies of silver
and gold. Copper output is less than before the World
War and is not adequate for local needs. Coal production
is about sufficient for domestic demand, some years showing
a slight excess of exports and other years an excess of
imports.

The country, then, is densely populated and is lacking in
resources. Numbers are growing and per capita wealth and
income are low. Sir Josiah Stamp's estimate of per capita
income for 1914 was $29, the lowest in his list given above
in Chap. III (p. 29). The Dresdner Bank of Berlin in a
recent compilation uses instead the estimates of Gini, the

Italian statistician, giving 188 marks (about $48) for 1913 to 1914 and 374 marks (about $93.50) for 1925. Adjusted to prewar prices, this latter amount would be 252 marks (about $63).

It is to be noticed that these figures indicate a gain. Although the country is poor and numbers are increasing and although per capita income is distressingly low when compared with that in Western countries, there is some improvement recorded. It is conceivable that if estimates were available for earlier dates progress would be shown over a long period of years.

When we inquire how such a gain has been possible, we encounter the familiar facts of growing manufactures, increased importations of food and raw materials, and expanded foreign markets. And, of course, there is the same growing dependence on other parts of the world.

Notice the growth of industry. From 1909 to 1922 the estimated agricultural population changed but slightly, although total population grew nearly 10 per cent. The percentage of the total engaged in agriculture consequently declined, the reduction being from 53.8 to 45.7 in the 13 years. This has meant a concentration in industrial centers and a greater reliance on manufacturing and mining. The number of workers in factories has increased and the number of mine employees grew from 193,000 in 1906 to 467,000 in 1918, declining, however, to 296,000 by 1927 because the pressure of war activity had been relaxed.

In spite of this emphasis on urbanization, the production of some foodstuffs has grown, especially that of rice, although that of other products has actually declined, especially since the war period. At the same time the importation of many articles of food has greatly increased. The accompanying table shows this for a number of leading foodstuffs.

[267]

Value of Certain Foodstuffs Imported into Japan
(In Yen)

	1914	1927
Rice and paddy............	24,823,933	78,906,550
Wheat....................	8,488,997	53,929,125
Sojabeans................	10,200,376	41,198,334
Sugar....................	21,678,634	75,804,004

There has been no corresponding increase in the exports of foodstuffs. The only gain worth recording is in the exportation of refined sugar from 13,382,809 yen in 1914 to 28,917,437 yen in 1927. With the world sugar industry in its present state of overexpansion and demoralization, sugar is hardly a product upon which to rely heavily. Japan is moving in the same general direction as other industrialized countries. Her growing population is being fed more and more on imported foods.

There is also a growing reliance upon imported raw materials. Some of them are included in the accompanying table.

Value of Certain Raw Materials Imported into Japan
(In Yen)

	1914	1927
Raw cotton...............	217,872,619	623,919,938
Flax, hemp, jute, and China grass....................	7,938,656	23,575,466
Wool....................	14,783,797	101,676,733
Woollen yarn.............	4,219,533	43,552,326
Iron: pig.................	6,595,242	20,975,480
Iron: plate and sheet not coated with metals..........	6,942,091	35,824,427
Lead: pig, ingot and slab....	2,950,068	15,210,984
Tin: block, ingot, and slab...	2,063,106	10,989,619
Pulp for paper making......	4,574,212	11,930,159
Leaf tobacco..............	1,355,737	9,465,285
Oil cake..................	34,864,678	98,979,213

These raw materials are substantially the same as those imported by the other countries which we have studied but with the significant difference that to a large degree the products manufactured from them are sold within Japan. As yet, foreign markets have been developed for only a few articles, which will be noted. A large part of the raw materials are worked up for domestic uses. They must be paid for, of course, as must the imported food, and an examination of the exports shows how this is being done, at least in part.

Value of Certain Articles Exported from Japan

(In Yen)

	1914	1927
Green tea............................	11,755,140	10,755,312
Sugar: refined........................	12,382,809	28,917,437
Raw silk............................	161,797,411	742,533,693
Cotton yarn..........................	78,554,500	38,794,408
Silk tissue...........................	30,890,488	38,149,722
Cotton flannel........................	1,087,022	19,338,925
Shirtings: grey, and sheetings...........	12,596,493	105,661,123
Cotton undershirts and drawers: knit.....	8,408,089	25,093,472
Paper: European and Japanese...........	2,781,136	19,290,782
Coal...............................	23,914,591	25,508,373
Iron manufactures.....................	1,213,505	12,059,623
Porcelain and earthenware..............	5,988,575	30,491,395

This table includes all items amounting to 10,000,000 yen or more in 1927. In it tea, cotton yarn, and coal are of declining importance as is also silk tissue if allowance is made for the altered price level. The others have increased rapidly, but the most noticeable fact in the list is the significance of two items—silk and cotton. In fact if all the exports of these two materials are brought together— those in the table and others not included—the result is even more striking. For the year 1927 the following is revealed:

	Yen
Total exports	1,992,317,165
Tissues, yarns, and materials of:	
Silk	900,466,297
Cotton	435,981,617

Exports of silk chiefly in the raw form were 45 per cent or nearly one-half of the total exports, and exports of cotton goods were another 22 per cent. The two combined were about two-thirds of the total.

Thus far we have a vivid picture of a densely populated and poor island country which has developed its foreign economic contacts with an amazing rapidity. But with it has developed a dependence for food, raw materials, and markets. The chief exports, it has been noticed, are of silk and cotton in manufactured or semimanufactured forms.

To this now must be added another highly important fact, *viz.*, the heavy economic dependence of Japan on the United States. Notice, first, that Japan does not raise raw cotton but gets it from abroad. In 1927 her total imports of raw cotton were valued at 624,630,000 yen. Of this, 202,282,000 yen came from British India and 343,563,000 yen from the United States. Over 87 per cent came from the two countries—32 per cent from British India and 55 per cent or over one-half from the United States. Since this raw cotton was nearly 29 per cent of the total imports, it will be noticed that the country is heavily dependent on a single raw material and on the two countries from which it is secured—particularly the United States. If all commodities are included in the calculation it is discovered that over 30 per cent of Japan's imports come from the United States and over 12 per cent from British India, or about 43 per cent of the total from the two sources.

When exports are examined, an even more important and potentially serious condition is revealed. Total exports in 1927 were valued at 1,992,317,165 yen. Of this total, 900,466,297 yen were of silk and 435,981,617 of cotton—"tissues, yarns, and materials thereof." In other words, over 45 per cent of her exports were of silk and silk products and nearly 22 per cent were of cotton products. About 67 per cent or over two-thirds of the total were of these two items.

The destination of the exports is also of importance. An analysis for 1927 shows that 833,804,256 yen or nearly 42 per cent of the total went to the United States. In the same year China took 334,183,608 yen or over 16 per cent of the total and British India 167,580,191 yen or over 8 per cent of the total. The three combined bought from Japan in that year 1,335,568,065 yen or more than 67 per cent of her total exports. And the United States took 42 per cent of her total exports of which 698,883,000 yen was raw silk. Since total exports of raw silk in that year were valued at 739,929,000 yen, the United States took over 94 per cent of her raw-silk exports.

Observers are often tempted to compare Japan and the United Kingdom. Both are island countries, one at the western edge of Europe and the other just east of Asia. Both are densely populated and both have developed a high degree of industrialization. Each is dependent on the free movement of commerce. Each has a large navy, the Japanese strongly urging that if the United States and Great Britain are to have parity in navies the fleet of Japan must be at least 70 per cent as large as that of either of the others.

But there are differences. Japan has developed an empire but her control has been extended to areas relatively near, while the British colonies and dominions are scattered all over the globe. British manufactures for export are concentrated to a considerable degree on iron and steel, textiles, and shipbuilding, but Japan has thus far limited herself closely to silk and cotton. Great Britain has large excess supplies of coal, considerable reserves of iron ore, and some other minerals and raises a large amount of wool. British control over distant sources of supply, moreover, is considerable. Japan has only a moderate amount of coal and but little else. Her important raw material is silk, which can be and is being produced elsewhere and must suffer increasingly keen competition from substitutes, especially artificial silk. Japan, like Great Britain, has control over external sources of supply, although they are chiefly on the mainland of Asia. But her influence there is bitterly contested and her ultimate ability to have her way is not clear. Her troubles with dependencies are fully as great as those of the British.

In some respects Japan should instead be compared with Italy. Both have limited natural resources. In both, the population is rapidly gaining, with Japan in the lead— in total numbers, in numbers per square mile, and in annual rate of increase. Per capita income is low in both, but with Japan far behind.

From 1882 to 1895 Japanese exports exceeded imports in value, with the exception of 1890 and 1894. Since 1895 the balance has been the other way, with the exception of 1906 and 1909 and the war years 1915 to 1918. But the excess of exports from 1915 to 1918 aggregated only 1,408,000,000 yen, while the excess of imports from 1919 to 1928, inclusive, was 3,269,403,000 yen. Unless this deficiency in commodity trade is offset by invisible items it is evident that the country is going behind.

Before turning from the balance of commodity trade to the balance of payments, which includes the invisible items, the trade for two recent years, 1926 and 1927, may be presented in summary form.

Foreign Trade of Japan
(In Thousands of Yen)

Imports:	1926	1927
Food, drink, and tobacco.......	350,280	323,540
Raw materials.................	1,341,918	1,201,982
Partly manufactured............	357,181	348,160
Wholly manufactured..........	314,990	290,365
Miscellaneous.................	13,115	14,996
Total imports	2,377,484	2,179,153
Exports:		
Food, drink, and tobacco.......	147,295	145,562
Raw materials.................	140,250	137,324
Partly manufactured............	881,863	852,183
Wholly manufactured..........	852,118	831,221
Miscellaneous.................	23,201	26,021
Total exports..............	2,044,727	1,992,302

This table gives in a broad way evidence of the usual state of dependence of an industrialized country—need for foreign food and raw materials and for foreign markets. It also shows for the two years covered an excess of imports and the consequent need for invisible exports to fill the gap unless the Japanese economy is accumulating a debt abroad.

Invisible exports are neither numerous nor large. Estimates by the Japanese government show for 1926 only 35,400,000 yen spent by foreign tourists, 103,400,000 yen earned as commissions, etc., 52,200,000 and 176,800,000 yen from shipping, freights, etc. And against these must be set invisible items on the other side amounting on the whole to about 60 per cent as much.

In a brief summary like this one the numerous details may be omitted and the general result as given by the Japanese government noted. The net deficits were 309,800,-

000 yen for 1924, 116,300,000 yen for 1925, and 232,200,000 yen for 1926. These amounts are important but not enormous and if the government estimates are correct the annual interest and dividend payments due abroad less the similar payments due from abroad are not burdensome. As given, the net amounts due from Japan on this account are only about 10,000,000 yen—a surprisingly small item. Perhaps it is to be explained by large Japanese investments on the adjoining continent.

In the field of government finance there has been a rapid growth in expenditures from 593,000,000 yen in 1912–13 to 1,578,000,000 yen in 1926–27 and a budget estimate of 1,709,000,000 for 1928–29. But revenues are given as more than adequate both in the ordinary budget and in the extraordinary budget, and unless one is in a position to criticise the construction of the budget, as the writer is not, no adverse comments can be made.

The monetary situation is quite different and calls for explanation. The monetary unit is the yen, which is worth 49.85 cents at par. As in other countries, prices were inflated during the war period and the return to a gold basis has been long and hard. In 1920 the wholesale price level was 259 (1913=100). It fell to 195 in 1922, rose again to 206 in 1924, and since that time has gradually fallen, until it was 148 in March, 1930. Retail prices of foodstuffs did not rise so high and have fallen less, resting at 182 in April, 1930.

This fall of prices has been the result of two influences in Japan. One is the general downward movement in all gold-standard countries. The other is the decision of the Japanese government to bring the yen back to its old par, a decision comparable to that of England and similar except in degree to that of Italy. In discussing England and Italy as well as in the general discussion of the subject in Chap. VI, the effect of this procedure has been pointed

[274]

out. By forcing down prices the burdens of all debtors have been increased. Since inflation at no time proceeded so far in Japan as it did in Italy, the consequences of deflation were less serious. And since debts, *e.g.*, those of the government, were not increased so much as in England, the effect of the downward fall in prices has been less pronounced. The public debt was 2,560,000,000 yen on Dec. 31, 1914, and 5,397,000,000 yen by 1928. Most of the increase had occurred in the domestic debt.

If Japan's economic problems are summarized, the first to receive attention is her food supply. With a population increasing at the rate of 1.5 per cent per annum, more food is needed. To secure constantly increasing amounts from her own soil is probably not possible. About 48 per cent of her area is forest land. There is a population density of 154 per square kilometer of superficial area and 993 per square kilometer of arable land according to the estimate in the League of Nations document that we have quoted. This means that only about one-sixth of the soil is arable and only a little more is to be classed in the broader category as agricultural.

This of necessity means an increasing reliance on outside sources of food supply unless domestic production can be encouraged by better agricultural methods or with the aid of a tariff. It seems improbable that the former can be adequate, and any help given by the latter involves of course, the diversion of productive effort to the raising of food but only in case the price of the food is raised. In other words, more food can be produced in Japan under tariff protection provided the general public is willing to meet the burden of a higher price. Presumably food imports will grow rather than diminish.

They can be paid for only with exports of some kind and these exports are of two sorts. First are products which are not dependent on imported raw materials. But these are few in number because of limited natural resources. At present silk is the only one of importance and, as we have noticed, it is 45 per cent of the total exports in value.

There are several disadvantages in this. Prices of raw materials are particularly subject to extreme fluctuations, a fact that definitely helps a producer when prices are rising in a seller's market but places him at a sharp disadvantage when prices fall. It is hard to support the decline and the consequences are apt to be serious. In Japan some direction is exercised but it seems to be effected through control of bank credit, a method that forces closing of plants and much unemployment.

Another disadvantage that especially affects silk is that it is a luxury article. It is not so much so as diamonds but more so than cotton or coal. As such, its use may expand rapidly in times of prosperity but contract sharply during periods of depression like the present one in the United States. In March, 1929, the price was 1,420 yen a bale but fell to 1,124 yen in July, rose to 1,400 yen in December, and then collapsed to 1,100 yen. Of course silk has been under constant pressure, even within Japan, from the competing textile, rayon, and there is a final disadvantage because of its extreme dependence on the American market. As we have noticed, the United States took over 94 per cent of the raw-silk exports of 1927.

A second class of exports is those that are manufactured from imported raw materials. In this class Japan is relying mainly upon cotton goods of the cheaper variety. As shown here and there in earlier chapters, this puts her in competition with an overdeveloped industry whose plants have expanded in number and in spindleage in all parts of the world. Also, it makes her dependent on foreign supplies of raw cotton—particularly on the United States and, to a lesser degree, on India.

It may be argued that there is an advantage in the plentiful supply of cheap labor, but it must not be forgotten that low wages do not necessarily mean low labor cost and that in any case the important fact is not labor cost alone but total costs. Besides, if there is any advantage in cheap labor that advantage is to be found also and perhaps to a greater degree in China and in British India which are Japan's leading markets for cotton goods. And both of them can raise obstacles against the Japanese product either through tariffs or through boycotts.

We may conclude that Japan has a difficult problem. There need be no surprise at her weakness in 1920, in 1927, and again in 1930. A depressed foreign exchange, heavy exportations of gold, and similar phenomena are only barometers. They merely reflect a poorly balanced economic structure. With Japanese life organized as it is today that country should be among the leaders in attempting to secure world economic stability and in supporting all feasible methods to avoid war. Imagine the consequences of a war with the United States from which she secures 30 per cent of her imports including 55 per cent of her raw cotton and to which she sells 94 per cent of her raw silk which is nearly 38 per cent of her total exports.

Chapter XV

THE PROGRESS OF THE UNITED STATES

WHEN Alfred Marshall in his "Industry and Trade" wrote of Britain's "drift toward massive production," of France's "individuality and refinement in production," and said that Germany was also a leader because she employed "science in the service of industry," he attributed the strength of the United States to what he called "multiform standardization." Today we hear much of "mass production" and find the whole world eager to learn "the secret of high wages" in "America, the golden."

There is a double peril in these formulæ. In some cases they are suggestive but it is easy to misuse them. First, they oversimplify a highly complex situation and, second, outside observers are at times prone to seize upon them and to attempt their application to equally complex conditions in Europe. There are, of course, many similarities in the two continents, and much that is helpful in one may, properly modified, be used in the other. Yet there have already been disappointments because of hasty conclusions and because of hurried attempts to adopt American methods in very different countries.

Those who seek interpretations of the country and its present status can find them in almost embarrassing numbers and diversity. Americans are trying more than ever before to understand themselves, and the people of other countries are visiting, studying, and writing about America with results that range from Beverly Nichols' "Star Spangled Manner" to André Siegfried's "America Comes of Age."

If the interpretations are diverse, and even contradictory, there need be no surprise. There is a huge area and there are few, even in the United States, with a sufficiently comprehensive and exact knowledge to grasp and portray the country accurately. Its area and its complexities are so great that any generalizations must be presented cautiously. We may be warned by the foreigner who read in one book dealing with the South that there are large numbers of negroes in the fields and in another book describing Boston that negroes are seldom seen in the streets. Accordingly he announced as one of his observations of America that there are large numbers of negroes who toil there in the fields but are seldom seen in the streets—a statement rather puzzling, at least to a resident of the great area south of the Mason and Dixon's line.

Notice a few broad facts about the United States. The continental area embraces 3,028,789 square miles in which there reside over 120,000,000 people. There are accordingly only about 40 per square mile compared with the much larger numbers that we observed for Italy, for Germany, for France, and for England and Wales. In this huge area there is a great diversity of climate and there are highly varied and extremely rich supplies of coal and minerals. The documentation of the World Economic Conference stated that the United States in 1924 contributed 17 per cent of the world's production of wheat, 75 per cent of the maize, 32 per cent of the oats, 38 per cent of the tobacco, 24 per cent of the hops, 50 per cent of the cotton, 53 per cent of the cotton seed, 44 per cent of the coal, 70 per cent of the petroleum, 81 per cent of the sulphur, 40 per cent of the natural phosphates, and 35 per cent of the aluminum. In smelter production it furnished 18 per cent of the pig iron and ferro-alloys, 52 per cent of the steel, 60 per cent of the copper, 46 per cent of the lead, and 46 per cent of

[279]

the zinc. The United States led the world in its production of iron ore, copper ore, lead ore, lead-zinc ore, zinc ore, natural gas, and artificial silk.

This list and others like it may be used, and they sometimes have been, as an excuse for lauding American power and self-sufficiency and as a means of boasting. Needless to say, this is not the excuse for such a recital here. No merit attaches to the people of America because these resources are located in the United States. The people of Switzerland did not construct the Alps nor did the Americans create the natural resources of their country. They are merely fortunate in having them and charged with a heavy responsibility as to their proper use. Unfortunately they may show no more intelligence and altruism in doing so than have the peoples of other countries and at other times. They may even be less wise and less considerate. If so, it is to be hoped that others will show to Americans a little of that tolerance and patience which Americans have often lacked in their harsh criticisms of the alleged faults of other countries in their times of dominance.

Expressed by reference to the factors of production, it may be said that in the United States there is an immense supply of natural resources owned by a relatively small number of people. One hundred and fifty years ago this was even more true than now, but capital was then lacking. A great area rich in timber, oil, coal, gold, and other minerals and with almost unlimited acres of fertile soil had a small labor supply and few tools. These two limiting factors have been increased. Population which was about 5,300,000 in 1800 is now over 120,000,000, a gain in numbers due to immigration both "from abroad and from heaven." Although immigration from abroad has been checked by legislation starting many years ago and made closely restrictive in the last few years, the natural increase in numbers due to the excess of births over deaths still continues. Vital statistics for the United States are far from perfect but the available figures show for 1926 a birth rate of 20.6 and a death rate of 12.2 per 1,000. The difference is 8.4 per 1,000. Although the birth rate is declining, the population gain is still rapid.

Supplies of capital, too, have been rapidly augmented. For many years these supplies came chiefly from abroad, supplemented by savings at home. As time has passed, domestic sources of capital supply have been increasingly used. This trend away from foreign borrowings was hastened by the World War during which earlier loans were largely repaid and the former borrower turned lender on a vast scale. In the postwar years these loans were continued and it is estimated that today the private loans abroad by American investors total perhaps $15,000,000,000. Each year they are growing, the amount named being in addition to the "political" indebtedness of some 13 foreign governments to the government of the United States. These debts arose, largely though not entirely, out of the financial operations of the World War, and their principal amount is difficult to state. This is because of the adjustments made under the funding agreements which call for the payment of various sums per annum amounting at present to less than $250,000,000 and increasing to a maximum of about $450,000,000 just before the end of the 62 years for which the agreements run.

The estimated wealth of the United States at the last federal census was $320,000,000,000 and is now probably $400,000,000,000 or more. The aggregate national income is perhaps $90,000,000,000 per annum or about $750 per capita, by far the highest in the world. A population of some 120,000,000,000 in a vast and very fertile area which, with its capital improvements, is worth perhaps $400,000,-000,000 has the greatest economic power ever known.

Several aspects of this situation call for elaboration. The mere possession of vast supplies of physical equipment means nothing. In the Ruhr area of Germany in 1923 there was an abundance of wealth. There were mines, factories, railroads, stores, and other forms of physical property in abundance. But their operation was paralyzed. Only an occasional factory chimney was smoking, few trains were running, hundreds of thousands were out of work. The masses of brick and stone and steel were of no importance in themselves—they were merely the aids by which production might be carried on, through which production might be possible. As long as they were idle they were useless. Their value was dependent on the possibility that at a later date they would again be in operation and would produce an income for their owners. The value of any property is found by capitalizing the potential income that may be derived from it. Anything that checks this operation, that hinders the free functioning of the productive factors cuts down income.

In the United States there are, of course, many elements of friction but there is one fact of the highest importance. Over an area of slightly more than 3,000,000 square miles there is one political control—that of the federal government. The various states cling tenaciously to their constitutional rights but the trend of events is strongly against them and in any case they have not been able under the federal constitution to restrict the movement of people and, except in very minor ways, of commodities throughout the country. No passports are needed by travelers and no customs duties on goods are imposed. As a consequence the vast area with its 49 states functions as an economic unit. Its productivity is enormous.

The $400,000,000,000 of physical equipment is able to work freely.

Perhaps we should add that this is not meant as a suggestion that European countries can quickly or easily create an economic United States of Europe by means of a customs union or otherwise. This may come but the obstacles to its realization are tremendous.

A second feature about the United States is the momentum attained in capital accumulation. Capital is increased by the consumption in a given year of less than is produced, this difference appearing in the form of an addition to physical equipment—more buildings, railroads, canals, machinery, etc. In a poor community this process is difficult and often painful. Saving under such conditions means sacrifice, often serious sacrifice, and economists are led to formulate theories accordingly, *e.g.*, the abstinence theory of interest—that interest must be paid in order that people may be induced to undergo the hardships involved in saving, in abstaining from consumption.

But as the supply of capital increases, and with its aid productivity is enhanced, further accumulations become easier. To set aside additional dollars from income is less and less difficult. A momentum develops and supplies of capital become larger and larger. The individual or country that acquires a lead finds it possible to maintain its advantage. The principle or law of increasing returns is an aid and other countries find it difficult to catch up. England could maintain the lead with comparative ease in the nineteenth century. Today the United States has vast accumulations of capital, whether stated in absolute figures or per capita, and in addition has natural resources in abundance.

A further significant fact is the character of the American population. It is extremely heterogeneous in its ancestry, in its cultural background, in its aptitudes, and in other particulars. This diversity has many advantages in carrying on production. But this same population furnishes a highly homogeneous market. There are many millionaires in America and a distressing amount of poverty. Yet the great mass of the public have incomes sufficiently near together to create an immense market for goods of any given quality. Tastes, also, are more uniform than in many other countries, a fact which is an invaluable aid in encouraging mass production. A manufacturer who can win the market for his product has opened an almost limitless opportunity for sales. If he succeeds, as has Henry Ford, his output may be so huge that his unit costs are very low.

America has great natural resources, a population large in the aggregate but small per square mile, with an average income at present of about $750 per annum and owners of wealth worth perhaps $3,333 per capita. To this may be added a leadership that is aggressive and probably stronger than it would be otherwise because social strata in America are comparatively unimportant. There are no "untouchables," though, in the minds of some, the negroes are nearly so. There are references to "classes" and "masses" but speaking quite broadly a young man or woman of ability and determination has a better chance of rising than in most of the older countries. The ranks of leadership are constantly being strengthened by the appearance of new recruits and the descendants of the giants of the past do not always maintain their positions on top. Emerson's dictum that in America these are but "three generations from shirt sleeves to shirt sleeves" is still more than a clever expression.

With such a combination of factors and with a considerable momentum, American advantages are clear. A theoretical economist might say that marginal productivity is bound to be high. Output per machine or per worker or per anything else is necessarily large. If the economic organization can be kept working smoothly, American leadership seems fairly certain.

But the world economic struggle is not between groups that are rivals because they have low living standards and are desperate. Apparently the poorest groups lack the incentives to struggle or else they do not have the qualities needed. At any rate, as we have repeatedly pointed out, the leaders are those whose living standards are the highest and whose economic lives have become dependent on external conditions. The United States faces no population problem like that of Italy or Japan or England. Its difficulty is not that of a large number of persons per square mile, since its population density is only about one-tenth that of Italy and about one-twentieth that of England and Wales or of Belgium. Instead, the problem is a lack of cultural homogeneity and a need for time to absorb the heterogeneous groups that have been pouring into the country so rapidly in the last 50 years. Even if we ignore the annoying demands of extremists, it is necessary to admit that the task of adapting so many newcomers of varying standards to the peculiarities of their new home is not easy. These difficulties are not appreciated, however, or even realized by most people in other countries, and the American decision to restrict immigration has created an abundance of ill will.

It is possible to trace for the United States the growth of large-scale production, since the reports of the Department of the Census furnish in a convenient form the data needed. One finds, for example, (as pointed out in an earlier chapter) that in 1850 there were 1,094 establishments manufacturing cotton goods. There were on the average

84 employers in each of these plants. The average capital investment was $68,000 and the average value of the product was $55,500. By 1910 the number of establishments had increased slightly to 1,324 but the average number of workers had become 286, the average capital $681,000, and the average product $475,000.

In the iron and steel industry the number of establishments had increased only from 468 to 654 but the average number of employees had grown from 53 to 426, the average capital from $46,700 to $2,282,000, and the average product from $43,600 to $2,119,000. For all manufactures the increase from 1850 to 1920 was from 7.7 to 31.3 in the number of employees, from $4,330 to $153,200 in the average capital investment, and from $8,280 to $215,100 in the average annual product.

This statement of averages tells little or nothing of the size of the largest plants, of the famous "billion dollar" corporations. The changing averages show a trend but to what they reveal there should be added a reminder of the heavy investments in the largest of the plants, of the huge annual liabilities which they have assumed, of the constant driving pressure under which they operate to meet their annual fixed charges. It is no reply to observe that they are wealthy, that their earnings are huge. No matter how large and powerful they may be, the pressure to which we refer is always present and the greater the size the more serious the problem.

In Chapter VIII emphasis was also placed on the significance of the corporate form of organization, on the anonymity thus introduced into business, on the large number of bondholders and stockholders and their incessant clamor for interests and dividends. In the United States as elsewhere the corporation has grown and now most business is carried on by corporations as distinct from individual and partnership management. In 1904 the corporations were only 23.6 per cent of the total number of business enterprises but they paid 76 per cent of the wages and marketed 73.7 per cent of the total product of the country. By 1919 they were 31.5 per cent of the total number of enterprises, paid 86 per cent of the wages, and turned out 87.7 per cent of the total production. The ownership of these enterprises, moreover, is not so concentrated in a few hands as is ownership in many other countries or as it was in the United States a number of years ago. Instead, it is widely scattered, so much so that some corporations have hundreds of thousands of stockholders whose average holdings are small but nevertheless highly prized. One writer has characterized this diffusion of ownership as the only really important revolution in the world in recent years and calls it a shift from Wall Street to Main Street. Even the forceful demonstration of another writer that the shift of control (as distinct from ownership) has really been from Main Street to Wall Street does not weaken the contention which we are urging. There are literally millions of Americans interested in the regular receipt of interest and dividends from the corporations in whose securities they have invested. The corporation is a *société anonyme*. As many a writer has urged, it is soulless. Most of its owners know little and care little regarding its operation, its attitude toward its employees, its sales methods, and its treatment of competitors, especially its competitors abroad. Many corporations, moreover, represent huge investments, are often unwieldly, and have heavy annual overhead costs to meet. Always some of them are on the margin of failure and hence are tempted to any method which will prevent bankruptcy. Those who are successful set standards of dividend payments which are difficult to modify and often issue new securities by stock dividends or otherwise that call for a permanency of dividend payments on a large par value.

There may be added a reference to business consolidations in the United States. For many years attempts have been made to prevent the formation of monopolies. The various states have their so-called "antitrust laws," and the federal government its Sherman Antitrust Law of 1890. This law does not declare all combinations illegal but merely "combinations and conspiracies in restraint of trade." Attempts to enforce this statute have brought dubious results. Even such spectacular decisions of the Supreme Court as those in 1911 against the Standard Oil Company and the American Tobacco Company did not result in any actual diminution of the alleged monopoly power of a small group of owners and in 1920 the decision in the case against the United States Steel Corporation ruled that mere size is no evidence of ill intent or of harmful action. Large combinations are thus not unlawful, even though powerful, so long as there is no improper use of that power. Corporations have accordingly grown in size and some of the greatest in the world are incorporated and largely owned in America.

To this should be added a reference to the fact that American concern over the large corporation—the monopoly or the "trust"—is primarily a fear of injury to Americans. While attempts are definitely made to restrict the power of "trusts" the attempt is merely to prevent injurious conduct in the domestic field. What they may do to the people of other countries is another matter. In fact combinations in connection with export trade are encouraged. The Webb Pomerene Law definitely authorizes their formation and the Edge Law permits active financial assistance.

Finally, among the influences at work there may be mentioned the heavy foreign investments of Americans.

Leaving out of account the political debts, these are very much less in absolute amount than the similar foreign investments of British nationals. In per capita terms they are of course far less, since the population of Great Britain is much smaller than that of the United States. Yet the amounts are now large and are continuing to grow. For the year 1928 the interest due from abroad to Americans on all private foreign investments, both long term and short term and including commissions, was estimated by the U. S. Department of Commerce at $882,000,000, while the corresponding amount due to foreigners on their investments in the United States was $359,000,000, an excess due to Americans of $523,000,000. In that same year it is estimated that $481,000,000 of foreign advances were made to the United States, while $1,443,000,000 of American funds were placed abroad, an increase in American holdings abroad of $962,000,000. Americans have, therefore, a heavy and a growing financial interest in other countries because of these investments; also because of their trade, since combined imports and exports now total over $9,000,000,-000 per year.

This statement of fact reveals the United States as in a very strong economic position. Just so long as the approach to world economic questions is organized along national lines the power of America must be reckoned with. If our previous analysis has been even approximately correct there is no question of the merit or the demerit of America. No matter what right, wrong, justice, and injustice mean in such discussions—and these words often lack precise content—it may be expected that Americans will behave about as other groups have always behaved when in a position of advantage and about as English, French, Germans, or Italians would behave under the same circumstances. To express the facts in this way solves no problems but it may clear the way for better and quicker solutions than could otherwise be found.

It is a fact that America's position at present gives that country a distinct advantage. Thus Americans may effectively protest against foreign capital holding a controlling interest in corporations chartered and doing business in the United States and see no inconsistency in the fact that American investments in German and British corporations are now very heavy. Yet the Germans and British apparently have no means of protecting themselves against this alleged American control. The United States may raise its tariff walls higher and higher and even provide government aid in dumping farm products abroad. In response the French and Italian governments may raise their import duties on wheat (as they have recently done) but it is probable that they will injure their own nationals more than Americans by so doing. French moving picture interests may fear the American invasion and attempt to change a 7:1 quota to a 4:1, but it is possible that more French than Americans will be injured if they insist.

This position of economic strength is gratifying to the nationalist, who finds in it nothing but a sign of the greatness of his country. And he holds to this view most tenaciously even though he criticizes the British pride in an Empire on which the sun never sets, the grandiloquent gestures of a Mussolini, and the equally extreme pronouncements of French, Germans, and others. But to those who are eager not only to avoid future military conflicts but also to soften the rigors of economic competition and to lessen the ill will against the United States which is now so noticeable the situation is both disheartening and baffling.

Before noticing some of the awkward problems that are calling for intelligent treatment let us add a few more facts

[290]

about the relation of the United States to the rest of the world. The foreign trade of the United States in 1929 included imports valued at $4,400,000,000 and exports worth $5,241,000,000. Years ago the volume of this trade was smaller, the imports were dominantly manufactured goods coming from Europe, and the exports were food and raw materials going to Europe. Today raw materials are imported in much larger amounts, particularly from non-European sources, and manufactured goods form more than half of the exports.

Forty years ago, from 1886 to 1890, imports were valued at only $717,000,000 and 56 per cent of this total came from Europe. In 1929 the total was $4,400,000,000 and only 30.3 per cent came from Europe. In the period 1886 to 1890, 22.6 per cent was crude materials, 15.8 per cent was crude foodstuffs, and 16.5 per cent was manufactured foodstuffs, a total of 54.9 per cent for raw materials and food. This left 15.8 per cent for semimanufactures and 29.3 per cent for finished manufactures or a total of 45.1 per cent. In 1929 the situation is vastly altered. Of the total imports, 35.4 per cent was crude materials, 12.3 per cent crude foodstuffs, and 9.6 per cent manufactured foodstuffs, a total of 57.3 per cent raw materials and foodstuffs, leaving only 20.0 per cent semimanufactures and 22.7 per cent for finished manufactures. The increasing importance of raw materials, of food, and the relative decline of manufactures is particularly noticeable.

Changes of great significance have occurred also in American export trade, but they have been summarized in Chapter VII and need not be repeated.

There are profound alterations in trade shown by these figures. The United States in spite of its own large supplies of raw materials and its vast areas of farm land is calling upon outside sources for huge supplies of raw materials, the most important being raw silk and crude rubber, and for important amounts of food, the most important being coffee and cane sugar. Instead of America helping to feed the world, her exports and imports of foodstuffs now tend to balance and in time the imports may be the larger. Greater and greater quantities of certain raw materials are needed for manufacturing which means participation by American interests in the scramble for available supplies. Exports are more dominantly manufactured goods which means growing competition with Europeans for markets, either inside or outside Europe.

The balance of trade of the United States has been favorable most of the time since 1873 and all calculations of the balance of payments (which are available only for recent years) show a favorable balance at least since 1914, *i.e.*, an excess of exports, including both visible and invisible items. It is not possible to analyze and explain the balance of payments for many years but trade figures are available. And since these trade or "visible item" figures were in the past of greater relative importance than now, they will furnish a fairly accurate picture for the earlier years.

Prior to about 1873 the United States was in the immature debtor stage. The country might have been developed from domestic savings alone but the process would have been slow. Growth was hastened by importing "capital" from abroad, *i.e.*, by receiving from Europe shipments of tools and machinery the value of which was greater than the value of the foodstuffs and raw materials exported in exchange. This annual excess of imports was possible because Europeans were willing to take American promises to pay later, *i.e.*, the bonds and the stocks of various American states, cities, and private corporations. The stocks of tools and machinery thus acquired permitted a rapid development of a vast territory rich in resources.

Borrowing abroad did not cease after 1873 but continued and even today has not stopped, since every year foreigners buy many American securities. But by 1873 annual interest payments on accumulated borrowings had become important in size. Also, the American merchant marine had nearly disappeared and each year we had to pay foreigners large freight charges for carrying our goods. Along with other items the net result was one under which more goods were shipped out of than into the United States. There started an export balance of trade which has been maintained ever since. America had entered the mature debtor stage in which exports were necessary to pay interest on accumulated debts. In fact some of our citizens soon began to lend abroad but the amounts were for years very small.

In the period just before 1914 another change was noticeable. More and more Americans were buying foreign securities while relatively at least fewer foreigners were investing in America. The immature creditor stage was starting, a movement which stimulated exports. Foreigners sold securities in the United States and with the proceeds of the sale bought commodities. From 1914 on, this process swelled to huge size because of war and early postwar demands. Europeans sold back securities formerly purchased, taking commodities in exchange. They sold their own new securities to Americans for still more commodities. Exports rapidly grew and American credits abroad increased enormously.

It is now possible to speak of a possible fourth stage—that of the mature creditor. If such a stage should develop, it would be one in which American investors would modify at least slightly their purchase of foreign stocks and bonds. Interest and dividends on past purchases might be so large as to exceed these new investments and payment of that excess be pressed upon us. This means that imports would tend to grow and might even exceed exports.

Some observers have rather hurriedly argued that such a change will come promptly but we need not be too sure. Just how long New York will be the best place in which to sell new issues of stocks and bonds and to arrange bank credits is not clear. Nor can we know how persistently Americans will privately invest abroad in ways not appearing in public security flotations. Then, too, there is a mass of invisible items including tourist expenditures, freight earnings, commissions, and what not, all of which must be allowed for.

It seems correct, however, to say that there will be some pressure of imports and that as a consequence a definite economic policy would be helpful.

It is to be emphasized that at least two tendencies are clear and may be expected to persist. One is an effort to export goods. The analysis of previous chapters, especially that of Chapter VII, indicates the strength of this force. Under our present economic organization all of us must strive to make money and to do this we must sell our goods and services, at home or abroad or both. American manufacturers will attempt to sell abroad just as much as possible.

A second influence that will doubtless continue is the desire of the American public to collect the amounts due from abroad. Private investors will demand interest as it falls due and in many individual cases will seek repayment of principal. Taxpayers will probably insist that the public or political debts be honored according to the terms of the debt-funding agreements.

It will be noticed that these two desires are alike in one particular. Both call for payments from abroad. Exported goods are presumably to be paid for. Payment of debts due means remittances. At least two groups of Americans—exporters and investors—should be anxious to facilitate payments from abroad.

In opposition to these two groups whose interests are similar are the interests of other groups. Payments from abroad though directly made with drafts or bills of exchange must ultimately rest on the importation of something into the United States—either commodities or services or both. Yet there are groups adversely affected by the receipt of these possible forms of payment.

Notice services first. One form used extensively in the past is freight service. Foreign ships carried the larger part of American commerce and were paid—a means by which a part of the obligations from abroad to the United States were settled. Now we have a large merchant marine and propose with various forms of national aid to make it still larger.

Another service was rendered by immigrants who worked in America, lived sparingly, and sent home large sums as remittances. But our restrictions on immigration are reducing these amounts. Similarly, the fact that American bankers and insurance companies have taken over much of the financial work formerly done in London and elsewhere lessens the commissions and premiums formerly earned from us by the people of other countries.

One by one we insist that these services must not be performed for us as in the past. Only as we tour abroad are we content to pay outsiders for services rendered. These amounts have been growing rapidly but may not continue their rapid rate of gain.

After all, the main form of payment is commodities and our imports of these are of necessity growing. Yet there are many objections from the groups that feel the pressure and every effort is made by them to check the movement, especially by higher tariffs.

These conflicting interests place the United States in an awkward position. Some groups demand payments and other groups oppose. The result is a strain which might have serious consequences. A country so large and dependent to so slight a degree on the outside world may be able to meet such losses as occur without any considerable harm. Yet a better adjustment of these contradictory influences would be better not only for other countries but for the United States as well.

Chapter XVI

SOLVING THE DILEMMA

Pʀᴇᴄᴇᴅɪɴɢ chapters have presented a dilemma. Economic life is often characterized as a struggle between man and nature in which man is continually striving to wrest more and more of the necessities, comforts, and luxuries of life from a reluctant Mother Earth. His victories are sometimes great and sometimes small but they never satisfy him, since his desires are in the aggregate insatiable. The more he secures the more he demands.

Emphasis on this fact has permitted us to evade the broader population question and to ignore the controversy between those who fear that population will outrun food supplies, and perhaps the supplies of power, and those others who believe that nature is bounteous enough to care for many times the numbers now in existence. We have stressed instead the 1,900,000,000 or more already on the earth, their congestion in certain areas, their extreme dependence on each other, and their incessant demands for maintaining existing standards and for attaining constantly higher levels.

Attention has been called to the fact that the most aggressive peoples in modern world controversies are the ones whose standards are the highest, rather than those whose standards are the lowest. It is not even true that the most aggressive are the ones whose dependence is greatest or whose somewhat high standards are most seriously threatened. Notice, for example, the United States of America. Her people have the highest per capita income in the world, and in spite of the existence of a numerous millionaire group, the distribution of income among the American people is probably less uneven than that of the British. While of course American life is interrelated with that of the rest of the world, her dependence is much less than that of any of the other countries whose status we have surveyed. Yet the United States is aggressively active in world affairs. In spite of many formal denials and the use of peculiar and at times ludicrous subterfuges, she is participating to an enlarging degree in the political and economic life of the entire earth.

What we have seen is a curious mixture of real economic dependence and of restlessness. Thirty years ago we spoke of manifest destiny and the white man's burden. Fifteen years ago in the United States it was called "dollar diplomacy." Today we talk of "imperialism" and usually avoid its definition. But from all this the careful observer should draw at least one lesson, *i.e.*, that mere condemnation of others and of ourselves is futile. Whatever be our statement of the causes of the world struggle, it has persisted for centuries. Men have surged back and forth striving to secure more of the good things of life, seeking a larger and better supply of food, clothing, shelter, security, recreation, and leisure. In the quest there have been ruthlessness and greed, there have been oppression, warfare, piracy, slaughter, and slavery. The strong have lorded it over the weak.

Apologies, when offered at all, have been varied and often have been specious. At times there has been a frank avowal of greed; again, religion has sufficed as an excuse; the necessities of defense against aggression have been urged. But with ample warrant or with little warrant or with no suitable defense of any kind the movement has continued. Start where you will in history, and give such interpretation as you prefer. Alexander extended his conquests, Greece enlarged her borders, Rome hemmed in the Mediterranean, Spain, Holland, England, Belgium, Germany, Italy, and even little Portugal have developed their empires. For over a century the United States has been adding to its area and today her political and economic influence is widespread and growing so rapidly as to create apprehension and arouse criticism in all parts of the world.

To call attention to this is not to voice approval but is merely a reminder that it is useless for Americans blindly to condemn the alleged errors of the British in South Africa, the Belgians in the Congo, the French in Syria and Morocco, the Germans in Africa, the Dutch in the East Indies. And it is just as useless, we may hasten to add, for the people in other parts of the world merely to condemn the attitude of the government or people of the United States toward Latin America. Occasionally some unusually vigorous protest has resulted in an adjustment of public policy and a slight modification of private behavior but the general movement has gone on. Those who condemned Cleveland's attitude toward England in the Venezuelan controversy found little consolation in the McKinley administration during the Spanish-American War, in Roosevelt's policy with Colombia, and in the dollar diplomacy of Taft and Knox. Nor was there satisfaction among these critics over Woodrow Wilson's treatment of Mexico, Haiti, and San Domingo or Coolidge's policies in Nicaragua and elsewhere. Yet these various national leaders were as different in temperament and in ideals as men can well be. Roosevelt boasted that he took the Panama Canal area and let Congress debate it later. Taft was good-natured and easy-going. Wilson was still different. And the Coolidge outlook was in contrast to them all. But the expansion has continued.

To repeat, this is not an endorsement nor is it the voice of despair. Instead, it is a reminder to Americans not to condemn the conduct of others when their own is so similar and it is a suggestion to others that the United States is doing today only what they and their predecessors have always done and what they seem to Americans still to be doing in Asia and in Africa wherever and whenever they can, in colonies and in mandated areas as well as against peoples presumably independent. For pots to call kettles black is a poor use of time.

If we can recognize that the problem is a general one and not the peculiar iniquity of any one country or people or government, the next step is a reminder of the powerful forces at work as we have sketched them in preceding chapters. There are the desires to maintain present or higher standards of living; to secure food and raw materials and to safeguard markets; to prevent heavy overhead costs under modern large-scale production from precipitating bankruptcies; the ruthless pressure of falling or of rising prices, first on debtors and then on creditors; the necessity for everybody to make money under our kind of price economy; the imperative need that markets be kept open if the industrial machine is not to crash; the intricate structure of the modern corporation and the persistence of the great masses of security holders in demanding interest and dividends; the huge and growing international movements of capital; the way in which governments seem inevitably drawn in to safeguard and extend trade and to protect investments in other countries. Such a list of facts and forces is formidable. To deny their existence is impossible. To approach with mere condemnation a situation so complex is worse than futile. Not only does denunciation fail to improve conditions, but also it makes them worse by rousing resentment, by encouraging recriminations, and by creating ill will when patience and goodwill are imperative.

Unfortunately we have found that economic strain is not diminishing. England has the largest population in her history and is more dependent than ever before on maintaining her contacts with food, raw materials, and markets. But she faces a world that has imitated and improved upon her industrialization and that can produce many articles more cheaply than she can. Her foreign trade has been reduced and the airplane, the submarine, and poison gas threaten to crush her in future wars.

For decades before the World War, Germany was advancing with great strides. Defeated in 1918, deprived of her merchant fleets, reduced in area and in population and with her economy demoralized, a quick recovery seemed impossible. Today, however, she is rebuilt. Her new fleet is almost as large and is far better than the one she lost. Factories are equipped with the most modern machinery, whole industries, and in fact nearly the entire country, have undertaken rationalization. This should be a gain for us all. More and better commodities can be produced at less cost. But unfortunately there are accompanying disadvantages. The world is strongly competitive and along national lines. If there were some way of adjusting production in other countries to the fact of a reorganized Germany, of quickly agreeing upon a national division of labor, of deciding calmly and promptly upon the articles in whose production each country has a comparative advantage, we might feel more complacent. Instead, no such division exists and Germany is still asked to pay as reparations annual remittances just as heavy as can be collected from her even though those payments should cause economic havoc and create ill will and though Germany is borrowing the funds with which to make them. They continue to be demanded even when money rates in Germany rise or when a general business crisis is threatened.

The French situation, too, is a difficult one. Government finances have been regularized but government indebtedness is still crushingly heavy. Taxes are burdensome, foreign debts must be met or the serious consequences of defaults and repudiation must be faced. By stabilizing the franc at less than four cents, or 124 to the pound, the burden of internal debts has been lessened for the government and for other debtors but at the cost of much ill will, especially among foreign holders of French internal bonds. French industry has been reconstructed, especially in the areas that were devastated by war, and today her railroads, her farms, and her factories are highly efficient. But their output also competes in many lines with the products of other countries, including Germany. Yet the burden of the French debt seems to compel collections from Germany that if really made may imperil the markets of France and also those of her former allies.

A review of similar problems as we found them in Italy and in the United States is not necessary in this chapter. Our survey might have been extended. Belgium, Czechoslovakia, and other European countries might well have been added. China and India might have been included. India is industrializing with a desire to lessen her reliance on other areas for manufactured goods but with the certainty that her gains in this direction will be in part offset by an ultimate increase in her dependence for food, for raw materials, and for markets. China, too, is building factories—as are many countries in Latin America and even in Africa.

All this does not compel pessimism. Much of it is a gain for humanity. More economy in the utilization of coal and the discovery of less expensive substitute fuels means a saving of capital and of human labor. Operating only the most efficient plants while the poorest ones are closed likewise means getting more of the good things of life with less effort—which is highly desirable. If cotton piece goods can be manufactured at less cost in the southern part of the United States or in India than in Lancashire, that ought to be a gain for the world. It would be a gross error to deny the importance of increasing efficiency, of lowering costs, and of locating industries where they can be operated most advantageously.

It would also be wrong not to point out that a considerable amount of capital and labor have been shifted from some industries to others. This has been particularly true in the United States where numbers of workers employed where they are now not needed have been absorbed by the newly developed automobile, radio, and moving picture industries and in some of the older lines which have continued to expand while others have contracted. In Germany where the rationalization movement has created a large amount of unemployment the discharged workers have been taken up in other industries more rapidly than could have been expected. In Great Britain, too, the huge amount of unemployment in coal, textiles, and ship-building has been slightly relieved by the expansion of miscellaneous new industries, particularly in the south of England.

But while there are reasons for satisfaction over the growth of human knowledge, at the increase of our power over nature, and in the better location and improved organization of our economic world, the elements of strain are too serious to be ignored. We have enumerated them at some length and shown their operation in a half-dozen leading countries. Only last year an illustration was presented in the resolutions adopted at Paris on June 4, 1929, by the presidents of 500 French chambers of commerce, in which a vigorous protest was made against the proposed raising of American tariffs, and the formation of a European economic *bloc* against the United States was advocated. Later in the year there came renewed discussions of a United States of Europe and of proposals for higher European tariffs and for cartels against certain American products, especially automobiles.

It may be assumed that the existence of strain has been demonstrated; that the forces causing the strain have been pointed out and that their strength is recognized. The dilemma has been presented: a world whose economic life is highly interdependent and whose economic welfare can be advanced only by close cooperation, but a world whose economic life is almost of necessity organized along national lines, an organization which to a degree helps in each country to stabilize the local economy but often does it in a way that injures other countries and reacts directly or indirectly against itself. To work our way out of the dilemma is not easy. The forces are powerful and the political organization along national lines performs many useful, in fact necessary, functions. "Political myth" is a misnomer and so to characterize it is to underrate its importance and to invite defeat.

Yet progress along what may be called "nationalistic lines" is difficult, if not impossible. And for this there are cogent reasons which may be made clear by noticing, first, the difficulties in one or two other fields of world effort. The attempt to secure disarmament is one of them. For many years now under the provisions of the Covenant of the League of Nations and through efforts outside League direction, conferences have been held and diplomatic exchanges carried on. As yet the tangible results are scarcely encouraging.

Disarmament is a highly technical question and on most of its aspects a layman has no right to an opinion and cannot intelligently join in a discussion. But it is possible even for the layman to comment on at least one point, *viz.*, there is no logical limit to the amount of military strength any country needs or claims to need, and there is no such thing as a logical apportionment of military equipment between the various powers. In time of war every country desires all the strength that it can assemble and in time of peace the situation is pressing, though not equally so. As Señor de Madariaga has pointed out in his volume "Disarmament," armaments are instruments of national policy even in times of peace. And he has also pointed out very effectively that no matter how the problem is analyzed there is only one conclusion possible. Real disarmament can come only through the organization and development of a world community.

A similar predicament is to be found in other directions when nationalistic solutions are attempted. For example, there are but few illustrations of logical boundary lines between countries. The English Channel is often suggested and the Pyrenees mountains. With the development of the airplane and the submarine and with the probable use of poison gas on a large scale in future wars, even these frontiers will be no barrier against military invasion. But even in the past there have been few logical limits to the extension of national frontiers. The expansion of the United States in the last century and a half has continued relentlessly, as did that of the British Empire and as have all other empires. No single addition to American territory was quite adequate to perfect the national domain. Each new acquisition required still more to defend it or else created a new set of national needs which could be met only by securing additional territory. When the huge and somewhat regular continental domain was rounded out there still seemed reasons why Alaska should be added— then the Philippines and Porto Rico. In recent years and without a nominal destruction of their sovereignty the United States has extended its influence over Panama, Nicaragua, Santo Domingo, and others. And there are those who are vigorously urging the outright annexation to the United States of Lower California and even of Mexico.

To each of these steps in political expansion there are vigorous objections by the supporters of the political party not in power at the moment, and by numerous others whose moral sensibilities are outraged. But the process goes relentlessly on. There is no logical place to stop. Once accept the premises of nationalism, the right of self-defense, the importance of strategic frontiers, the necessity of coaling stations and the rest, and there are literally no limits that can be rationally set to the expansion movement. British trade called for coaling stations and trading posts, which needed hinterland for adequate protection, and this hinterland needed still more for its safety. This increased trade demanded a larger navy and hence more coaling stations and trading posts with their hinterlands. Even buffer states like Persia and Afghanistan crumble under the pressure of opposing political forces like those of England and Russia.

There is similarly no logical stopping place in economic expansion. If economic life is organized by groups those groups will compete with each other for advantage. No gain that is secured in the struggle brings final satisfaction; more is always desired. And just as long as economic organization is along national lines, strain will exist between the opposing national groups. This strain will be among the causes of war even though the immediate occasion may be a failure of the Abyssinians to salute the Liberian flag or the murder of an American in Mexico.

Probably the general picture is clear but it must be made vivid by illustration or it will fade too quickly. The science of economics, like others, is merely organized common sense and at times seems to be an elaboration of the obvious. But the obvious is easily overlooked even when it is most needed and this lesson is so important that emphasis on it cannot be too strong. The world's economic dilemma can doubtless be solved but it will not solve itself. Even with a complete appreciation of the issues involved there is no one simple panacea on which we can all agree and which can readily be applied. Instead, the problem itself is complex, the solutions adopted must be many and intricate, and we shall find it hard to agree among ourselves as to what ones to apply and when and where.

In the process of economic expansion and aggression there is no agreed natural or logical limit. Notice the growth in population. Numbers are still everywhere increasing. There are retardations in some areas, and in some there are even signs of a reduction in numbers. But on the whole the growth is still rapid in spite of what some observers think are dangers. Even the experts are not in agreement in their theories of population density. Some writers urge an "optimum" number but find it hard to agree on the meaning of the word. There are those who argue that the proper number of people in a given area is that number which can produce the largest amount of wealth in the aggregate; others say the largest amount per capita. Still others argue for reproduction only of those who conform to certain standards of physical or mental fitness, but as yet they disagree over the composition of those standards.

And as the numbers increase, the question of population density presses. There are more in some parts of the world than in others and many in the thickly settled countries wish to migrate to Canada, to Australia, or to the United States whose present inhabitants protest. They claim a "right" to keep out others who in their turn claim a "right" to come. At once we are in a maze of difficulties. Many urge that there is such a thing as national sovereignty and that the residents of any given country have certain political or legal rights; that among them is the right to control immigration; or, as the saying goes, that immigration is a domestic question. But is it? If by this expression is meant a legal right, the layman must defer to the political scientists and lawyers who alone are competent to answer. But as they ponder, we must remind them that time presses; that Italy must "expand or explode" unless something happens soon; that the Japanese are restless; that there are too many people on the British Isles unless a number of other problems can be adjusted. We may further remind them that, after all, laws exist for mankind rather than mankind for laws, just as the Sabbath was made for man, not man for the Sabbath. Legal concepts may have to be adjusted to the realities of the twentieth century.

Anyone who has even glanced at the literature of sovereignty appreciates the difficulties raised. But let us waive the legal issue for a moment or, still better, assume that the experts will find some way of settling it in accordance with what are often called "principles of equity and justice." What are those principles? What is meant by justice? After our concept is clear there will still be the difficulty of applying it to the problem at hand, *e.g.*, to the desire of Italians or of Japanese to emigrate to America. But what is the concept?

Shall we fall back on the voice of authority as it speaks through direct revelation to each of us through a sacred book or through some supposedly infallible spokesman of the Divine Will? Shall we rely on conscience, whose promptings differ so widely from one person to another and from one time to another? Many contend that conscience is nothing but a set of reactions determined for each individual by his heredity, his early education, his environment, his church, his political party, his club, his newspaper. Shall we fall back on etymology and remind ourselves that "moral" is derived from *mores* and that moral things are the customary things? If so, we shall come perilously close to alleging that whatever is is right. Perhaps then we can take refuge in the comforting expression "survival of the fittest" and attempt to apply it in this troubled world. But if so, we must guard against at least one fallacy in reasoning. The right to survive perhaps should be tested by fitness but there may be no way of testing fitness except by survival.

The layman may be venturing beyond his depth. Questions of ethics should be argued by experts. If so, the world is now in urgent need of their help. Many plead for the application of the Christian ethic, for the simple principles of Christianity. This may be the answer but it is difficult to avoid the suggestion that while in individual and domestic problems the success of Christianity is at least debated, in the international field it is seldom mentioned. Formal expressions of the brotherhood of man are frequent but in war and for practical purposes, even in peace, they are little used.

It is not inaccurate to urge that we have no settled concept of justice to aid us in international affairs. Or if we say that it is a struggle concept, if we go so far as to contend that "might makes right," if we relate it in some

[309]

way to survival, perhaps arguing with Professor Carver that "whatever inevitably tends to be" is right and that survival is the only final evidence of this tendency, we may have an ethical concept but it is not one which will make for harmony. It is one that invites competition and struggle during days of peace and one that may easily lead to war.

The difficulty appears in other fields than that of migration. The people in the densely crowded countries want food and raw materials from others. Are they to have them and on what terms? By all means let us have an equitable distribution. But what is equitable? What does the concept mean—an equal distribution on a per capita basis? If so, why? And are we ready to apply this principle to oil by setting aside the same number of gallons per capita for the people of China and of India as for Americans although the former have not adapted their social and economic life to petroleum so fully as have the people of the United States? Probably not.

It will be easy under these circumstances to accept the *status quo* or, in other words, to consider that whatever is is right in this best of all possible worlds. We may, of course, admit the difficulties in measuring needs and be tempted to use desires as the test. But desires are capable of indefinite expansion and the desires of the Chinese or the Germans or the British may be just as intense as those of the French, the Americans, or the Argentinians.

But there is no simply stated economic limit to the amount of oil or rubber or sisal or coffee or nitrates that the people of any country, *e.g.*, the United States, may desire. Under the stress of economic forces the amounts wanted are unlimited, or if there are real limits somewhere, they are not easily reached and are of little help in practical affairs. Human wants expand indefinitely. The higher our standards the more vigorously we are wont to affirm them or even to try raising them. The more we have the more we seem to want. Shall we then distribute oil according to needs? If so, there is the awkward task of calculating needs, possibly by noting the economic organization of the country, the number of automobiles in use, the factories and homes and ships that use oil. But after making the calculation the problem is not much clarified. For perhaps the existing adjustment is due to a past advantage in the possession of oil, an advantage that is rapidly disappearing. And because of this advantage there may have been a neglect in the development of substitutes, such as available water power. If so, shall this temporary advantage and this neglect be overlooked and other countries kept at a permanent disadvantage?

The obstacles to progress by a continuing contest along nationalistic lines are just as serious, and perhaps more so, in the scramble for markets. There is no limit to our desire for them. The difficulty is peculiarly vivid in the postwar years. All of us want more and more of the good things of life; to lower our living standards no matter how high they are is cruelly hard and we can easily justify any opportunity to raise them. We do it by making more money. Money is made by selling commodities (and services) for a price as high as one can get and through a margin between costs and selling prices. One builds a plant, hires labor, buys raw materials. He must pay for the materials and make huge expenditures for wages, interest, depreciation, insurance. Having a plant of a given size, he has every reason to operate it at full capacity. Overhead expenses are large and unit costs are high when output is small but small when output is large. Bondholders must be paid if bankruptcy is to be avoided. They can demand only their fixed return but stockholders are insatiable.

[311]

They want the highest dividends that they can get, while to reduce or to pass dividends is in their eyes almost unforgiveable.

But to make money one must sell goods in markets. There are no satisfactory limits. A business man must sell all he can. To gain a market is often the only way to ward off failure, while to lose a market may be to invite bankruptcy. Domestic markets may be large and able to absorb a huge output. But, if so, plant capacity is soon extended sufficiently and often far more than sufficiently to meet this domestic demand. To meet a temporary increase in orders, plants are built that prove far greater than are needed in ordinary times. The inevitable result is a scramble for markets here, there, and everywhere, both at home and abroad. And no extension of markets either at home or abroad is a solution. As fast as these markets are secured, plants to supply them are built and the old scramble is renewed. There is no limit to be rationally set for the steel market or the textile market or the coal market or for any other market so long as an unrestrained competition is the only determinant. And with government support and perhaps public subsidies for each national group no peaceful adjustment is possible.

Within any given country relief from destructive competition may be found in combination but as long as combinations are intranational this intensifies the struggle in the international field. Each national monopoly may seek and may secure the support of its own government in its contest against the similarly fortified monopolies of other countries. The nationalistic approach gives no answer. Señor de Madariaga sees no possibility of military disarmament unless there can be the organization and development of a real world community. Perhaps in this there is a suggestion that will aid in economic disarmament.

Solving the Dilemma

One approach through international effort may be emphasized. In May, 1927, the League of Nations directed a World Economic Conference at Geneva, attended by the representatives of nearly every country in the world, even those not members of the League. The United States sent a strong delegation. There was a certain amount of disagreement but under the circumstances a gratifying unanimity. World illness was readily and accurately diagnosed. Remedies were urged. It was found that in spite of a growth in world population and in productivity, trade languished. Restrictions on the movement of goods were too numerous. Tariffs were everywhere rising. It was time for a movement in the opposite direction. The resolutions were clear and enthusiasm ran high. Upon the delegates was pressed the importance of influencing public opinion and governments in every possible way when they returned to their respective countries.

Two years passed. In May, 1929, was held the second meeting of the Economic Consultative Committee which had been organized "to follow the application of the recommendations of the Economic Conference." Its chairman was M. Theunis who had also been chairman of the Economic Conference. His opening address, though constrained in tone, clearly reflected his own disappointment and that of his fellows. Notice a few brief extracts:

Two years of experience have clearly shown . . . that the policy recommended at Geneva in 1927 corresponded to economic necessities and to the deepest aspirations of the different groups of world activity.

And yet, as far as the commercial policy recommended by the Economic Conference is concerned, it must be recognized that the efforts made to carry this policy into effect have met with varying fortunes . . .

The events of the past year mark a slowing down in the progress achieved.

These brief extracts may convey a slightly wrong impression. M. Theunis found some grounds for satisfaction and urged his associates to still greater efforts. Yet the general discouragement was clear. The year 1928 had seen some retardation in the upward movement of trade restrictions. But 1929 was witnessing another forward surge. In many directions tariff increases were being made or threatened. Especially was the attitude of the United States viewed with concern.

In so far as this discouragement was warranted the reasons lie in the nature of the problem—a competitive world organized on a national basis, a price economy, a fierce need for markets. And the solution proposed was for each national group to apply the golden rule for the sake of the general welfare. Although increasing a tariff seems to give each national group an advantage, the same action by all of them is "collective suicide." The answer seems to be through an appeal to common sense. Resolutions that each should consider the welfare of all had been passed but the resulting reactions were far from gratifying.

There were many undoubted gains from the conference of 1927. Its statement of principles was vigorous, its diagnosis of world ailment and its indication of what should be done for relief calls for no dissent. But there was a double weakness. First, its proposals were of the negative sort. Governments were urged not to raise tariffs, not to impose restrictions on trade. Secondly, no action was proposed or even clearly endorsed that made a direct appeal to the self-interest of any powerful group concerned. An undue reliance was placed on altruism and on alleged indirect advantages supposed to accrue from considering the general welfare. Tangible results to date are few and the prospects for real gains in the near future are not encouraging.

Four suggestions may be made for constructive effort. They are not spectacular, they cannot be immediately

[314]

applied in a wholesale manner, and each may have accompanying disadvantages. We have several times referred to Alfred Marshall in this volume, and we may again mention him by noting his fondness for the motto: *Natura non facit saltum.* In economic life as elsewhere evolution is gradual. Progress is often so slow as to try one's patience and is often not fast enough to prevent disaster. On occasion it may perhaps be hastened but for the most part so tardily as to be discouraging.

First is the gain through commercial treaties. Treaties may be bad as well as good. Their results may be to create ill will rather than to lessen it. Yet the converse is more often true. Through treaties better relations may be established and difficulties adjusted. Reductions in tariffs may be agreed upon through mutual concessions which bring a definite and prompt gain to the industries of both countries—an appeal to the self-interest of influential groups within the territory affected. And if the most-favored-nation clause is incorporated in such treaties the advantages secured in any one treaty become generally available.

Second is the form of international cooperation found in the trust or cartel. There is not space to describe particular cartels. The title itself is vague and tne activities of the business groupings to which the name is applied are numerous. But they have one advantage—through them business disputes, quarrels over raw materials and over markets, are adjusted. Marketing areas are divided, output quotas are determined, and prices are agreed upon. Business peace is secured. The huge industries concerned settle their differences without appealing to their governments and through governments to their fellow nationals for support. Patriotism is not invoked to aid Belgian steel or American sulphur.

[315]

Of course the international trust raises problems. But it is here and cannot be conjured away. It must be accepted. At its worst it is a blessing compared with war and through it at least one cause of international friction that may lead to war is eliminated. Prices will doubtless be adjusted with some reference to the law of monopoly price—at the level that will yield the highest net return. But that level is not necessarily a high one. It may be low, and, although high, it is better than military conflict and probably better even than an economic conflict between the opposing groups with all the demoralization that usually follows. The fear of potential competition, moreover, is a powerful deterrent against putting prices at too high a level—a lesson recently and forcibly presented to the world in the operation of the Stevenson Plan and one that constantly influences the attitude of the Brazilian government in its attempts at coffee control. Then, too, we must not forget that prices can be raised only by curtailing sales and hence output. This sets free labor and capital for use in other directions.

Financial consortiums through which bankers cooperate in their dealings, *e.g.*, with Mexico and China, can be given only a passing mention, with the reminder that the results for the borrowing country are apt to be better than if money lenders engage in a wild competitive scramble, each national group appealing to its own government for support.

One of the valuable developments of the postwar period has been the organization of the International Chamber of Commerce. The problems which we have been discussing are business problems. There is everything to gain if business men of different countries can meet each other, talk over their differences, argue out their views in mixed committees, pass resolutions covering the points on which

[316]

they can agree. Between biennial sessions their work goes on through committees and with the aid of resident commissioners at various large business centers.

Finally, and all too briefly, the League of Nations must be added. One need of students today is for a competent and thorough analysis of the economic work of the League. Our earlier criticisms of the approach made by the Economic Conference should not be misinterpreted. The conference itself was most worthwhile. It was merely not a heaven-sent panacea through which the world's difficulties will be resolved. Nor are any of its other efforts. But step by step the League is leading us to cooperate in treaties, in finance, and in almost countless other ways. For economic ill will and friction it is gradually helping us to substitute sanity and a spirit of adjustment.

It is in these four ways but not only in these four ways that the world is working its way out of a dilemma that might easily become an *impasse*. Though the gains are at times slow, there is ample reason for believing that progress is really being made.

INDEX

Index

Index

Prices, effects of fluctuations, 94ff.
  fall of, in 1921, 83
  fluctuations since 1790, 92ff.
Production, large-scale, in Great
  Britain, 71
  influence of, 70ff.
  need for diversification, 237
  relation to foreign trade, 81, 125
  tendency to expand, 86
Protection, 117–119

Q

Quick, Herbert, 33, 162

R

Rathenau, Walter, 148
Raw materials, demand for until 1920,
  12
  relation to overhead costs, 79
  in trade of Belgium and Germany, 43
  unlimited desire for, 310
Redfield, W. C., 67
Rights, legal, 46
  to migrate, 308
  moral, 47
Rist, Charles, 209
Rubber, control by Great Britain, 49
Russia, as a source of food, 11, 56

S

Seligman, E. R. A., 30
Shipbuilding, 83
Smith, Adam, 86
Smith, J. Russell, 13
Sombart, Werner, 144
Sovereignty, 4
Stamp, Sir Josiah, 28
Standards of living, differences in 20
  varieties of, 14, 30, 34
Stoddard, Lathrop, 37
Sundbörg, W. G., 32
Switzerland, coal imports of, 67

T

"Trusts," in Germany, 82
  international, 315, 316
  in the United States, 49, 82, 288

U

Unemployment, in France, 242
  in Italy, 252
United States, area, 279
  balance of payments, 292ff.
  birth rate, 281
  capital accumulation, 283
  corporations in, 286ff.
  creditor status, 293
  death rate, 281
  diminishing source of world food
    supply, 11
  economic strength, 289ff.
  economic tendencies, 294ff.
  exports of cotton, 67
  foreign investments in, 150
  foreign investments of, 281, 288
  foreign investments and trade, 158
  foreign trade analyzed, 123ff., 291
  freedom of trade in, 282
  immigration restraints, 36
  income and wealth, 281
  Japan's dependence on, 272
  large-scale production, 72, 285
  population, 279
  resources, 279
  "trust" control, 49

W

Wages, deflation and, 105
  iron law of, 10, 21
  overhead costs and, 87
War burdens not postponed, 215
Water power, 66
Wheat, world dependence on, 54ff.
Wiggam, Albert E., 37
Woolf, Leonard, 134
World Economic Conference, 122, 313
Wright, Harold, 13